ARE GOD AND THE GODS STILL THERE?
HOW POETRY MATTERS

John Newton studied for his Cambridge degree in English under F. R. Leavis and H. A. Mason. He then went on working in universities, for longest in Cambridge but also in the US. Following Leavis's and Mason's examples, he has always preferred to speak of his relation to younger students of literature as a matter of his reading and thinking with them rather than of his 'teaching' them. He was one of the two principal founder-editors of *The Cambridge Quarterly*, where the greater number but by no means all of his many articles and reviews have been published. These have ranged widely in their subject-matter, which has included film, painting and religion as well as English Literature of all periods from Chaucer to the present day. In 2000 he edited for Penguin's the Complete Poems of the great but long neglected early 20th-century poet, Charlotte Mew. He has now retired from his active university positions and is concentrating more fully on his writing. He is a Life Fellow of Clare College, Cambridge, though now living in Wales where one side of his family comes from and where he spent some years of his childhood.

Are God and the gods still there? How poetry matters

John Newton

ARE GOD AND THE GODS STILL THERE?
HOW POETRY MATTERS

Olympia Publishers

www.olympiapublishers.com
OLYMPIA PAPERBACK EDITION

A CIP catalogue record for this title is
available from the British Library.

ISBN: 978-1-905513-77-2

Olympia Publishers part of Ashwell Publishing Ltd

First Published in 2009

Olympia Publishers
60 Cannon Street
London
EC4N 6NP

Printed in Great Britain

Dedication

To the memory of the late H. A. Mason
and his quite outstanding mind and spirit

Acknowledgments

The already printed articles and reviews that are reprinted here with some revision originally appeared in *The Cambridge Quarterly*, the *New England Review*, *The Sewanee Review* and *Tears in the Fence*. Acknowledgment is made to Faber and Faber for permission to quote one poem by Philip Larkin in its entirety, to the Oleander Press and Sue Lenier for permission to quote one poem by her in its entirety, to John Freeman for permission to quote one poem by him in its entirety, and to the late F. T. Prince for permission to quote his translation from John of the Cross. Acknowledgment is made to Joanne Weiss for permission to quote a number of complete poems by her.

Contents

SOME SUPPORTING ARGUMENTS

PREFACE

I give this book its main title because I don't believe the book simply falls in the 'literary criticism' bracket.

It has its second part because I like both the way it plays on the title of Dana Gioia's timely *Can Poetry Matter?* and the coincidence that, before that book's appearance, these words were already at the head of the talk of mine on which the first chapter's first section is based.

Most of the chapters added as supporting arguments to the main one were written independently of each other and of that main argument. (Most of them were also written before the latter, in some cases long before it.) I hope readers may find that the book, nevertheless, does very much hang together, and that it gains more in liveliness by being based in the main on separate talks, articles and reviews, written at different times and on different occasions, than it loses by not being a series of strictly consecutive chapters. It's long been a belief of mine that written literary criticism's natural length is that of the article or review.

Another longstanding belief about literary criticism is that the real thing is relatively uncommon and its natural readership a general one and that almost everything that academics in university literature departments write at such great length for each other and/or for their students is in need of a different description. At the beginning of Chapter VII I identify as 6th-formers in England the audience for which the original talk was written, but the same is true of Chapter II, most of Chapter V and much of Chapter III. Such an audience is much closer to a general audience than the specialist audiences in a university department of literature, and I'm profoundly grateful to the schoolteachers who, by inviting me to give those talks, helped me to have that general audience in mind as I wrote. For the same reason I'm grateful for the invitations I had when in Boston University to address audiences made up of colleagues and students from a great variety of different departments. Each of the first chapter's first two sections began life like this. If I do write more as an academic 'specialist' in the long chapter on Marvell's poetry, I hope that for the general reader the chapter will have some of the interest of a historical detective-story, besides whatever interest its relevance to the book's main argument gives it.

The little tenth chapter is a previously unpublished review of a 1995 London exhibition of paintings, and I add it not only because I believe there is another fight to be fought over this painter's neglect. It is also a small acknowledgment: that the faults of the provincial English poetry 'scene' probably have a parallel or two in the English 'scenes' in the other arts.

Finally, I need to acknowledge the personal relationship that there is between myself and the main poet whose work I seek to draw attention to here, Joanne Weiss. But I also need to say that this relationship began many months *after* I had first been shown essays and poems and a play by her – and had my breath taken away by them.

You have given me praise for having reflected faithfully in my poems the feelings of human nature. I would fain hope that I have done so. But a great poet ought to do more than this: he ought to a certain degree to rectify men's feelings, to give them new compositions of feeling, to render their feelings more sane, pure and permanent, in short, more consonant to nature, that is, to eternal nature, and the great moving spirit of things.

William Wordsworth (letter to John Wilson, 7 June 1802)

[Poetry] purges from our inward sight the film of familiarity which obscures from us the wonder of our being.

Percy Bysshe Shelley (A Defence of Poetry)

The future of poetry is immense, because in poetry, where it is worthy of its high destinies, our race, as time goes on, will find an ever surer stay. There is not a creed which is not shaken, not an accredited dogma which is not shown to be questionable, not a received tradition which does not threaten to dissolve. Our religion has materialised itself in the fact, in the supposed fact...

Matthew Arnold, The Study of Poetry (where he is quoting, with some changes, words first written by him in his Introduction to the first volume of a publisher's compilation called *The Hundred Greatest Men*).

THE MAIN ARGUMENT

Introduction.
Poetry and 'faith'

"The world will be saved by beauty"
And nothing else
At all. *

It is tempting to begin with the proposition that every human being is
religious in the sense of having some religious experience and faith
except the person who believes what the doctrines of the Christian
Church say he or she should believe. Though I'm immediately going
on to qualify, I do offer the proposition seriously. It is an unfair one in
that the 'believer' is not only as much of a human being as the rest of
us but can sometimes be a better one. It is just that the abundance, if
not preponderance, of irreligious moments that he or she experiences,
again like the rest of us, probably includes most of his or her moments
qua 'believer'. It's likely that such irreligious 'belief' also exists aplenty
in other established religions of the world.

The positive part of the proposition is the more interesting part,
and the negative is added to it only because irreligious 'belief' so
insidiously leads to the obscuring and even denying of the religious
experience and faith that we all have, and of the truth and soundness
in them, and thereby does damage.

Unless there are some exceptions among the insane and the
psychopathic, in ways I'm not qualified to say anything about, all of us
have been deeply moved by beauty. And in that experience, however
fleeting it is, or however incomplete is our consciousness of it, or
however disregarded it may be by us, we have for the moment come

---

* The poem from which these lines come will be quoted in full on a later
page. The first of the lines is a statement by Dostoevsky that was quoted by
Solzhenitsyn when he was accepting his Nobel Prize.

through to a state of exceptional inner stillness and peace and, in that state, to what can feel something like a revelation. Though the love and awe felt may initially be more exciting than peaceful, such a stillness does follow when interruption or distraction doesn't stop it from doing so, and the experience does then seem to become that of a calmly certain knowledge. This includes a rare sense of ourselves as we really are. And that can be accompanied both by some apprehension that in those real selves of ours we are somehow intimately linked with all other living things and even with everything in the universe and by some recognition of an unmistakable though finally incomprehensible wonderfulness, both in the smallest things and in the great sublime and terrifying thing that the immense whole is. On those occasions when beauty does suddenly and without our premeditation catch us so deeply – in a landscape, a night sky, silence, a flower, an insect, a work of art, an old cathedral, the face of a sleeping beloved, a deathbed – we are taken out of ourselves more completely than at almost any other time yet simultaneously feel that we are ourselves more completely. And the consequences for our thought, feeling and behaviour could hardly be more fruitful, even if in their degree they obviously vary according to the fullness and duration of the experience and the attention we allow ourselves to pay to it. We are no longer so governed by the cares, fears and wishes that we otherwise tend to be all too governed by. These now strike us as optional or smaller than we imagined, or even pointless. Altogether, we see and feel more disinterestedly, from what feels like a more impersonal and permanent centre – from what can even feel as if, though it is the deepest thing in us, it somehow hasn't anything to do with what we normally think of as our 'selves'. Then, if it is true that for however short a time we are then more 'moral', that is not so much to do with any consciously dutiful heeding of supposed ethical rules as a matter of our being more surely inner-directed in our behaviour, from fundamental disposition, and with an exceptional freedom, ease and confidence that are not at all manic but completely sober.

I want to put all this to the test of a beautiful new poem that, because of its bold sexual subject, could seem even shockingly distant from almost any conventional idea of religion (in spite of the Bible's having *The Song of Solomon* in it and the old church marriage service the words "With my body I thee worship"). But I should first clarify the objection to Christian 'belief' by saying that that 'belief' not only treats as matters of fact what almost certainly are not matters of fact and quite certainly cannot be known to be such: just as seriously, it tends to be a set of dried-up, merely intellectual *notions*, more or less drastically cut off from whatever poetic truth they may originally have had and from whatever religious experience and faith were once expressed in this poetic way. (The reader who knows Matthew Arnold's *Literature and Dogma* will recognize my debt to it here.) Main examples of what has become thus horribly and blasphemously ossified are the related Christian doctrines of the Trinity and the Incarnation. How many ministers of any Christian church seek to guide their flocks back to the origin in experience of the former doctrine and thus to whatever poetic truth it has, thereby making contact with and in that way clarifying and strengthening apprehensions we may all still more or less dimly possess – guide them back to this origin in experience by having some such go as this at expressing those apprehensions?

> About the universe though beyond our ability to understand there seems to be something extraordinary which, while it certainly terrifies us, also awes us in a further way by seeming to be something extraordinarily beautiful and good. At our best moments we can feel we are profoundly united with this great beauty and goodness and recognize them as working inside us as well as outside. A few extremely rare individuals can strike the rest of us as being at one with them with a quite exceptional completeness, distinctness and efficacy.

Then, how many ministers guide their flocks to understanding how the tribute and recognition that were given to one of those extremely rare individuals when he was called the "only begotten" Son of God, a tribute and recognition that at that date were almost certainly natural and meaningful ones to give, is now more or less arbitrary and meaningless, or else an offensively arrogant false claim for its own unique supremacy by just one of the world's major religions? (Not that there are no ministers who give such guidance. While the Anglican

Prayer Book is unreformed in this respect, a Church of Wales church near where the author lives has inside it representations of Vishnu and the Buddha as well as of Christian figures, and its rectory has a beautiful room, over the garage, called an ashram and with many more such figures, for anyone to meditate in.) Such Christian doctrine has become so dried up because the intuitions and apprehensions it derives from have gradually over the centuries not been able to resist being so hardened in people's minds as to become only those all too hard-edged, mere intellectual notions. As such, they have not only their spiritual as well as intellectual bankruptcy but are bound to have a somewhat confused and confusing relation (and sometimes a rather wilfully managed one) to whatever religious experience and faith that modern 'believer' is like every other human being in having.

Real religious faith is evidently the stronger the more any person values the experience of beauty, treats it as significant, and seeks consciously as well as unconsciously to do something about it, with one result of this being a proportionately greater ability to have that experience counting at more difficult times.

Now to the shock-test beautiful new poem (which I confess it took me some time to see is a sonnet):

> You whom I love lift my heart to a height
> I never have felt and yet when I feel
> Below your belt, delirious in delight,
> Again that wound I never want to heal
> Breaks me to my knees – there my heart lifts high
> To your hard-on. Happily I unzip
> Your trousers, happily I reach in and pry
> You free, tongue wet encircling with each lip
> I suck. Throbbing needing you now inside take
> Me lift me high let this cold world crawl
> Through sleeping nights, in this our love I ache
> And feel the universe awake. This ball
> Of spinning fire and, my love, my love, each day.
> Who needs more? On this passionate earth let's play.

Here my proposition is that for most people this can touch the spirit both more freshly and more deeply that almost any of the words in, for example, *Hymns Ancient and Modern* or the Anglican *Prayer Book*, though an exception may be made for the best of the poetry in some of that *Prayer Book*'s readings from the Bible. In fact, such language as the following sits well with this sonnet:

> Let the heavens rejoice and the earth be glad: let the sea roar and all that therein is.
> Let the fields be joyful and all that is in them: yea, let all the trees of the wood rejoice before the Lord. (*Psalm* 96)

Another claim for this sonnet may follow a little reflection on its boldness in disregarding the uncomfortable and/or scornful feelings that some readers could have in response to it: that the writing of the poem required some unusual purity and intensity of faith. Not that the touch isn't light: the poem is obviously written with a wonderfully easy good humour. That comes with that rare degree of faith, just as it contributes to the final little moving realisation and its peace.

Perhaps I can give some support to these claims by first trying to say in general terms something more about that stillness that all deep experiences of beauty can take us to. It seems almost invariably to involve some finally truthful and happy resolution of contrary feelings. For example, by being so 'other' or foreign the deeply appreciated landscape or insect is challenging and almost threatening us at the same time as it is also attracting and delighting us. Both reactions are true, and can easily co-exist with each other and create together the more complete and final-feeling truth that brings with it that unusual peace and satisfaction. This idea first occurred to me in connection with poetry, and specifically in connection with a disappointment that I have sometimes experienced when reading poems by John Donne. (It can have me doubting whether he is really one of the great poets). Many of his poems have long seemed to me too short on contrariety of feeling or impulse, to be all too much one way, in one direction, and to be this in an assertive and all too ego-governed way. At its end one of his poems can leave us still too much up in the air, very possibly feeling some heady excitement but not the beauty, resolution and stillness that in their countless different ways are created by purer works of art. (There is clearly some relation between this general idea about beauty and the idea of catharsis that is specifically associated with tragic art – though also sometimes with comic. There will be some discussion of catharsis in more than one of the chapters that follow.)

But isn't that sonnet all one way? What are the contraries being resolved in it when it expresses nothing but loving delight at the sexual activity? First answers to this doubt are that, nevertheless, there is no sense at all as there is with those poems of Donne's that are all one way of a triumphantly assertive ego; and then that the existence and resolution of contrary feelings or impulses in every good work of art and deep experience of beauty may often be a relatively subtle matter.

Of the conflict in this sonnet it may be enough to say that the poem begins by somewhat shocking the reader but finally needn't shock the reader at all. But one can say more. Isn't there some play on "high" and "height"? Implicitly the words admit that it is quite other things that we ordinarily and conventionally think of as lifting human beings to sublime heights, and at the same time the words are expressing their surprised as well as delighted wonder at the fact that such lusty desire can do this too. The play is partly created, with some humour, by the close juxtaposition of the lofty language with the disconcertingly frank details, as in the play on "felt" and "feel" in the second line or in the later alliteration of "heart", "high" and "hard-on". At the same time, there is the coexistence of the passionate eloquence of the voice's moving forward in the poem with moments of joky-feeling jauntiness in its music, as in the internal rhymes and particularly that of "belt" with "felt". In addition, "height" plays against and yet successfully combines with "Breaks me to my knees", which words themselves involve a play and combination with the idea of prayer – and perhaps at the same time, given what follows, with the idea of taking Communion! Later in the sonnet there is the conflict between the statement that this "world" is "cold" and the description of "the universe awake" as "This ball/ Of spinning fire", with the resolving of this conflict completed and enriched in what follows when the serious-sweeping quality both of the question asked in the last line and of the phrase "this passionate earth" is combined with that line's ending with the so active verb "play". (If the idea of passionate play in sex is familiar enough, and if the intimate connection made in the preceding lines between microcosm and macrocosm is also traditional, made in so much love-talk as well as love-poetry, there is surely no doubt about either's being given fresh power again here.)

The beauty of the lovers' experience is felt with the kind of calm finality that goes with truthfulness. The ardour for it has no narrowness, since the peace would not be achieved in the complete way it is achieved if the poem was not utterly wide open. The reality of other kinds of experience of the heights is not questioned but, rather, taken for granted and effortlessly and gladly lived with, and the only questioning is the implicit, confidently gentle and good-humoured questioning of the blindness that people can show when fear and over-solemnity make them insist that quite different routes to those heights are the only ones. That aggression is known about by the poet but no trouble to her, simply seen as a little absurd, perhaps somewhat touchingly so, in a suddenly much larger perspective that is both more generous and more religious.

That the experience of beauty when we respond to it at all adequately can seriously be thought of as the essential religious experience may be suggested by something else: the fact that beauty is ineffable, finally inexpressible in words – in the case of a poem's beauty in any words other than those of the poem itself. How laboured my own comments on this light-hearted sonnet haven't managed to avoid being though its beauty is simple as well as ineffable!

While "ineffable" tends to support my general thesis, it also introduces something else. Poetry's being ineffable may be the main thing that makes it also vulnerable, like other religious experience and faith. The wind blows where and when it wants to, and no one can know for sure, and certainly not as a matter of hard, provable fact, exactly where and when that is. Good new poetry can go unrecognised for a time, as can also its complete absence from all too many new volumes of verse. This is partly what this book's main argument is about. (Like the gifted unknown poet quoted in both of the first two sections of the chapter that follows, the writer of that sonnet is also unknown.) And the vulnerability of at any rate all man-made beauty is clearly one of the reasons why people value coming together with each other in the enjoyment of it. Hence in part the creating in 'official' religion of communal forms of all kinds, with the regular Sunday comings-together the most familiar. Hence in part, too, the terrible sadness in both Britain and the U.S. of poetry's near-invisibility and near-inaudibility to the community at large – a sadness both for that community, through its serious impoverishment, and for the few scattered good new poets and lovers of good new poetry, through their serious discouragement. It seems all too significant here that, while poetry has its fullest life and beauty when it is delivered aloud, the practice of reading poetry aloud in the ordinary family circle or circle of friends has declined so markedly over the past century and more. We also seem to have lost some of the conviction that became conspicuous in the 1960's about the possibility of inspired public readings. (A brief tribute to the late Allen Ginsberg comes in my first chapter.) If the existence of the theatre is obviously significant here, along with that of the concert-hall, pop and classical, our current theatre does not have much poetry in its new plays, and in these two countries there has never in any case been anything to match ancient Athens's special communal valuing of the theatre, for the rare wisdom in its power and beauty.

But, finally, why on this last page, and previously with the sonnet, have I been pressing "new" poetry? So much of the language heard in churches is ancient. That also answers the question. In any new generation the spirit cannot always be awakened and nourished just by the old words, whatever valuable life some of these may still have, and whatever valuable life different people may also give to still more of them by feelings and associations that they bring to them. To believe the opposite, that the spirit always can be awakened and nourished just by the old words, is idolatry, and the temptation to such idolatry is evidently enough another thing to which religious experience and faith are peculiarly vulnerable, from that very insecurity that is caused by their object's being ineffable.

I hope readers will find it making sense that the fuller argument that now follows starts from scratch again, as if nothing had yet been said about any relation between poetry and religion.

Postscript The special beauty of spirit of the current Dalai Lama is an inspiring example of beauty's involving the happy-wonderful resolution of seeming contraries. "How can such goodness be human? Yet at the same time it's so especially clearly nothing but human!" I thought of this after reading his *The Art of Happiness*, in which his co-author, Dr Howard C. Cutler, wisely devotes space to more than just the recording and discussing of things said by the Dalai Lama, also describing the latter's demeanour in meeting people and talking to them. A reason for mentioning the example here is the fresh and excitingly living (and excitingly untheological) meaning it gives to the idea of 'Incarnation'. Other new reading has given me words that could have been an additional epigraph at the beginning of this introduction, from the great Sufi, Ibn al-Arabi: "If you love a being for his beauty, you love none other than God, for his is *the* Beautiful Being." (Quoted in Karen Armstrong's *A History of God*)

Chapter I
The grace of poetry and its disgrace

Though poetry is one of the greatest gifts and needs of the human race, I believe that there are these two sad interdependent facts about the current poetry 'scenes' in the U.S. and Britain: poetry has nothing like the central, valued place in the general community that it has had before and still has elsewhere, and it is difficult to believe that the vast quantity of new verse that gets published every year has any claim to such a place. However, this book is partly written in the belief that some poetry of our time that is at present hardly known does have a strong claim to a central, valued place in the general community and, though it will take time, as often in the past, will eventually get that place. Then there will again be poetry quite outside our enclosed and dry – socially and spiritually so small – poetry 'scenes': being heard and read and cared about by people who now rarely or never hear or read or care about poetry.

In the nature of the case, this poetry is likely to win that place not with the help of the current poetry 'scenes' but by somehow contriving to by-pass them. The element of anger in this chapter's title is not only at the low standard of published new poetry, with the hungry sheep looking up and not being fed – and for so long that the very idea of such food and of looking for it is discredited and there is a widespread, if unconscious, starvation. Another consequence of the standard's having become so low is that, when the real thing does turn up, it just does not look right in either of those poetry 'scenes' – as if it belongs in either or can really be any good therefore – and it can be slow even getting into print.

The anger is more at the situation than at the people involved. Tenth-rateness or worse in poetry clearly need not be a matter for anger, nor enthusiasm for tenth-rateness or worse, in someone who does not know any better new poetry, or is so unused to seeing it that its sudden appearance is difficult to recognise.

This chapter's argument is about ways in which poetry that meets a much higher standard can be described, and is illustrated with one or two well-known classic poems as well as with some of the new poetry that I believe meets this standard too.

I. THE SUBLIME, OR HOW POETRY MATTERS

Does the serious use of the word 'sublime' need to be revived, in order to signify something essential both in poetry and in art in general? The lack of the idea which this word represents both means that we are probably losing something essential in the great art of the past and helps explain the common failure to recognise and even know about the art of our own time that is that art's successor.

I begin by translating a few sentences by the great 17th-century French poet and critic, Boileau, who was himself reviving the word and idea of the sublime and, incidentally, doing so as an embattled advocate of the best new poetry of his own time, particularly his friend Racine's. In 1674 he published with a Preface his translation into French of the little treatise on the sublime by the writer in ancient Greek known as Longinus. There is the more point in going back as far as Boileau because it is too easy to think of the idea of the 'sublime' as belonging peculiarly to the later, Romantic period of art, whereas what actually took place in that Romantic period was, among many wonderful other things, some special development of it (so that in painting, for example, it tended to be associated with great mountain landscapes). This special development may eventually have deprived the idea of much of its meaning and made the word what it is now, a difficult one to use seriously. These sentences from Boileau's Preface seek to clarify Longinus' idea:

> You have to know that by sublime Longinus does not mean what the rhetoricians call the sublime style but, rather, that extraordinary and wonderful thing in the writing that hits you hard and makes a work take you out of your own possession, enrapture, transport. The sublime *style* always wants big showy words, but the sublime can be found in a simple single thought, figure of speech, turn of expression. Something can

be in the sublime *style* and nevertheless not be sublime – that is, not have anything in it that is extraordinary or surprising. For example, "The supreme Arbiter of Nature with a single word formed the light." That is in the sublime style, but is nevertheless not sublime, because there is nothing in it that is really wonderful and could not have been produced by anybody. But "God said, Let there be light, and there was light." This extraordinary turn of expression... is in truth sublime and possesses something divine.

I like and take seriously Boileau's use of the word "divine", and so am the more anxious to avoid the confusion over it that could be caused by his having chosen his example from the first chapter of *Genesis*. A different word that is sometimes used to describe the same kind of breathtaking poetic success is "magical". That word can certainly be used, for example, about extraordinary things done with the simplest words by Dante. At the same time, neither "divine" nor "magical" is only a superlative about a poet's powers of expression. The sublime poem may not be religious poetry in the immediately recognisable way that the first chapter of *Genesis* is, but it *is* an expression of the ineffable and, whatever its subject, communicating something of the divine, terrible-wonderful beauty and mystery of life and death, and is capable of doing so to any kind of believer or unbeliever. Especially in its context, immediately after the first verse of *Genesis*, "God said, Let there be light, and there was light" can fill the mind and feeling of even the agnostic or atheist with all the chastening wonder and mystery of the sheer fact of light: its presence in our lives and in the universe. Or it can do so if its poetry is read as the great poetry it is.

Another word of Boileau's that I am evidently taking seriously is the word "wonderful" (*merveilleux*), and perhaps the general idea that I am arguing is best stated with the help of the word "wonder". How poetry and art matter is (1) that most of the time we are cut off from the feeling and knowledge that at exceptional moments we do have, of the wonder of the divine terror, beauty and mystery of life and death, and (2) that, in spite of this, that feeling and knowledge are almost as necessary to us as our breath and our blood, indispensable for our sanity, let alone wisdom, and for any full living of our lives. While poetry and art are not, of course, the only means of access to this feeling and knowledge, they are a potent means of access to them and – I am suggesting – at their greatest and most authentic that is what they most essentially are.

A sublime poem is an expression of the ineffable whatever its subject – whether Creation or (say) the death of a pet dog. Anything and everything can be seen *sub specie aeternatis*, and in the end needs to be. This is a short poem of our time, on the death of a pet dog:

> Our world's a little breath of day
> That breathes our little world away,
> Yet play and laugh, beauty did dare
> To live so boldly, unaware.

Such words as those of the last line and a half here could hardly be simpler, or their meaning clearer. Yet their meaning could also hardly be richer. The word "beauty" is at once an emphatic loving tribute to the dog and the statement that her beauty is what every living creature possesses, at least potentially, including we human beings who are thus being encouraged and inspired to have play and laughter as the cheerfully innocent core of our lives too. The dog dared all this "unaware" not only of mortality, her own and everyone's and everything's, but also of her own courage and beauty in living as she did, and of the eternity of this beauty as of all beauty. The negative word "unaware" clearly gains a powerful positive force here.

But this is only part of the meaning. More could be said. Clear and rich, the poem's meaning is also a meaning we feel and know we can never come to the end or the bottom of. In the nature of the case. That is what the liberation and sublimity of it are. The presentation is, breathtakingly, of something *of* the wonderful mystery, beauty and terror of life.

"…that extraordinary and wonderful thing in the writing that hits you hard and takes you out of your own possession, enraptures, transports." In a later work, the *Réflexions critiques* of 1715, Boileau expanded on the passage from his Preface to Longinus, to insist that the sublime in poetry can often be in the simplest words, with that almost constituting the sublimity: striking words are so far from being the point that, even, "there are sublime passages in good writers whose grandeur comes from the energy of the words' very smallness and ordinariness." If we have our breaths taken away by

> beauty did dare
> To live so boldly, unaware.

or by

> That breathes our little world away...

these sublime effects would almost certainly not have been achieved if the writing were not so simple and straightforward, and so effortless-seeming. A kind of swiftness seems to be of the essence.[*]

This may come out more clearly by a comparison with another poem of our time and of some distinction (I think it may be one of its writer's best): a poem, though, that I would never think of attributing sublimity to. It is another poem about the death of an innocent, this time of a young child, a younger brother of the poet: "Mid-Term Break" by Seamus Heaney. Neither its greater length nor its handling of the death by the mainly external narration of key moments in the poet's experience of his bereavement is in itself, of course, any sort of weakness, though they may seem more significant if the poem then does not take things anywhere near so far as the other poem does. These are the first six and last seven lines (the whole poem is in Heaney's first book, *Death of a Naturalist*):

> I sat all morning in the college sick bay
> Counting bells knelling classes to a close.
> At two o'clock our neighbours drove me home.
>
> In the porch I met my father crying –
> He had always taken funerals in his stride –

---

[*] For a swift surprise not dissimilar to the quoted ones Dante actually uses almost the same words as this poem's "play and laugh", suddenly springing them on his reader as *the* description of what was lost in the Garden of Eden: "*onesto riso e dolce gioco*" (*Purgatorio*, Canto 28).

And Big Jim Evans saying it was a hard blow...

Next morning I went up into the room. Snowdrops
And candles soothed the bedside; I saw him
For the first time in six weeks. Paler now,

Wearing a poppy bruise on his left temple,
He lay in the four foot box as in his cot.
No gaudy scars, the bumper knocked him clear.

A four foot box, a foot for every year.

If a certain kind of swiftness is of the essence of the other poem's sublimity, that does not necessarily mean that it is literally read faster than "Mid-Term Break". It feels swift because the large amount that is happening in the interactions between its words does not for a moment stop those words from following each other simply and straightforwardly and at an easy, normal-seeming pace. A lot of ground is being covered fast. "Mid-Term Break" does have its own simplicity and straightforwardness, which contribute a lot to such success as it has in being a touching poem. But the reader is aware of these qualities being achieved carefully and deliberately, not effortlessly, and certainly not with the breathtaking effortlessness of the other poem. If that poem is swift, this one is plodding.

It plods in, among other ways, the prosy way it tells its story item by item. The emotional reticence that goes with this is a strength of the poem, but the absence of any subtle interaction between the separate items goes with the poem's taking things so much less far than the short poem does. Just about, we can be touched by the poet's grief over the terrible killing, but we end the poem not really knowing anything about it, each of us almost as much imprisoned in his or her little shell as before we started to read, cut off almost as much as we usually are from feeling and knowing anything of that wonderful terror and beauty and mystery.

I suggest that we are only "just about" touched by the poet's grief because the poem is in some danger of becoming sentimental here. If we think about it for ourselves, we may well be deeply moved by the killing of a four-year-old child in a road accident and the pain of his sibling. But that thinking about it for ourselves is something we would have to be doing at some distance from the poem, not simply as part of reading it. For the poem does not itself lead or enable us to do that thinking about the death that could take us to full moving realisation. And if we then fail to stay clear in mind and feeling, recognising that just about touched is *all* we can be by what we are told, the poem can begin to trade on our knee-jerk, cliché reaction that 'of course' such a death is a deeply moving one – a reaction that, uncontrolled and unilluminated by full realisation, is going to be sentimental.

If it is possible to avoid this, and so feel some relief and gratitude at the absence of any sentimentality that is compulsory, the poem is still an uncomfortably limited one, emotionally both a bit thin and a bit clumsy. On such a subject who wants to plod? In its light swift way the shorter poem is moving about the dog's death, and it is no coincidence that at the same time it gives its sublime apprehension of that divine beauty and mystery – divine, or whatever anyone wants to call it. What grief is full that does not in the end, in one way or another, take the griever to such an apprehension? That strange deep peace might be thought of which, with and through all the pain and all the violent inner protest, so often surprises a person at the bedside of a dying loved one or at the funeral.

The proposition is that at its greatest and most authentic poetry is sublime, and that there is a proof of this in the fact that the more poetic the way in which a poet succeeds in using words – the more magically the words in a poem interact with each other – the more sublime the effect. Heaney's writing is being used as a contrast to set off more clearly the example of this that I believe we have in the other poet's writing. On the basis of only these two poems does it even seem likely that Heaney could never write a sublime poem – and therefore, on these terms, never be much of an authentic poet – whereas there must be a lot to expect from the other poet? This can be put to further tests by comparisons between further poems by these poets (with a minimum of comment).

First, beside Heaney's well-known "Digging" (also from *Death of a Naturalist*), which readers may remember begins with the lines –

Between my finger and my thumb
The squat pen rests; snug as a gun.

Under my window, a clean rasping sound
When the spade sinks into gravelly ground;
My father, digging.

– may be placed both the following shorter poem by the new poet and the longer poem quoted later on her grandmother's 80th birthday:

A man in a yellowing field
Rakes the last cut grasses in the summer light
It's all I remember of the place
In a train I saw the waves of blue twilight,
The hills, fold over him.

Remembering the hills, the drifting light,
The man without a name, there is faith.
The curl of yellow fingers around the rake,
Blue trousers, the face I never saw

Another way of talking about the poetic sublime: while "Digging" never takes off, never leaves the ground, this poem is somehow never on it. And is this another point: that, when this poem about a briefly glimpsed stranger is compared with "Digging", partly written as a tribute to the poet's father and grandfather, it actually seems to have much more love in it, not less?

In this respect Heaney may do better in another poem, the "Sunlight" that is one of two poems with which he dedicates his *North* collection to his mother. There is some beauty here, as on the special peacefulness with which time is passing in the kitchen –

here is a space again,
the scone rising…

– but can the reader fully enjoy this beauty when in so much of the poem the writer is so self-conscious about putting things 'well', so fussily and ploddingly deliberate in expression? It begins:

> There was a sunlit *absence.*

Full stop. Clunk. And it immediately goes on:

> The *helmeted* pump in the yard
> *heated its iron...*

(My italics.) In the poem's last stanza -

> And here is love
> like a tinsmith's scoop
> sunk past its gleam
> in the meal-bin.

– anyone might love to be reminded of the thrill of suddenly seeing the part of such a scoop that usually stays in the meal, thus perfectly and amazingly preserving its shine and avoiding the tarnish of the rest of the tin. And there is a potential beauty in the comparison between this and the poet's thrill of suddenly realising afresh the love in his tired and dowdy-looking mother. But this latter thrill is, I think, difficult to feel in most readings of the poem, the general plodding deliberateness tending to kill the possibility of being caught and surprised by any such magic.

The other poet on her grandmother's 80th birthday:

I

So now a moment of celebration long anticipated comes
In this surprise birthday party today.
Strangers, near family, stand gathered around
Mingled at the table strewn with pastries, while
Here and there a scattering toast to the beauty of time.
Dear Nana, we squander unknowing the hours of our vanishing
Let me summon one moment honored in stillness. Let these word
                                                                    wrap
As sleep around a dream embracing your time grown wish.

From these still words let life spring touched for ever
In depths untouched by the winter air of this November day.

II

Curled upon a chair, fingers clasping the pink soles
Of both feet, once I watched you make an apple pie.
One by one you peeled each surface skin away into its white
                                        fresh roundness
Then, paring each fruit into moist slices, you spoke to me of your
                                        childhood in Poland
Of the encircling valley below the summer farm where you
                                        would run
Gathering up the wild apples for a feast
Where the young sheep grazed beside the sun's white image
Reflected in the still water of the pond
And where in those yellow fields ripening, you would lie so still
                                        listening
To the gathering sounds, until the air's cooling light brought you
                                        to sleep.

III

With each childhood memory, you fingered each apple slice into
                                        the pastry shell
Then, lowering the top crest over the swell, you pressed
Deep furrows around the dough with the yellow tips
Of your four fingers. Your movements were too beautiful for
                                        speaking, Nana, I
Could not be with you. Looking away through the kitchen
                                        window
Misting with warming winter steam, I saw the air of the yellow
                                        sun's fingering
Move into a beauty twilight brings.
In the kitchen, pushing the finished pie aside, looking outwards,
You sighed. Outstretching a still moist hand you wiped the
                                        window with your fingers

And the room filled with the yellow light of winter.

IV

Now I too sigh as the day sinks down
Down into the stillness of the evening.
Yet here in this birthday gathering
Let us not forget
Moving in happiness and joy
Amid the encircling limits of death.
Dear Nana, I reach out my hand to you
I will remember your wish
Lengthening in the unfolding dusk
Of shadows of gathering light.

The words "stillness" and "still" might be picked out and set against that fussily deliberate writing in "Sunlight". Perhaps these lines –

Dear Nana, we squander unknowing the hours of our vanishing
Let me summon one moment honored in stillness.

– say what Heaney at his best is always trying to say but can hardly be imagined proving able to.

A last poem by the new poet is something of a small manifesto, evidently written after suffering in a university English department. (It was Cambridge's.) Though the poet does not use the word "sublime", is her idea of poetry the same? and even in this little squib of a poem is there again something of the thing itself?

They speak a sophistry for want of some
Intention in their words, teaching us
That poetry is just a clever bag
Of tricks. And all the while one
Can hear them calculate the words they say
Into the consequence and measure of
Their own ambition's
Gain.

But death gains nothing, just the fragile soul:
"The world will be saved by beauty,"
And nothing else
At all.

I choose Heaney's poems to help set off the sublime in the new poetry because they are well-known and easily looked up – and because I can hardly do this Nobel-Prize-winner much harm. Of this new poetry no one has yet heard because, the interest in sublime poetry being what it currently is in the U.S. and British poetry 'scenes', it has not been in print. The writer is American: Joanne Weiss.

2. THE REVELATORY: "*POETS* ARE *PROPHETS*? NOT IN *OUR* SMART POETRY SCENE!"

This second argument is almost exclusively, like the latter part of the first, argument by juxtaposition. One of the reasons for including it is that this particular use of the word "sublime" comes out of the artistic and literary world's talk about itself, so that the question whether all authentic poetry is sublime could seem to be one only likely to concern those already reading poetry and thinking about it. Fully to bring out how poetry matters to everybody requires the further step of suggesting how poetry is revelatory. Much has already been said on this apropos of the sublime, but the idea may be worth some full statement and illustration by itself – partly because it seems a laughable idea in relation to the present little U.S. and British poetry 'scenes'. It is, of course, an ancient and a worldwide idea. I doubt that the renewal of poetry that is always needed from time to time and is certainly needed now can take place without it.

A further preface to this section is five simple words of Wordsworth's describing revelation. He is not writing directly about poetry but, here and in the whole long sentence that ends with these words in his Tintern Abbey "Lines", is describing something that we all of us wish and need to do and have our lives centred by doing: "see into the life of things."

The section is an invitation to read four poems, both with each other and in a setting made by certain quotations in prose, the latter from texts I was at the time of writing reading with students in a 'great books' course.[*] Its title invokes a proposition put forward by a colleague in that same course, in a lecture on the Prophetic Books of the Hebrew Bible or Old Testament: that not only are those prophets great poets, but also all great poets are prophets. One might even use a word that, like many faculty as well as students, I first learnt the meaning of in that course, and contend that every great poem is a theophany, an appearance of God, the gods, the divine life of the world, whatever you want to call it – every great poem and not only the great poetry that directly presents itself as a theophany, spoken out of the whirlwind in Chapters 38 to 41 of *The Book of Job* or giving Arjuna's vision in the Eleventh Teaching of the *Bhagavad Gita*. By themselves the poems that are going to be juxtaposed here are also, obviously, too special a case to support the whole general contention. Its application to another kind of great poetry, the outrageously comic, is treated in later parts of this book.

The first prose quotations are from Augustine's account in Book IX of his *Confessions* of certain special moments enjoyed with his mother shortly before her death, and from his discussion of eternity in Book XI:

> As the flame of love burned stronger in us and raised us higher towards the eternal God, our thoughts ranged over the whole compass of material things in their various degrees, up to the heavens themselves from which the sun and the moon and the stars shine down upon the earth. Higher still we climbed, thinking and speaking all the while in wonder at all that you have made. At length we came to our own souls and passed

[*] That 'great books' course was the Humanities section of Boston University's Core Curriculum. This little piece on the revelatory was first put together for an informal evening occasion when, as used to happen most years, some of the professors read favourite poems to students and colleagues. The piece is dedicated, in warm intellectual tribute and gratitude, to the person who is probably more responsible than everyone else put together for that Core programme's having been one to treasure being involved with, and who was retiring after his many years of directing it: Brian Jorgensen. He was the lecturer I am about to cite on the Hebrew prophets.

beyond them to that place of everlasting plenty, where you feed Israel for ever with the food of truth. There life is that Wisdom by which all these things that we know are made, all things that ever have been and all that are yet to be. But that Wisdom is not made: it is as it has always been and as it will be forever – or, rather, I should not say that it *has been* or *will be*, for it simply is, because eternity is not in the past or in the future. And while we spoke of the eternal Wisdom, longing for it and straining for it with all the strength of our hearts, for one fleeting instant we reached out and touched it.

[Some people] do not yet understand how the things are made which come to be in you and through you. Try as they may to savour the taste of eternity, their thoughts still twist and turn upon the ebb and flow of things in past and future time. But if only their minds could be seized and held steady, they would be still for a while and, for that short moment, they would glimpse the splendour of eternity which is for ever still. (The Penguin translation by R.S.Pine-Coffin)

In its own way each of the following four poems creates such a moment. Another poem that does so and also at some length discusses such moments is, of course, T.S.Eliot's "Burnt Norton".

The first poem is by the great 16th-century Spanish poet, John of the Cross, translated by the South-Africa-born British poet, the late F.T.Prince, one of the very rare good British poets of our times (though probably more appreciated in New York than in London)[*]:

Songs of the Soul

Darkness covered all,
But for my heart with flames enwound,

---

[*] Prince's translation from John of the Cross was published in his *Soldiers Bathing and other poems* (1954) and subsequently in *The Cambridge Quarterly* IV 1, each time with other translations by him from the same poet.

When I went free from thrall -
O happy chance! – and fled unfound,
For all the house and household slumbered sound.

Darkness covered all,
But I the secret ladder found
In safety, by the wall -
O happy chance! – and reached the ground,
And still the house and household slumbered
                                                           sound.

So in the dead of night
I won my way, by none discerned,
Nor by myself, for light
Nor guide could show the way I learned -
Unless the light that in my bosom burned.

Led on by that alone
As if by noonday's bright degree,
I came where one unknown,
Whom yet I knew, waited for me,
And there none saw, for there were none to see.

O night that was my guide,
More lovely than the dawn of day!
Whose darkness brought the Bride
To her Beloved, showed the way,
And changed one to the other where they lay!

For there upon my breast
Whose flowers for him alone I kept,
He laid his head in rest;
And with my arms about him slept,
Lulled by the airs that from the cedars crept.

From the dark tower the air
Came softly down, and blew aside

The soft locks of his hair:
And then when he had touched my side,
I felt a wound so sweet, it seemed I died.

Forgetting and forgot,
My face I buried in his breast:
Abandoned to my lot,
I cast off all that I possessed,
And lay and with the lilies took my rest.

The momentary touching of eternity can also occur (perhaps in a degree always does) in an experience that may sometimes be thought of too slightingly, nostalgia, and is created in Tennyson's well-known poem on the subject:

Tears, idle tears, I know not what they mean,
Tears from the depth of some divine despair
Rise in the heart, and gather to the eyes,
In looking on the happy Autumn-fields,
And thinking of the days that are no more.

Fresh as the first beam glittering on a sail,
That brings our friends up from the underworld,
Sad as the last which reddens over one
That sinks with all we love below the verge;
So sad, so fresh, the days that are no more.

Ah, sad and strange as in dark summer dawns
The earliest pipe of half-awakened birds
To dying ears, when unto dying eyes
The casement slowly grows a glimmering square;
So sad, so strange, the days that are no more.

Dear as remembered kisses after death,
And sweet as those by hopeless fancy feigned
On lips that are for others; deep as love,
Deep as first love, and wild with all regret;

O Death in Life, the days that are no more.

(To those who may doubt that there is anything prophetic in Tennyson's poem I would recommend suggestive statements the poet himself made on his poem, quoted in Christopher Ricks's edition of *The Poems of Tennyson*.)

A few more words from Augustine's *Confessions* preface the last two poems. In Book VIII he records how he and a companion were first told about the great saint of the Egyptian desert, Antony, and writes, again addressing his God, "For our part, we… were astonished to hear of the wonders you had worked so recently, almost in our own times…"

This next poem, of our own times, starts from a sudden ecstatic noticing of ordinary human movements and actions and of that extraordinary pure thing in them, life.

From every gesture breathes a god so beautiful
He dies into the delicate invisible
And so we weep, or touch, or laugh, unaware and lovely
In a vanishing of miracles.

Oh my beautiful, stay with me
Do not let the world again fold into darkess
Open each word like a wing into flame
For I want to hold and remember this vanishing hour.

Oh beauty, oh memory, carry me into your silence
I will tell no one where you take me
I will keep you buried in some secret, sacred ground
In the light-tipped loveliness of a stranger's eyes

In this moment of perfect remembering.
Here, the wilted leaf of the pansy, here red wine,
       chrysanthemums
In water blooming. I want no more.
Years of striving become a moment poised upon infinity.

In the following poem, by the same poet, the special moment does not come with any sudden ecstasy but is something quieter and calmer, even subdued: eternity somehow apprehended as the perspective within which to look back on one's life to date, the inner strength and clarity and beauty of doing this perhaps come upon by the poet in a struggle with grief and the confusion attending it. (I suspect the poem may be a little influenced, probably unconsciously, by what happens to have been another text in that 'Great Books' course, the *Tao Te Ching*.)

My mind has been a clear stream flowing.
In the winter it has been sparkling icy, piercing to touch, and
                                                                hard.
But in the summer it changes into a fragrant balm of sensual
                                                pleasure unparalleled
When I dip my body naked into its curling waters.
In the spring it strokes my stiff limbs like a healing hand
Softening, melting the ache of effortful days,
And in the autumn the dying summer sky lays its colours down
Into its playful reflection, shimmering still with a youthfulness
Lost by all else.
Yes, my mind has been a clear stream flowing
And I dip my pen into its waters
Remembering.

This poet is Joanne Weiss again. My closing prose quotation from another of that course's 'great books' puts the indictment of the tenth-rateness and fraudulence of the present U.S. and British poetry 'scenes' that are represented by the fact that almost nothing of her extensive writing is even in print.

But woe to you, scribes and Pharisees, hypocrites! for you shut the kingdom of heaven against your fellow human beings, neither entering yourselves nor allowing to enter those who otherwise would...
Woe to you, scribes and Pharisees, hypocrites! for you are like whited sepulchres, looking good and impressive enough but

inside containing only matter that is dead and stinks.

Woe to you, scribes and Pharisees, hypocrites! for you erect splendid tombs to the prophets and elaborate monuments to the other great moral heroes and heroines of the past, saying, If we had been alive then, *we* would never have been among those making life miserable or impossible for these wonderful people. In so doing and speaking, you are only witnessing against yourselves: that you are all too recognisably the direct descendants of those who murdered the prophets.

Or, in other words, very slightly adapted from words of W.B. Yeats's about all the experts on poets and prophets:

Lord, what would they say
Did their Catullus walk *their* way?

3. POETRY IS NOT FOR THE LITERATI BUT FOR PEOPLE IN GENERAL: IN HONOUR OF THE LATE ALLEN GINSBERG

In Britain and the U.S. it is not so long ago that poetry did again, for a time, both command large general audiences and deserve to do so.

A consequence of this was that a self-appointed young doyen of the British poetry scene wrote, in an anonymous though, I think, all too easily identifiable review in the *Times Literary Supplement*, that Allen Ginsberg, it was now clear, had more to do with the history of advertising than with the history of poetry.

I cite the major example and inspiration of Ginsberg, and add two little bits of anecdotal evidence in further support of the proposition in this section's title.

The director of the distinguished and popular film, *Four Weddings and a Funeral*, had the delivery of a sixteen-line poem of W.H. Auden's "Stop all the clocks, cut off the telephone" recited by one of the characters at the funeral of his gay lover. When it came out, I saw the film in a fairly crowded popular cinema, and was aware that this beautifully created moment was far from turning most of the audience off and, on the contrary, was intensifying concentration. That special stillness was unmistakable.

In the larger family and acquaintance of the grandmother for whose 80th birthday Joanne Weiss wrote the poem quoted above on pp39-41 there is either very little reading of poetry or none at all. There was nevertheless the strongest wish that she should give another public reading aloud of the poem after her grandmother's death, at the funeral service.

4. THE REVELATORY: AN ANCIENT AND WORLDWIDE IDEA OF POETRY

I offer illustrations from ancient Greece, not in the form of explicit statements made there about poetry but in a very elementary description of things its actual poetry does. Here it is the surviving poetry of its tragedians, including the 'Homer' whom Plato writes of as one of them. The first is a main powerful effect that is made as *The Odyssey*, in Books 17 to 20, approaches the climax of the story it is telling, and the second is that paradox of tragic drama whereby, at an adequate performance of a great tragic play, the audience's spirits are raised rather than cast down.

(1) At the beginning of Book 17 of *The Odyssey* the hero, at long last back in Ithaka, has just been reunited with his now more or less grown-up son Telemakhos, and is making the extremely dangerous move of going to his own house. In it his loyal and loving wife Penelope is beleaguered by the large host of unwelcome suitors, who for years have been plundering the house with endless feasting in it, as guests who will not and cannot be got rid of. Because of the danger from them, Odysseus is having to go there in his disguise as a battered old beggar. While those suitors number well over a hundred, he has finally arrived back on the island completely on his own, having lost on the terrible journey home every one of the fellow-Ithakans who had gone with him to the Trojan War and survived it.

From the beginning of that crucial move towards his house one dramatic irony follows another. These are most powerfully at the expense of the suitors, and of servants of theirs, equally assured, brutal and insolent in their attitudes to the house and family that are being ripped off by them all. But some ironies are also at the expense of Odysseus himself and his family. In one episode, in Book 18, he in his disguise has observed that one of the suitors is behaving quite a bit less obnoxiously than the others and he therefore, admirably, wants to try to save him from the slaughter he knows has to be made. So he takes the risk of making a speech to him that, without giving anything away, warns him of the likely consequences of the appalling behaviour of himself and these other predators. And he does get through to the man, who feels the deadly chill of the truth he is being reminded of. But he does not feel it quite enough – to act decisively on it by straightaway getting out of that house. There is the dramatic irony that the fate this suitor is being warned of in vain is actually imminent, since the seemingly powerless beggar who is giving him the warning is himself the extremely powerful and resourceful person he is being warned against. But there is also the dramatic irony that Odysseus himself does not know how vain his attempt to save this life is, since the goddess Athena is determined that all these predators should get killed and is actually paralysing this particular suitor's impulse to get away.

At the end of Book 20, Odysseus in his disguise, Penelope and Telemakhos are all, separately, watching and hearing the suitors as they go to new extremes of outrageous blind assurance and insultingness, laughing uproariously as they drink and crow and mock – even as they are being warned by a stranger, who is not in the know about the disguised beggar but has prophetic powers that are enabling him to see that destruction is just round the corner for them. The gap between the suitors' actual position and their extreme confidence is a dramatic irony of tremendous effect. But also frightening and awe-inspiring is the fact that none of the Odysseus family knows that it is Athena again who is at work, driving the suitors to be more and more outrageous so that in the impending showdown there will be no question of either Odysseus or his son not being utterly determined or anything but merciless.

Nobody now believes there is literally a goddess called Athena, but in each of these passages what she is said to be feeling and doing is profoundly 'true', vividly and powerfully making manifest something deep in the nature of things. While a good person like

Odysseus does not want to have to kill such a person as this less obnoxious suitor, whose life he therefore tries to save, the nature of things, or the justice of life, can be much less merciful. The good family man or woman who is normally kindly and principled enough gets caught up like many others around in, say, Nazi activities and, though both warned about how evil the activities are and feeling much of the warning's force, is nevertheless not courageous or decisive enough to get out of his involvement in time, and is among those rounded up at the end of World War II and punished as a criminal. In the episode at the end of Book 20 the new extreme of outrageousness that the suitors *en masse* are led into, their hearts hardened by Athena as Pharaoh's heart is said in *Exodus* to have been hardened by God, makes sense because these men cannot be wholly unaware of the new things happening at this time in Odysseus' house but, choosing not to attend to them, are led by them only to act the more defiantly. Often the way that the gods harden the hearts of sinners?

In a brief description, and without all that Homer does in the way he composes this whole part of his poem, with, among other things, his wonderful control of pace, little idea can be given of just how deeply thrilling these and other dramatic ironies are. But enough may have been said to suggest how a part of what is so deeply thrilling is the sense created of a powerful and terrible inevitability. Nothing can save any of these suitors. Their blindly confident defiance only makes that the more certain. And the admirable decency and humaneness of Odysseus also cannot make any difference, or allow there to be even a single exception. Things have gone too far, and the forces and laws of life that are involved are beyond the ordinarily human – and are this in spite of the fact that the vengeance life takes on the suitors is mainly going to be enacted by human beings: by Odysseus, his son and two loyal servants, and by the Penelope who does not even know who the beggar is but somehow comes out with the all-important idea about how, in the showdown, the overwhelming disadvantage in numbers may be overcome. She makes a striking contrast with the suitors because, equally in the dark, she has nevertheless been picking up the kind of hints that something is afoot which they have been blithely disregarding, and she then courageously, hardly knowing what she is doing, makes her crucial, brilliant contribution. The dramatic ironies are thrilling because they are revelatory of the deep forces and laws of life, mysterious and beyond us and most of the time unknown to us but made manifest to us here. We are seeing into the life of things.

(2) The paradox of tragic art is that human beings find pleasure and reward in contemplating and imaginatively living through something that is terrifying and heart-breaking. Members of the audience leave the theatre with their spirits raised rather than cast down when the creation of the terror and heartbreak has conformed with the laws of tragic art and thus brought them through to some ultimate – however intangible and inexpressible – 'truth', a truth apprehended with a wonderful sense of both release and peace. This evidently does not happen when, as it all too easily can be, painful subject-matter is handled *un*truthfully – sensationally or sentimentally or clumsily.

Two of the explanations that have been offered for this paradox are clearly non-starters: that at a tragedy we avoid sheer painful distress by making the secret reflection to ourselves that none of these terrible and heart-breaking things is happening to us, or else by reflecting that what is happening on the stage is not really happening. These options we have, insofar as we really do have them, are certainly no more than negative pre-conditions of the positive effect of tragedy. They are not even absolutely necessary pre-conditions, since the positive cathartic effect can exist not only in the experience of art but also in life, where there are no such options at all and the distressing thing is both really happening and happening to us. While our use of the word "cathartic" must in the main derive from Aristotle's writing in the *Poetics* of the "catharsis" of painful emotions effected by tragic drama, we do evidently give the adjective a wider application – and, in fact, now use it much more often of experiences in life than of experiences in art.

But, if "catharsis" is a better explanation for that paradox of tragic art, how exactly does it explain it?

Aristotle doesn't elaborate on what he means. His idea is probably, among other things, an implicit answer to Plato's criticism of tragic drama (in *The Republic*) that it feeds and waters the emotions that we human beings should be concerned to control and check. No, Aristotle answers, those plays do arouse terror and upsetting concern for someone but they do so with the effect of purging these emotions.

He writes no more about how this "catharsis" is a positive effect. The Greek word *was* used not only of physical purging but also of psychological, moral and religious purification, and Aristotle does briefly use the word in this way, apropos of music, at the end of his *Politics*. But we cannot be sure just how close his idea of the positive effect is to ours. It is our definite if not perfectly clear idea that from a cathartic experience a person emerges not only with some release from the painful emotions involved but even feeling better than before the suffering of them, and better *for* having suffered them. In addition to the feeling of a purified and enhanced life and a rare deep peace, there is also, and even if little or nothing can be put into words, more understanding. The person can feel that in a blessed way, and for a moment, he or she is seeing into the life of things.

One law of tragic art is that it must create a special sense of finality. The fact that many tragic plays end with the deaths of their protagonists is clearly no coincidence, even though such a death is not an indispensable requirement and the finality may be achieved in another way. The sense of it seems to be a sense of an ultimate limit having been reached and crossed and of something being thereby broken in us. The terror and heartbreak go clearly beyond the limit of what would ordinarily seem tolerable, and yet the powerful tragic art is allowing us no option or desire but to go through with it and not pull out. We are being simultaneously broken and made whole, or (in another metaphor) are stopped dead in our tracks – in our ordinary thought and feeling and whole way of apprehending life – and are into something different that we do not normally know about.

I will end on this with a joke of an equation:

Catharsis = having one's mind blown in an exceptionally decisive and complete way
= the death of the ego
= seeing God.

The "ego" here is the part of us that is consciously in control and looking after us, and hoping and fearing and being anxious. "God" is an optional shorthand for the pure and eternal essence of things, "the life of things".

A final note here and a qualification. The note goes back to Athena in *The Odyssey* as well as to that shorthand in the equation. All the presentation in great poetry of the workings of God or the gods is a presentation not only of the permanent conditions and laws of life but also of the mysterious coherence and sense these conditions and laws are felt to make, for all the powerful things that seem to contradict and cry out that they do not make any sense at all. The coherence and sense that they make are mysterious because we feel and even, at our fullest stretch, know that they make them but never fathom how. We can hardly begin to find words for it. Or the only words for it are the words of poets.

The qualification is that, if all tragic art is fundamentally religious, it is not religious either in a conventionally and comfortably doctrinal way or in a conventionally and comfortably 'pious' way. It implicitly challenges the claims in conventional religious doctrine to know more than human beings can know, and it is evidently much too tough-minded and emotionally unsparing to be compatible with anything that is the least bit cosy.

5. THE MISLEADINGNESS OF THE WORLD'S 'SACRED TEXTS', AND ALSO OF SHAKESPEARE

Besides the low standards dominating those current poetry 'scenes', there are much older things that have also helped to obscure the revelatory nature of good poetry: notably (1) various religions' separating off certain writings as 'sacred texts' and (2) Shakespeare's relative lack of any great interest in wisdom. The former cannot help suggesting that there is nothing sacred or revelatory in *other* texts, and that can seem to be confirmed when the best-loved poet of the modern West is at once bardolatrously treated as the supreme poet of all time and, with some encouragement from him, thought of all too commonly and readily as almost wholly a secular poet.

Justice needs to be done to the large measure of historical accident that there has been in some great poetry's finding its way into 'sacred texts' and some great poetry's not doing so. As in the Bible, poetry sometimes finds its way in alongside the writing of law, of legend and history, and of moral and other practical precept; and it must be acknowledged that, for all the great differences, there cannot be a quite absolute and clear-cut distinction between that poetry and these other kinds of writing in such a 'sacred text'. Nevertheless, the poetry of the first stories in *Genesis*, the *Psalms*, *Job*, *The Song of Solomon* and the Bible's prophetic books is writing that has very much *more* in common with the poetry of Homer and the Greek tragedians, and it is not sacred or revelatory in a different sense or in a different way from their poetry – or, in fact, from Shakespeare's.

It is the general modern assumption about poetry, not only about Shakespeare's, that it is mainly something secular. A kind of separate compartment tends to be made in the mind, sometimes a bit condescendingly, for what then gets called 'devotional poetry' – with that condescension sometimes partly merited because much of this poetry is less powerfully beautiful. But that very fact means that it is also *less* sacred, *less* revelatory. Ever since coming across it, I have been delighted by Leslie Stephen's writing in a letter that he dislikes George Herbert's poetry because the poet seems "always to be skulking behind the Thirty-Nine Articles" of the Church of England. Stephen was not only being his sturdy late-Victorian agnostic self here: he was also writing of a serious limitation that the poems have, for all their charm and touchingness, in poetic and religious power.

If Shakespeare is less interested in wisdom than most great poets, that does not mean that his outstanding gifts are finally for anything else or that his work does not yield much impressive wisdom. He is certainly among the supreme poets who set the standards, and he is naturally the one turned to first by someone whose language is English (as he is turned to by me in the next chapter). But turning to him first too easily becomes turning to him as if he were *the* unique supreme poet, with a greatness somehow quite beyond that of any other of the world's unique supreme poets, unlimited while the greatness of all the others is limited. And that makes the limitations that his own work has the more seriously misleading, particularly the main limitation that all over his work he shows himself in favour of playing around and taking relatively easy lines.

It is difficult to put this point fairly because there can be so much great and sublime wisdom in that very unseriousness of Shakespeare's, as also in his celebration of unseriousness. But perhaps this is suggestive: that, at the height of his powers, his compelling inspiration to return to tragedy seems to come upon him against his will and to be resisted and struggled against even as it is also being followed. The revelations of the great tragedies from *Hamlet* to *Macbeth* are wonderful ones and increasingly complete and clear as the series of them goes on, but the fact that he is being dragged into writing these plays shows in some serious uncertainty, unevenness and unclarity in the writing, and there is hardly the easy sureness and confidence that revelation is what each of the plays is being written for that can be found in Greek tragedies – and that Shakespeare himself has already shown in comedy, exceptionally, when at his fullest stretch and most profound in it, in *A Midsummer Night's Dream* and *The Merchant of Venice.* (I write on this last play in the next chapter and on Shakespeare's tragedies in Chapter V.)

Here I insert a little anecdote about the grace of poetry and the misleadingness of conventional ideas of the sacred. The first time I went to an Episcopalian church in the U.S., which was the first time I had been to any church for many years, was fairly recent and for a Christmas Eve service that my wife and I were being taken to by the good friends who had invited us to spend Christmas with them. I cannot do enough justice to what an attractive occasion the service was in many respects, in a church that was fairly large and absolutely packed: there was plenty of warm good feeling, and dignity without any strained formality; the priest struck no false or pretentious notes and seemed an almost ideally genuine, sensible and decent person to be leading things; the Nativity story was read, sung and listened to with affection and respect; the music, instrumental as well as sung, may have been a bit short on power but was pleasant, and it was pleasant that time was being given to it; the communion seemed to be taken by the large number of people who did take it with some quiet and deep pleasure in the fact that, while each person took it individually, they were all at the same time joining each other and being a community as they did so.

It could not help coming over me, however, how completely cut off I felt from anything holy. As something of an agnostic outsider, I was likely, of course, to be slower than most of the other people to feel anything special that was there to be felt, but I am sure that I would not have been completely unaware of real power if there had been any. I am thirsty enough for that, and I knew fairly quickly that its absence here was coming over me so particularly clearly and strongly because of a contrast: with the great closeness to things holy that I had often experienced in the university semester I was just then coming from, reading and thinking and talking about great poetry – about that in the early *Genesis* stories and in *Job*, and about that of the Greek tragic poets, Plato (in his *Gorgias* as well as *The Symposium* and *The Republic*), Virgil and Dante.

A further illustration, from Virgil, can be brief. Down in Hades to meet the shade of his father Anchises, Aeneas exclaims in disbelief in the Elysian Fields when his father tells him that certain long lines of shades are waiting to cross the river Lethe and be reborn into life on earth. How could anyone possibly be willing to experience life again? In suddenly sharp focus for a moment, in Aeneas' short but vehement three-line speech, is all the bitter blackness there is in Virgil's representation of human life, both in the long half of the poem that precedes this moment and in the long half of it that is to follow. To his son Anchises explains the cycles of death and rebirth and, as he does so, we are suddenly into one of poetry's most thrilling 'theophanies', and into the core of the whole long epic poem. It is the more powerful because of the combination of, on the one hand, the surprise with which it is suddenly and completely there for us and, on the other, our strong if obscure knowledge that what we are now apprehending has actually been there all the time, as somehow the most essential thing in all the terror, heartbreak and weariness. In these lines, at any rate when they are read in the full context and in the Latin, there is no doubt that we are, in the very depths of our beings, meeting and knowing the pure holiness of life and feeling ourselves at one with it. Even in translation and in extract, separated from all the rest of the tremendous tragic vision of life presented in the epic, which is needed for the lines' full power to be felt, the lines may still be found sublime.

> First, then, the sky and lands and sheets of water,
> The bright moon's globe, the Titan sun and stars,
> Are fed within by Spirit, and a Mind
> Infused through all the members of the world

Makes one great living body of the mass.
From Spirit come the races of man and beast,
The life of birds, odd creatures the deep sea
Contains beneath her sparkling surfaces,
And fiery energy from a heavenly source
Belongs to the generative seeds of these,
So far as they are not poisoned or clogged
By mortal bodies, their free essence dimmed
By earthiness and deathliness of flesh.
This makes them fear and crave, rejoice and grieve.
Imprisoned in the darkness of the body
They cannot clearly see heaven's air; in fact
Even when life departs on the last day
Not all the scourges of the body pass
From the poor souls, not all distress of life.
Inevitably, many malformations,
Growing together in mysterious ways,
Become inveterate. Therefore they undergo
The discipline of punishments and pay
In penance for old sins: some hang full length
To the empty winds, for some the stain of wrong
Is washed by floods or burned away by fire.
We suffer each his own shade. We are sent
Through wide Elysium, where a few abide
In happy lands, till the long day, the round
Of Time fulfilled, has worn our stains away,
Leaving the soul's heaven-sent perception clear,
The fire from heaven pure. These other souls,
When they have turned Time's wheel a thousand years,
The god calls in a crowd to Lethe stream,
That there unmemoried they may see again
The heavens and wish re-entry into bodies.

I think the translator here, Robert Fitzgerald, does particularly well with certain poetically crucial phrases: "fed within by Spirit," "fiery energy from a heavenly source," and "Leaving the soul's heaven-sent perception clear."

The same pure holiness of life is being met and imaginatively united with, if in varying lesser degrees of fullness and intensity, in all the poems quoted complete in this chapter's first two sections – as also in this poem:

> Weekday commotion churns
> the surface of the lake.
> But on Sundays early, look
> deep into the still, clear,
> more than water till more than
> mysteries are disclosed,
> and the one watching has
> more than seen, become.
> Arrived at a better state.
> It is incorruptible: it can't
> be made use of or kept,
> only sometimes regained –
> but never impatiently.
> In tune for a time with what
> lies beyond reach of time.

Readers may have noticed another equation that is being proposed, particularly since the church came in: sublime = revelatory = sacred = holy.

6. PROPHECY IN COMEDY?

As suggested earlier, the actual thing, whatever it is to be called, can also be met and imaginatively united with in outrageous poetic comedy. It seems to me to be there in the high comedy and fantasy of, among other works, Plato's *The Symposium*, Chaucer's *The House of Fame* and *The Wife of Bath's Tale*, *A Midsummer Night's Dream* and *The Merchant of Venice*, *Così fan tutte*, perhaps Fellini's *8½*... It is also there – breathtaking, delightful and fulfilling – when, after all the very different creation that has preceded, each of *The Odyssey* and *The Book of Job* ends extraordinarily with a bold and brief light *presto*. "What on earth is going on here?" – or some exhilarated inner exclamation to the same effect – must be part of the response when, for example, the reader is told that Job's three new daughters are beautiful, is given their names (as does not happen with any of all his other children), and these beautiful names are from love-language, perfumery and cosmetics.

That actual thing can also be there in the comedy or wit of much shorter poems, as in the bouncy lightness and sublimity with which the older Dryden, in the last stanza of a poem on music, is suddenly writing of the end of the world –

> …So when the last and dreadful hour
> This crumbling Pageant shall devour,
> The TRUMPET shall be heard on high
> The dead shall live, the Living die,
> And MUSICK shall untune the Sky.
>> (From "A Song for St Cecilia's Day," 1687)

– or, in another poem, is dismissing the seventeenth century just as it ends:

> …Thy Wars brought nothing about,
> Thy lovers were all untrue.
> 'Tis well an old Age is out,
> And time to begin a New.
>> (From "the Secular Masque")

The same pure holiness of life… There is an obvious resemblance between the breathtaking swiftness of such a phrase as "This crumbling Pageant" and the swiftness in the first poem quoted in this chapter -

> That breathes our little world away

– a resemblance the more interesting and striking because the modern poem seems to be written quite independently, whereas "Weekday commotion churns" does have its echoes of Eliot's "Burnt Norton".

7. CODA

The poorness of the contemporary poetic 'scenes' in the U.S. and the

U.K. means that good poetry that does get into print may still not be heard of by most of its potential readers. I have to acknowledge this, and the fact that some qualification – I cannot know how much – must therefore be needed to the sweeping dismissal in this chapter's first sentence of "the vast quantity of new verse that gets published every year." The acknowledgment is in the quoting of the beautiful "Weekday commotion churns". It was sent to me by the poet, John Freeman, after I had written the rest of the chapter, in a group of not yet published poems but together with books of his poems and a collection of his reviews and articles on other off-'scene' contemporary poetry, *The Less Received: Neglected Modern Poets*. ["Weekday commotion churns" has now been published, in the sequence of poems it belongs to, "A Suite For Summer," which gives its title to Freeman's most recent collection of poems, published by the Worple Press.]

Chapter II
Our prejudice against poetry

This chapter's subject is not the particular prejudices of a particular time, but the permanent prejudice against poetry that arises from risk-taking's being at the core of the writing and reading of it. The following identification and analysis of this permanent prejudice are Shakespeare's in *The Merchant of Venice*, first of all in the play's fairy-tale test of the three caskets.

If I may remind the reader, the rich and beautiful Portia is courted by many suitors, but her late father has laid it down that she can only marry the man who chooses the right one of these caskets. They are of gold, silver and lead, and in the right one is a miniature portrait of her. The only clue that is given to any suitor attempting the test, besides the difference between the metals, is the different mottoes on the caskets' outsides: the gold one's "Who chooseth me, shall gain what many men desire," the silver one's "Who chooseth me, shall get as much as he deserves," and on the lead casket that contains the portrait: "Who chooseth me, must give and hazard all he hath." The choice is very much a leap in the dark, and the stakes are high. Portia's hand is to be won but, on the other side, any suitor attempting the test has to swear beforehand that, if unsuccessful, he will not only keep what he now knows to himself but bind himself never to marry at all. We are told of several would-be suitors who have decided not to take that risk and have simply backed out. Then we see two noble princes venturing unsuccessfully, one choosing the gold and the other the silver. While there is comedy here, I believe it is a serious mistake whenever in a production of the play these two unhappy princes are allowed no dignity and made simply ridiculous. In their love for Portia they are strong and generous enough to take the risk of losing all prospect of marriage and children and, if only in a small way in this comedy-fable, are moving in their failures. Taking the risk, they are nevertheless not able or willing to go right through with it and risk absolutely everything, as the eventual successful suitor is: Bassanio, the young man from Venice who is not put off by either the lead or its motto. We may be reminded of the New Testament: "He that findeth his life shall lose it; and he that loseth his life for my sake shall find it."

It could be said that the complete risk Bassanio takes is only a symbolic one, or that at best his choice of the lead casket expresses only a willingness to take that risk. In the plot of the play the real complete risk is taken by his good friend Antonio, the merchant of Venice who has lent him the money he needs for his expenses as a suitor and mortgaged his own life in order to borrow the necessary funds. These have come from the money-lender Shylock, who as a guarantee for the loan has required that, if it is not repaid by the right date, he can cut a pound of flesh from Antonio's body – which could be fatal and is certainly intended by him to be so.

Antonio and Shylock have fundamentally opposed attitudes to life. Antonio is loving, generous and risk-taking and helps young lovers; Shylock is fearful and mean, will never take any risk, and in his house locks up his beautiful nubile daughter as well as his money and jewels. Their very difference of profession is a symbol. Antonio is a wealthy merchant but with all his wealth out, hazarded, at risk – in the form of rich cargoes at sea that can at any time be lost to shipwreck or piracy. In the play's first scene there are lovely lines in which another Venetian tells Antonio how worried he would be if he was in the same position. When he went to church, the very stone of the building would make him think straightaway of

> ...dangerous rocks,
> Which touching but my gentle vessel's side
> Would scatter all her spices on the stream,
> Enrobe the roaring waters with my silks,
> And in a word, but even now worth this,
> And now worth nothing.

Shylock does not deal in beautiful spices and silks but in ugly-sounding "ducats", those sheer hard coins that he accumulates and hoards, and lends out only at high interest and on excellent security.

The only passion that overcomes his intense, fearful possessiveness is the passion to defend himself in it, the passion of murderous hate he feels towards the man whose scorn for it and very different conduct of his own life are a profound challenge and reproach. His loan to Antonio is one he prefers not to have repaid, because then he will be able, as he hopes, legally to kill him. (In a note at the end of the chapter I give reasons for questioning both the common sentimentalising of Shylock in performance and the excessive and distorting concern either to get Shakespeare off the hook of anti-Semitism or to make sure he is well hung on it.)

The character of Antonio has been thought to be something of a self-portrait by Shakespeare. In his love and solicitude for his young friend Bassanio, he has much in common with the Shakespeare who in the greater number of his collection of sonnets is addressing a beautiful younger man, sometimes pressing him to marry, often showing a striking selflessness in the love for him that he expresses, and often, too, just as Antonio is at the beginning of the play, deeply melancholy. Though this idea can be little more than speculation, it is attractive – among other reasons, because it could help to explain Shakespeare's readiness in this play to make material splendour and high social position symbols of spiritual worth. (The young man of the sonnets appears to be an aristocrat, and this at a date when the aristocracy could combine a magnificent style of life with a dubious or poor financial position, like Bassanio's.) I mention the speculation to introduce a different idea that seems to me more than speculation: that in this play Shakespeare, among other things, is meditating on the nature and value of poetry. Do those quoted lines about Antonio's possible loss of his precious cargoes at sea partly express a poet's fears about writing for that public theatre? It could be said that *prima facie* it is unlikely that Shakespeare would have been contrasting two such fundamental attitudes to life as Antonio's and Shylock's without thinking of it in some relation to his own life and work. But the idea is based on more than that.

That the characteristic subject-matter and inspiration of poetry is love is a common enough belief in the modern West and was peculiarly strong and serious in the later Middle Ages and Renaissance. One only has to think of Dante and Petrarch to realise that much more was involved than the cliché, which writers of the period themselves made fun of, that the poet is always a pining lover, or the pining lover always liable to fancy himself a poet. Chaucer says in some of his poems that they too have everything to do with love, though *he* presents himself as an unhappy poet-lover with a difference: he has been so hopelessly unsuccessful in love that he knows little about the subject but is devoted to the men and women who do know all about it if only through intense suffering. At the beginning of his great tragic love-story, *Troilus and Criseyde*, he says, as the somehow essential thing about himself, that he is the servant of the servants of the god of Love. That is, his poetry comes from his being the lover and servant of lovers.

But that is also what Antonio is in *The Merchant of Venice*. In a strange way, too, Antonio both stands right at the centre of the play and, in a sense, does not belong to it. He is not the active initiator of anything that happens and is somehow, for all his central position, standing to the side.

It is interesting that in his *Troilus and Criseyde* Chaucer, after describing at length the bliss of the lovers' first night with each other, immediately turns to and turns on the figure of the fearful grasping "niggard", the Shylock figure, as the scornful arch-enemy of lovers. The passage is lines 1373 to 1393 of the poem's great Third Book. Those busy wretches, who call love a madness or idiocy, are "full of woe and dread", and grasp whatever money they can get hold of and hug it to themselves, because they are so deeply and miserably distrustful of life. In contrast, these lovers whom the niggards would despise are often shown suffering from their uncertainty both of each other and of what fortune has in store for their relationship but taking the risk of losing everything. Chaucer is again on this sacred terror of love at the opening of *The Parliament of Fowls* –

> The life so short, the craft so long to learn,
> Th' assay so hard, so sharp the conquering,
> The dreadful joy, always that slit so yerne: [*slides so quickly*]
> All this mean I by Love, that my feeling
> Astonisheth with his wonderful working
> So sore, iwis, that when I on him thinke, [*truly*]
> Not wot I well wher that I float or sink. [*know, whether*]

– where he is surely writing also about poetry.

In *The Merchant of Venice* the identification with each other of the lover's risk-taking and the poet's may come finally home to the audience or reader, if not necessarily to full consciousness, in the sublime poetry that is part of the long night scene that ends the play, beginning with the duet of two further lovers who have risked everything, Lorenzo and Jessica. Now united and for the moment safe in Portia's garden, well away from Venice, this couple celebrate their love and implicitly pray for the protection of their elopement's fragile success, and they do this by recalling and associating themselves with the beautiful protagonists of poetry's great tragic love-stories (including Troilus). Their duet is notably musical poetry, and it is soon followed by actual musicians' entering and playing, by Jessica's being highly open and sensitive to their music and by Lorenzo's speaking more than thirty lines of beautiful and profound poetry about the spiritual value and significance of music. Shakespeare has this end with an implicit but emphatic reference to the Shylock possibility in human nature: general treachery and malice are almost inevitable in

> The man that hath no music in himself,
> Nor is not moved with concord of sweet sounds...

The scene goes on to some final teasing light-profound comedy on the subject of risk-taking, between Portia and Bassanio and between another pair of lovers, and it ends with the union and happiness of all the lovers. For the lover and servant of lovers, Antonio, there is the significant news that his ships, whose delay and reported loss had put him in danger of Shylock's knife, have now finally come in. The poetic treasure of *The Merchant of Venice* is complete and safe and, with a quick little note of gracefully humble relief and gratitude, hardly noticed among everything else that is going on, being rejoiced and almost triumphed in.

As I have said, this chapter is not about the prejudices against poetry that can arise from the particular circumstances in which different people may encounter it, meeting poetry that is bad or is made bad by the way it is presented – the poetry of those disgraceful current poetry 'scenes' or what much better poetry can be turned into in, for example, the classroom. (A main disgrace here is the frequency of a murderously pedestrian and inflexible direction of students to "say what a poem means" rather than feel and enjoy it.) But these other prejudices bring up a further point about Shylock, and about that permanent prejudice that could make a poet like Shakespeare feel in his blacker moments that there is something in all of us that would like to kill him. For it is unlikely to be a simple matter when we are put off poetry by bad or badly treated examples, with our alienation taking place only through our waiting passively and uncaringly to see whether or not we are attracted and then not meeting anything attractive. Some of the alienation must take place precisely because we do care. The potential love of poetry is a sensitive spot, like all our capacity for love, and there can inevitably be some fierce shyness about having it touched at all, let alone clumsily or disappointingly. Those bad examples can seem to confirm that something sacred is going to be betrayed, and in that case we would rather not know. In the very intensity of Shylock's fearfulness and hate are great sensitiveness and sensuality. Antonio's generous trustingness seems to him quite extravagantly careless, and he finds it a moral outrage that anyone should give so readily and fully and take such risks. There is always too much danger of disappointment and loss and, when anything may happen at any moment and everything new must be a potential threat, the only possible course is to clutch tightly to oneself the good that is already known and possessed and sure. The especially maddening thing is that Antonio is not only confident and at ease with that attitude to life that he has but actually looks as if he may be going to get away with it.

All this Shakespeare means by poetry and our prejudice against it. Some examples will illustrate his idea: short poems by himself and two of his contemporaries. I believe *The Merchant of Venice* helps make clearer than they otherwise might be some crucial differences of quality between them. This is like the test of the three caskets. In which of these poems is the spirit of Antonio most completely present and the spirit of Shylock most completely absent?

The question might be thought to be at best only a little like the casket test since, all of the poems being good ones, any mistaken choice is not going to be so deadly serious a matter. None is going to turn out to contain a skull, like the gold casket, or "the portrait of a blinking idiot", like the silver one. Yet it could, in fact, be serious if the choice of the wrong poem represented a decided and settled preference for a poem in which the Shylock spirit was less completely absent. Who is to know what the consequences might not be over a lifetime, in spiritual loss and secret disappointment and in the misery and even murderousness they can lead to? If this mistake is made, how many similar mistakes will be made and accumulate – and not only, of course, in the judgement of poems?

"Who chooseth me, must give and hazard all he hath." Besides "he that loseth his life for my sake shall find it" and also the parable of the talents, another passage from the Bible that Shakespeare might well have had somewhere in his mind when he wrote *The Merchant of Venice* is from *Ecclesiastes*: "Cast thy bread upon the waters: for thou shalt find it after many days." Antonio has cast all his wealth upon the waters. Which of these poets is doing that?

An Elegy

Though beauty be the mark of praise,
  And yours of whom I sing be such
  As not the world can praise too much,
Yet is't thy virtue now I raise.

A virtue like alloy, so gone
  Throughout your form, as though that move,
  And draw, and conquer all men's love,
This subjects you to love of one.

Wherein you triumph yet: because
  'Tis of yourself, and that you use
  The noblest freedom, not to choose
Against or faith or honour's laws.

But who should less expect from you,
  In whom alone love lives again?
  By whom he is restored to men:

And kept and bred, and brought up true.

His falling temples you have reared,
   The withered garlands ta'en away;
   His altars kept from the decay,
That envy wished, and Nature feared.

And on them, burn so chaste a flame,
   With so much loyalty's expense
   As Love, t'acquit such excellence,
Is gone himself into your name.

And you are he: the deity
   To whom all lovers are designed,
   That would their better objects find:
Among which faithful troop am I.

Who as an offering at your shrine,
   Have sung this hymn, and here entreat
   One spark of your diviner heat
To light upon a love of mine.

Which if it kindle not, but scant
   Appear, and that to shortest view,
   Yet give me leave t'adore in you
What I, in her, am grieved to want.

In the sixth stanza the idea that Love is gone into the woman's name is presumably the poet's making a compliment to her out of the fact that the letters of the word love are all in her name. No note is needed on this second poem.

The sovereign beauty which I do admire,
   witness the world how worthy to be praisèd:
   the light whereof hath kindled heavenly fire,
   in my frail spirit by her from baseness raisèd;

That being now with her huge brightness dazèd,
   base thing I can no more endure to view:
   but looking still on her I stand amazèd,
   at wondrous sight of so celestial hue.
So when my tongue would speak her praises due,
   it stoppèd is with thought's astonishment:
   and when my pen would write her titles true,
   it ravished is with fancy's wonderment:
Yet in my heart I then both speak and write
   the wonder that my wit cannot endite.

In this third poem the "canker" is the scentless dog-rose, and the last line's "vade" means "go away".

Oh how much more doth beauty beauteous seem,
By that sweet ornament which truth doth give.
The rose looks fair, but fairer we it deem
For that sweet odour which doth in it live.
The canker blooms have full as deep a dye
As the perfumèd tincture of the roses,
Hang on such thorns, and play as wantonly
When summer's breath their maskèd buds discloses;
But for their virtue only is their show,
They live unwooed, and unrespected fade,
Die to themselves. Sweet roses do not so;
Of their sweet deaths are sweetest odours made.
   And so of you, beauteous and lovely youth,
   When that shall vade, by verse distills your truth.

Let me for the moment go on playing the game of the parallel with the casket test. The first poem, by Ben Jonson, is the silver one: "Who chooseth me shall get as much as he deserves." In this vigorous, charming and dignified poem Jonson may still come over, by the highest standards, as slightly too sure that this love he represents as so rare and so ideal is, for all that, something he himself completely understands and has the measure of, as well as something he himself ought to be receiving. The extravagance of the compliments he pays the woman expresses a lively eloquent enthusiasm but is also fairly coolly calculated, so that the compliments feel a little hollow and cold, and Jonson seems less in any awe of the woman or feeling any very warm affection for her than interested in her as an opportunity for himself as a fine moralist in verse and witty courtier. The second poem, by Edmund Spenser, is the gold casket: "Who chooseth me, shall gain what many men desire." Here awe is certainly felt, and I confess I am reluctant to say any but enthusiastic things about the poem. The reputation of Jonson's poetry has probably been higher for some time than it deserves, benefiting a bit from the special strength of the prejudice against poetry in the twentieth century, and it will probably not last at quite that height; but the reputation of Spenser's poems, at any rate of his shorter ones, could well be much lower than they deserve and be due to rise again. Nevertheless, rather more is felt in this poem of the wonderful experience he has himself gained in his awe than of the beauty that is supposed to have inspired it. In contrast, in reading the third poem, by Shakespeare, our minds and feelings are full of nothing else but the profoundly and intimately thrilling loveliness of the young man and the roses, and we feel the love being expressed for it through the poet's very absence from our minds. At the end, it is true, he refers to his own poetry and, by implication, to its beauty, but that is because the poem is finally nothing else than the young man's beauty, its timeless quality and the love inevitably felt for it.

Now I drop the game. What I mainly have in mind when I propose that *The Merchant of Venice* has a bearing on our opinion of these poems is not unrelated to the above but has more to do with the process of each poet's creation than its fruit. Is it clear that some such phrase as "divine detachment and carelessness" applies to the way Shakespeare puts words together in his sonnet but not to the way Jonson puts his words together or Spenser his? I am haunted here by more than one image of hands. One comes from religious art, from certain sculptures of the Buddha: the difference that there is in a fist clenched in tension and distrust from a relaxed open hand that is somehow exquisitely gracious and giving, human and touchingly slender and vulnerable but at the same time strong and sure. Another image comes from cycling or acrobatics or ballet: "Look, no hands!" It is an image of the usual control that human beings rely on most of the time being let go because there is a more perfect invisible control. When their poems are read alongside Shakespeare's, it can almost appear possible to see how both Jonson and Spenser write their poems and, though it finally is not, we can certainly see more of the process than we can with Shakespeare's, which seems to come from nowhere and be a miracle or magic.

I can remember watching soccer on television and suddenly hearing what one team's supporters were chanting: "Dúncan Mackénzie is máa-gic!" On a different field and level, it is the same point. You could not tell what brilliant thing that player might do next or where on earth he suddenly got the idea of it from. There was the same fundamental Antonio quality of the genius trusting the unknown, the apparently blind inspiration of the moment, and with split-second decisiveness taking the full risk of acting on that sudden inspiration – with divine detachment and carelessness.

Both Jonson and Spenser are writing much more deliberately. In Jonson's poem there is no strong sense that ordinary control has been let go and, if in Spenser's poem it *is* let go, wonderfully, it is let go in a prepared and practised release and elevation, with an art that the poet has cultivated and is always using. I believe this can be felt even by somebody unacquainted with much or any of his other writing, and with the fact, for example, that the special excitement that he creates with the sound as well as the sense of the word "huge" – with the very way in which we pronounce it – works very well but is something that he is always doing with that word. It is similarly both a good and a standard Spenserian effect when there is the contrast of this excitement –

That being now with her huge brightness dazèd

– with the reduced, steady-even quality of the line that immediately follows:

base thing I can no more endure to view

The sound and meaning of "huge" do not create the excitement by themselves. There is also the fact that here Spenser is using another favourite device of his to slow the verse and secure extra emphasis and elevation: the placing of a strong-significant monosyllable like "huge" where, in the iambic verse, the accent does *not* fall, so that the reader, led by its meaning to give it something like an accent, is then forced to make the iambic accent on the following syllable ("bright-")

73

a more than usually strong one, in order to preserve the metre. This excited slowing down has already begun, of course, with the "h's" at the end of "with" and beginning of "her", which encourage the reader to make a more than usual separation and space between the two words. They also create more sensitiveness to the excitement created by "huge", a part of which has to do with the extra kind of breath that seems to be required in Spenser's verse by an initial "h". The person acquainted with little or no other Spenser can still tell that these strong poetic effects do not have the breathtaking spontaneity of the even stronger and seemingly careless poetic strokes that there are in Shakespeare's sonnet. The extraordinary "perfumèd tincture" and the lovely "When summer's breath their maskèd buds discloses" seem, like everything else in the poem, to come suddenly out of the blue and are not especially emphasised parts of the poem. There does not seem to be any feeling on Shakespeare's part that the effects made are anything special, and they can almost seem like accidents. They hardly seem 'intended' and there can even be moments when, in spite of having been caught by them, we doubt that they are really there.

Why is "perfumèd tincture" extraordinary?

> The canker blooms have full as deep a dye
> As the perfumèd tincture of the roses...

It is characteristic as well as wonderful that in that greatest kind of art that is created with complete risk-taking abandon and perfect invisible control it is not at all easy to identify or put into words what the effects and suggestions are that make up the profound beauty – and the reader feels quite sure that, even if some of them may begin to be identified with some accuracy, they are never going to be described either definitively or completely. There will always be something more there and something a bit different. There is nothing of this kind in Jonson's poem: what every word means and suggests is perfectly clear and limited – carefully and admirably delimited by the poet. There is a little of it in Spenser's poem but not so much, and it is not so subtle or mysterious. In the seventh line

> but looking still on her I stand amazèd

there is some special richness in the words "still" and "stand" and through their interaction with each other, so that "still" means both "motionless" and "constantly, always", and "stand" means both "stop, be brought to a stand" and "stay standing"; and perhaps, too, partly as a result of this richness, the word "amazèd" has more than an ordinary single sense. (And the Oxford Dictionary supports any inclination we have to see the idea of bewilderment and utter lostness being combined with that of powerful surprise.) In those fifth and sixth lines of Shakespeare's sonnet one main overall suggestion seems to be the magical one of something like the thrilling essence of the beauty, its very nature and living spirit. The combination of "perfumèd" and "tincture" has the simple prose sense of a reference to the coloured rose that is also, unlike the canker or dog-rose, scented, but in addition that combination contrives to suggest that the colour the roses are steeped in is somehow the very same thing as the scent, which is also felt as somehow pervading, going through and through them. The stem "fume" also suggests breath and, with "per", suggests that this single thing that is going right through the roses as both colour and scent is also some kind of living breath. (This effect is helped by the fact that in the Elizabethan pronunciation of "perfumèd" it is the middle syllable that is accented.) The sense of the word "tincture" seems just right, combining with and taking further the idea of "dye", but there also seems to be in that infinitesimally small difficulty or hesitation that there is in the pronunciation of the word, in the first syllable and the movement on to the second, a suggestion of the actual subtle operation of this phenomenon of the living pervading essence.

It is clear that all this could not have been deliberately and carefully worked out by Shakespeare. At some level of consciousness, in the split-seconds involved, he must have known perfectly well what he was doing, but by our ordinary understanding of consciousness he could not have had much idea at all and simply had to take the steps in the dark and cast his bread on the waters.

Another passage from the Bible that is relevant is one that can also sound almost a contradiction of "He that findeth his life shall lose it":

> For whosoever hath, to him shall be given, and he shall have more abundance: but whosoever hath not, from him shall be

taken away even that which he hath.

If someone with that love and faith acts on them, there will only be more and more of them and of the rewards they bring. If once the real spring is tapped and then stayed with, it flows and flows and seems never to come to an end. For example, not a word has yet been said here about the fact that in Shakespeare's sonnet this living and timeless essence or spirit or breath of beauty is also called "truth": while an account of what this does can be attempted, it is difficult to imagine that account's ever being quite finished.

If a poet does not tap that spring or stay with it, then the things he or she achieves may in some sense be real but become with time a little hollow and unreal, and fewer. Jonson's own good but limited poem – limited when it is the nature of poetry to be unlimited – illustrates this law of diminishing returns:

> Who as an offering at your shrine,
>   Have sung this hymn, and here entreat
>   One spark of your diviner heat
> To light upon a love of mine.
>
> Which if it kindle not, but scant
>   Appear, and that to shortest view…

The idea of a spark from the fire of this woman's powerful, faithful love inspiring the woman Jonson loves but being likely to ignite only a feeble little flame that will soon gutter out remains only an idea. It makes sense but that is all it makes. There is no impression of or apparent interest in the actual inward process whereby the woman might be inspired by this wonderful example, and this means that there is no depth here in the traditional metaphor of love as a divine fire. Using that same metaphor, Spenser immediately makes a difference and achieves some depth by combining the idea with the contrasting ideas of frailty and baseness and with the different metaphor of raising:

> the light whereof hath kindled heavenly fire,

in my frail spirit by her from baseness raisèd...

In the emphatic position it is given, "my frail spirit" immediately gives us some sense of the inward operation, partly through the sound of the word "frail", its tentative character and the slight uncertainty there can be as to whether it is one syllable or two, and through the relation of that sound to the sound of the word "fire" and then to that of "raisèd". The development of the weak dragging "frail" into the strong positive "raisèd" helps the change from the one metaphor to the other to work as poetry and to overcome any potential awkwardness it might have. The absence of anything like this from Jonson's lines means that the woman's "diviner heat" of constant love is not really divine at all and that that phrase not only fails to grow and, with time and re-reading of the poem, take on more and deeper meaning, but comes to mean less: "from him shall be taken away even that which he hath."

One major difference between Shakespeare's poem and the other two has been touched on only indirectly: it is profounder poetry but also, in the way it is written, lighter and less weighty than either Jonson's or Spenser's, and the pleasant paradox is that it is profounder because it is lighter. This is an aspect of the divine detachment and carelessness and of the resemblance to the lead casket. The lightness is felt immediately, in the way the poem has to be read. It cannot be read in the solemn big voice that has to be found for the Spenser or in the intent thinker's voice of the Jonson. There is even something that could be called perfunctory about the way Shakespeare writes here – about the way, for example, in which he uses the sonnet-form. He knows the simple metre and rhyme-scheme that he regularly uses in sonnets, and he seems simply to fill them up with the words that come. (I think again of how casual a brilliant flicked pass by that soccer-player could look.)

Here there is more to be said in justice to both Jonson's poem and Spenser's. The phrase "divine detachment and carelessness" cannot quite be used of them, but it would be unfair to say that either achieves nothing at all of the same order. For all the deliberateness of their composing, each in his different way achieves a beautiful naturalness, Jonson by giving so convincing an impression of a man speaking – speaking politely and gracefully and neatly but also firmly and very plainly and forcefully – and Spenser by putting such emphasis on simplicity, preferring to sound artless and ingenuous rather than be cleverly ingenious. The difference from Shakespeare is that in each case the beautiful naturalness is a studied naturalness, while Shakespeare does not seem to have to bother.

"...and he shall have more abundance" – and not only of power and beauty within the same short poem. It is surely no accident that the writers of these poems wrote Shakespeare's plays, *The Faerie Queene* and Jonson's plays, or that those great creative achievements, when compared in power and beauty, come in more or less the same order as these poems.

A reason not yet mentioned for the unusual strength of the prejudice against poetry in our time is that there is an extra difficulty about poetry's enjoying its natural strong place in the life of a community in which prose has come to be what stories, novels and plays are almost always written in – and in which, also, the connection between formal lyric poetry and actual music has become, at any rate in our current poetry 'scenes', so remote, only something in our literature's distant past. These changes have taken place over a long period, since at least the seventeenth century, though I do not believe that that is any reason to think that there cannot or will not be changes back in the other direction. Already, the dominance of prose naturalism in the theatre is much weaker than it was in the middle of the twentieth century. If there are any laws to be discerned in the history of poetry, the most definite one may be that an immense achievement in a particular form, like Shakespeare's in poetic drama, is going to make it both difficult for a long time for new great things to be done in the same language in that form and likely that new great things will be in different forms, like the novel. But, if anything, that law could make the prospect more promising rather than less for the future of poetic drama in English, our theatre now being very far away indeed from that of Shakespeare. The "abundance" shown by all of Shakespeare, Spenser and Jonson in their work on a larger scale also suggests how unlikely it is that any greatly gifted new poets will not be impatient of confinement to the slim volumes of short poems that have for so long been so much the rule in our current poetry 'scenes'. It is the nature of Antonio's giving in *The Merchant of Venice* to be fluent, and this idea of Shakespeare's about poetry could help, together with his own example, to restore belief in the beauty and worth that fluency can have in poetry, both locally in a short poem or passage and over longer works and a whole *oeuvre*.

I end this chapter with another casket-test and question. Here are three poets writing towards the end of the twentieth century. I quote rather more than half of each of the first two short poems and the whole of the even shorter third one. I believe two of the poems are beautiful, though one of them also somewhat hectic and hurried, the poetry piled on a little as if to make sure that a golden casket is being created, while the other poem is simply an ugly and absurd abuse of the English language. Does *The Merchant of Venice* help the discrimination to be made and explained? And is it clear that the two beautiful poems have a fluency that makes it no surprise that both these poets, unlike the other one, have readily written large-scale works too (in each case poetic plays). One poem is called "Argonauts" and was dedicated to Robert Conquest:

> Exotic stimulations!
> Our passions pulled so loose
> From anything we might
> Share with our congeners,
> Why should we not refuse
> Their craven fabrications?
>
> Conquest (what a name for
> The emulous and mettled!)
> How can you think the score
> Settled by mere good humour?
> Confess a covert wish for
> The Orphic, the unfettered.

One is an untitled sonnet:

> Mourn no more for the flowers you have broken,
> Lies you have told and clouds stirred on my face
> Roused from my dark to the moons you have awoken,
> In this fair night your blackness keeps no place,

When Winter holds her blue tongue to the trees
Licking them white, they cry not at their death
With tears like wings of flies washed in the breeze
And blown away, each sad and lonely breath...

And one is called "Last summer day":

A breath of summer still lingers
And fills the air of my room,
A bird still wings through silence
Past the rising, round white moon –

While worlds are whispering something
I cannot understand,
Dear summer sighs softly as sleeping
From the flush of warming land.

There is a story about these poems. The first poet is the best-known. His poem was printed in a well-established London literary paper and then, a few weeks later, in the next-but-one issue of the same paper, the writer of it quoted the whole of the second poem at the beginning of his review of the début book of poems from which it comes, as a main piece of evidence for a thoroughly damning verdict: "The truth is," he wrote, "that [this book] should never have been published." Could it be that this was Shylock again trying to put his knife into generously risk-taking creativeness? In the literary 'scene' in which this kind of thing happens, it is no wonder that the third poem is only printed for the first time here. Another part of the story was reported to me by the writer of this poem: that, very unlike that reviewer, she had been excited by that début volume more than by other new poetry she'd read, and found it both inspiring and a profound encouragement.

The late Donald Davie's "Argonauts" was published in 1982, like his review of Sue Lenier's *Swansongs*, in *The London Review of Books*. The description of Shakespeare's as a "more perfect invisible control" is originally Lenier's, in conversation. For a rather surer illustration of her own possession of such control see the poetry quoted later in this present book (pp91, 107). "Last summer day" is

Joanne Weiss's.

Postscript I have come to believe that there is some injustice to the sonnet by Spenser in this comparison with Shakespeare's. Since, if its music is fully re-created in a reading, it is a larger and weightier poem, with a dramatic intensity Shakespeare's doesn't attempt, I was to an extent comparing incomparables. But I hope and believe that that very special quality in Shakespeare's writing here remains a quality worth isolating and identifying.

Some further notes on *The Merchant of Venice*

(1) Strong feeling about anti-Semitism should not make it so difficult as it apparently does to recover from the old theatrical tradition of sentimentalising Shylock – at any rate not in a reading of the play. A performance may be a different matter. Spoken forcefully in a public place, the abusive references to Shylock's Jewishness touch a highly sensitive spot and must be very difficult to tolerate. And, as a result, it may be that *The Merchant of Venice* can no longer be played for its full beauty and wisdom. It hardly holds together if Shakespeare is not allowed the poetic licence of creating this villain and in him uniting the traditional oppositions of usury to trade and of avarice to sexual love (this latter found in Spenser's Malbecco in Book III of *The Faerie Queene* as well as in Chaucer's *Troilus and Criseyde*) with an opposition of Old Testament 'law' to New Testament 'grace'. It *is* clear enough in the last scene of the Third Act that the hostility to Shylock is ethical and religious, not racial, and there is possible further help with tolerating that hostility instead of either hating it or sophisticating it away: in the plausible speculation that behind Shakespeare's interest in a fanatical Old Testament legalism was knowledge less of Jews than of Puritans. (There were few Jews in Elizabethan London; Shakespeare would not have been the only writer before Dryden to associate Puritanism with Old Testament Judaism; Shylock's position in relation to justice and mercy is the same as the Puritan Angelo's in Shakespeare's later play, *Measure for Measure*; Puritan business-men in the city of London were enemies of the theatre and would not allow any theatre within the city boundaries.) Shylock is not, of course, a

moral monster just because his main attitude to life is profoundly wrong, and rightly a matter for such vehement indignation as we are told Antonio has always expressed. He is not denied all human worth and dignity, or a soul to save like everyone else, and there would clearly be a very serious inconsistency in the play if he were.

(2) One obvious reason for not playing as mere figures of fun the two princes who choose the wrong caskets is that two good speeches would then be thrown away, the speeches in which they work out and explain their choices. It is not as if their reasoning in them does not deserve and need to be taken seriously – for example, Aragon's argument that success ought to be the reward of merit. If the strength of this position is not felt as well as its folly, and the strength as well as the folly of the pride with which Aragon argues it, the religious idea of grace surely loses its difficulty and depth, and with them its reality.

(3) A point for the director of any performance of the play is that, in the comedy test of the rings at the end, it could and should somehow be clear – though possibly not till the very end, since the audience could then go through the ordeal with Bassanio and Gratiano – that the test is the opposite of what these two new husbands believe and fear it is. They have, in fact, proved their love for their wives by breaking their promises to them and giving the rings away. It is another case of giving, risking and trusting, and the Portia and Nerissa who tease and torment them over their broken promises must actually be delighted that by 'failing' they have passed the test, if only by the skin of their teeth. Not that the episode is not also chastening, modifying all the happiness and helping to stop it becoming heady. Its comic and cheerful image of 'failure', together with how close the two men have been to a real failure, is a playful reminder to everyone that it is impossible for a human being to keep all of the rules all of the time: as Portia has warned Shylock, "in the course of justice, none of us / Should see salvation," and, if there is no mercy, everyone would be terrified of ever taking the slightest risk.

Chapter III
All-out poetry and poetry all too English, with some incomplete English steps towards all-out poetry

The poetic must finally be unknown in the sense of indefinable, however alive, compelling and illuminating, and however strongly felt and treasured by us. Those who treat the poetic as known are the academic poets and all too many academics. To them poetry has come down from the past, with its prestige but also time's patina on it, and no longer its full spirit and vitality. When felt, the latter make the poetry still new however old, and thus make it fresh, mysterious and dangerous again. But it is the definition of academic poets that their work is not dangerous, while to tame poetry can be what academics actually take to be their job. In one way or another, both bid to make it a known quantity.

These facts are affecting the way in which this book's Main Argument is argued. In the first place, there is unorthodox argument like the simple quoting of poems in a given context and in juxtaposition with each other (as on pp34-41, where it is only the copyright laws that stop me quoting each poem by Heaney complete, and on pp44-48). Then there is the argument's developing, as I hope, a little from chapter to chapter but at the same time, and perhaps rather more, going from one variation on a theme to another, arguing the same fundamental point but in different words and with different illustrations. The general argument clearly needs to be tested against a wide range of illustrations, within the limits of the arguer's knowledge. In this chapter some illustrations are even going to be from art-forms other than poetry. Also, if in one chapter certain words are used to describe the poetic only in the next to be dropped in favour of other words, the integrity of the poetic as finally unknown will be easier to leave intact.

In this chapter there will be little more talk of the sublime or the revelatory, or of generosity, love and risk, but a pressing of the description "all-out" and of words explaining it. After the preceding chapters, readers may particularly enjoy the first of these words.

1. SIGNS OF ALL-OUT POETRY: (i) DEVIL

It is probably common for admirers of the wonderful John Cleese to be just a little disappointed by the main full-length films for the cinema that have had him at their centre. An example is *Clockwise* (1985), a wonderful film that, in my experience, was even more enjoyable the second time than the first, and is touching as well as very funny. But it may not be quite so unmistakeably a work of genius as his best *Monty Python* sketches or the whole *Fawlty Towers* series. Clearly the shorter-length television farce did have to be adapted for the different medium, and in *Clockwise* the adaptations were intelligent and resourceful. But the result was still that the farce was not quite so mad, so extreme or so outrageous, was a little more ordinary, did not have quite so much of that devil in it that, like all great art, great farce needs. Other ways of expressing the point are: the farce of *Fawlty Towers* has a peculiar intensity; it has no holds barred; it is dangerous, wicked, too much. During one of the funniest episodes (I believe it was the one in which a hotel guest is suddenly found dead) I can remember a young teenager running out of the room with a muttered exclamation of vehement repudiation. Great art goes to that utter limit of the credible and the tolerable that is always beyond where we think it is.

A not dissimilar point is made, according to Lorca's famous lecture on the *duende* (given at the end of the 1960 Penguin selection of the poems), when that word is used in Andalusia with reference to Flamenco dance and music: to describe a great impersonal and irrational power, primitive, sensual, amoral and thought of as coming up from the soles of the feet and right through the whole body. (A Spanish-teaching colleague gave me this description of how it is thought of.) Lorca gives one or two stories to illustrate the importance attached by connoisseurs of Flamenco to the difference between the dancer who has the *duende* and other dancers, describing, for example, how an eighty-year-old woman won a dancing contest against much beautiful young competition "merely by raising her arms, throwing back her head, and stamping her foot on the platform." In the English and American theatre something similar happens on those special rare occasions when, in a ballet, opera or play, a great artist-performer can suddenly electrify an audience almost without doing anything, by a quality of sheer presence and a quite exceptionally intense and complete concentration, being absolutely on that spot and in that moment and with not the slightest shred of thought or feeling anywhere else.

As I mentioned earlier, 'magical' is often another word used to salute the power of all-out art. "It's just *magic!*" is said when a person is trying to salute the tremendous achievement the art is felt to be while acknowledging that it is quite unaccountable (and may not even be an 'achievement' by the ordinary idea of what an achievement is). Unaccountable, for one thing, is the abrupt character of the power. Suddenly, as Lorca described in another story, the famous dancer who had been dancing all evening with great energy and skill but failing to excite her expert audience was at last dancing with the *duende* that made all the difference, and those experts were suddenly absorbed and wildly enthusiastic. The artist is suddenly completely into the work and its power, not travelling from A to Z like ordinary human beings but at Z straightaway.

The abrupt manner is at the same time one of unusual authority. Ordinary mortals, sitting in an audience or, even more, when silently reading, can hang back and be slow and reluctant to yield to the effect of such power. Most of our lives we like to see where we are going, have things as much as possible our own way, be able to pick and choose, stay wary. Yet, when more open and not too blocked by fear and prejudice on meeting the real thing, as we especially can be when the real thing is also new and unknown, we can quickly feel this special authority. And then we know straightaway that we have had it and the game is up, and are thrilled and delighted.

Very similar, again, to the devil of all-out art is what Artaud means by "cruelty", in his argument in the 1930s that Western theatre had to learn to be cruel to its audiences again – disturbing them profoundly and putting them under the most tremendous strain – if it was ever to recover its true power and value, satisfying audiences as deeply and completely as it had in the past. Art does not possess its truth unless it is simultaneously terrible and wonderful, and it is greater art the more of such truth it has; and the power that is felt and enjoyed so deeply is the sheerest and purest possible animal and spiritual energy, and the peace of that. That is what is so releasing and fulfilling about it, and that is why, before it can be this, it can be felt to be fierce and extreme and disturbing. Human beings are rarely living at this level, and we cannot be taken to it without first having everything inside us shaken up. (I call the energy both animal and spiritual not with any idea that those words are here describing different things, but with the idea that they are describing the same thing, which either word by itself would be in danger of misdescribing.)

All this helps bring out how the possession by *Fawlty Towers* of a little more of that indispensable devil than *Clockwise* has is the same thing as its having a little more of the universality of great art. I should not have been surprised, though I confess I initially was, as I picked up from people from various parts of the world that the *Fawlty Towers* series had been bought by their different countries' televisions and been a great success. *Clockwise* is a little more limitedly English, with not quite so many unforgettably vivid images of our essential human folly.

Yet it still does have many such images, and I will make one my illustration of how real mad and all-out farce is universal farce: the image of the stiff, would-be dignified and important and in-command John Cleese headmaster at one point, when he is already in a very tight spot and is now frustrated by three faulty public telephones in a row, finally breaking – and suddenly and furiously trying to hammer the third phone to pieces. People seeing the film in other parts of the world might know little about the English class-system and nothing about either the vandalising of public phones in England or the frustration of the whole British people at that time with a type of pay-phone now happily phased out, and just conceivably they might not know of close equivalents of any of these things. But the farce here does not depend on any such knowledge. For one thing, it is more immediately physical, and the sudden break from the tightly self-controlled professional person into the absolutely raging adult behaving as uninhibitedly as a very small child at the peak of a supertantrum – yet doing so sternly and deliberately as if he were somehow performing a responsible public duty of punishment – makes an image of universal power and appeal.

The emphasis here has been on the sheer energy and power. What about the grace, sweetness and beauty of art? Is there the short answer that these qualities are simply the most precious manifestations and fruits of that devil of all-out pure energy? What is more terrible and cruel than the most perfect pure beauty, or puts a more tremendous strain on us before we can see and accept it? and what requires a greater vitality to create? It is one of the main things that make it seem a miracle that, when it *is* at last there, it feels and is so easy. That can move one to tears.

2. ALL TOO ENGLISH: (i) POETRY

The all too English subject-matter of *Fawlty Towers* does not stop it from having the devil or *duende* of all-out art, and it has not stopped it from travelling all over the world. The 'all too English' that is incompatible with all-out art is obviously something not in the subject-matter but in the attitude or spirit, and I believe that that limitation affects and provincialises almost all of the English English literature[*] of the second half of the twentieth century. When this literature is in mind, the elementary things just written about all-out art can seem a satire.

The purpose in now focussing on only that literature is to identify such a limiting attitude or spirit by isolating the one specific example. The provinciality in one country's literature is not the same as that in

---

[*] Though the word "British" has come to be used to distinguish English English writers from English-speaking writers from other parts of the world, it will not do here because the distinction also needs to be from the Welsh, Scottish and Irish. If Heaney is mentioned and quoted again, that is because as a poet he is nothing but English – unlike, for example, Dylan Thomas, Hugh MacDiarmid or Patrick Kavanagh.

another, even when the language is the same. And twentieth-century English English is the provinciality I know best. It is for this reason that the phrase "all too English" has been coming into my mind for a long time, always in connection with English English writers of the twentieth century, never in connection with English writers of previous centuries, expressing a sharp embarrassment. Of course, those writers of earlier centuries have been sifted out and separated from what was most provincial in their time. But it seems to me likely that time's sifting out will leave, as really classic, very little late-twentieth-century English English writing at all. And the provincialising seems to have started in the first half of the century. George Orwell is all too English, and so also to a degree is the much more gifted and less crippled W.H. Auden, and even the still more gifted and still less crippled D.H. Lawrence. If I myself would argue that Charlotte Mew is more completely free of the limitation than these other writers are, I would also have to admit that it is probably no accident either that she is older or that her work was almost completely forgotten for much of the century. Her sex is also, almost certainly, no accident, since in this context "all too English" seems always to be referring to qualities of rather limitedly masculine – sometimes all too boyish – English *men*.

I believe the phrase came to my mind first not in connection with poetry at all but when I was trying to understand why, for all my respect, liking and gratitude for Orwell's best work, in his essays, I would tend to get a bit irritated when I met other readers of his who were treating him as more than a very good second- or third-order writer, somehow as one of the great significant writers of the century and of the world. "But he's so terribly *English*!" Made too much of, Orwell's very virtues of conscience and clarity in incisive plainspeaking can become a little maddening: he can seem all too 'honest' and 'decent' and 'sensible', and too content to be nothing else. It is as if absolutely everything in the world simply has to be straightforward and rational – and this even though there is so evidently something irrational at work in his own writing, producing a certain shrillness. Also, his imagination is somewhat asexual and unsensual, and there is pervasive impression of deep unadmitted self-dislike.

Auden does not have exactly the same kind of limited Englishness, and Orwell was no great admirer of his work, but is there still a kinship?

> Lay your sleeping head, my love,
> Human on my faithless arm;
> Time and fevers burn away
> Individual beauty from
> Thoughtful children...

This is 'honest', 'decent', 'sensible', and everything is straightforward and rational, and unsensual. And, at the same time, self-dislike, not so unadmitted but still not fully admitted, shows in the strange, uneasy self-consciousness of Auden's wording.

It is not, of course, that all-out art has no place for self-dislike. This can evidently be a source of material, as in *Othello*, and what, after all, about *Fawlty Towers*? or the Prince poem *Memoirs in Oxford* that I will be saluting later? But then the self-dislike is not governing and inhibiting the art.

I go to Auden and to the not very good, though significantly popular, Auden of "Lullaby" because of that self-consciousness in its words. In what I have not quoted from it the poem has still further adjectives that draw attention to themselves. And its word-choices illustrate the way in which Auden helped to set an all too English style in poetry, or vice of style. In his own work it is not simply a vice since something is being expressed by his use of a smart knowing manner: a raging unease that elsewhere, when he is at his best, as in, for example, the eleventh and twelfth sonnets of "The Quest" sequence, means that there are a kind of silent scream just beneath that manner and at least a teasing hint, thereby, of the possibility of some devil and of something all-out. Comparably, perhaps, in Geoffrey Hill's partial adoption of the same vicious style there is some sense of an unusual even though lumbering and often obscure emotional force and intensity:

> Centaury with your staunch bloom
> you there alder beech you fern,

midsummer closeness my far home,
fresh traces of lost origin.
(From "Two Chorale-Preludes" in Tenebrae)

The vice by itself can be seen in the quotations earlier in the present book from Heaney and Donald Davie (pp35-39 and 79), and it can sometimes look as if it is all over Philip Larkin's early collection, *The Less Deceived*:

> Beneath it all, desire of oblivion runs:
> Despite the artful tensions of the calendar,
>
> The life insurance, the tabled fertility rites,
> The costly aversion of the eyes from death...
(From "Wants")

It is an influential vice when so good a poet as Larkin certainly became can pen phrases like "the artful tensions of the calendar" and "the tabled fertility rites" and use "costly" like this. And the vice does not only appear in adjectival words, though it is often most conspicuous there. It can appear in a verb –

> As you plaited the harvest bow
> You *implicated* the mellowed silence in you
> In wheat that does not rust

– or in a noun-adjective combination (the same poem continues):

> But brightens as it tightens twist by twist
> Into a *knowable corona*...
(From "The Harvest Bow"in Heaney's
Field Work. My italics.)

And consider what Craig Raine says he has seen of an orderly "In the Mortuary":

> He calls the woman 'Missus',
> an abacus of perspiration
>
> on his brow, despite the cold.
(Penguin's 1982 Contemporary British Poetry)

It is fundamentally the vice of plodding composition, separate step by separate step, all too visibly deliberate and careful and 'precise', and inevitably neither very musical nor very passionate. Each thing mentioned in a poem seems to be buttoned up all by itself, and in a deadly way buttoned down.

The vice can sometimes seem to run through English English verse of the later twentieth century almost as much as the not dissimilar vice of "poetic diction" runs through later eighteenth-century English verse. "From this hubbub of words pass to the original," Wordsworth wrote as, in his famous Preface's Appendix on "poetic diction", he followed his quotation of an eighteenth-century verse-paraphrase of a Biblical passage with the beautiful words of the Authorized Version. From misuse of the language turn to use of it. In the four-line poem by Joanne Weiss quoted on p34 and again in the following four-line poem from Sue Lenier's *Swansongs*, it is clear that the meaning has not had words laboriously and showily sought out for it, dogged and would-be clever step by dogged and would-be clever step. The meaning unfolds seamlessly and with apparent effortlessness: clear, simple and mysterious.

> Rainbuds sparkling on the ground
> Splash over the tumbling nerves of snowdrops,
> Pale and wilful they droop and shudder
> Cold maids under the colder ground.

In these two examples one mark of the poetry's being all-out is that the fluent words slip and slide into each other, interacting in more and subtler ways than can be readily identified, and thus create something that the same words cannot be imagined creating in ordinary prose. With the first poem I made initial suggestions about this. With this poem a start could be made by observing how "sparkling" develops into "Splash over the tumbling nerves..." By being partly present again in that second line, "sparkling" helps, together with the vivacity of the new "sh" sound, to ensure that those nerves are almost unbearably alive though so helpless, even while that near-inert helplessness is itself more precisely known from the simultaneous change of sound from "spark-" to "tumb-" and "nerves".

3. SIGNS OF ALL-OUT POETRY: (ii) TEARS AT BEAUTY

The twentieth century got a long way from the Tennyson whom his son Hallam reported as saying this about time he had spent with his fellow-poet, Clough: "Clough had great poetic feeling: he read me then his 'In Mari Magno' and cried like a child over it." Of Tennyson's reading of his own *Maud* Dante Gabriel Rossetti is quoted by Hallam as saying: "whilst the fiery passages were delivered with a voice and vehemence which he alone of living men can compass, the softer passages and the songs made the tears course down his cheeks." He also quotes his father as saying of three short replies made by characters in Shakespeare that they "always bring tears to my eyes from their very simplicity."

Is this more satire on the English English poetry 'scene' of the later twentieth century? I think so, even when allowances have been made for the fact that behaviour has undergone some general changes since the Victorian period, with tears, especially male ones, less common. Beauty in art – as well as other beauty – still brings tears into eyes, among the audiences of music, opera, ballet, play and film, and it is only in that poetry 'scene' that eyes seem always to be quite dry.

Towards the end of the evening the leading female dancer and the leading male enter, dressed in shining pure white or silver, and they stand still as Tchaikovsky's or Prokofiev's music moves to a melody that has either not been heard before or not been heard with this new swelling emphasis. The wedding is about to take place, or the great final *pas de deux*. An inner shock can be felt, arriving apparently out of the blue but taking complete possession of anyone in the audience, like a sudden extreme tightening of the mind, an almost unbearable concentration of it in the one spot. And the body, too, seems to be held extraordinarily still in the vice-like grip of what is taking place – even while in its depths it is being helplessly and amazingly shaken and the tears coming into the eyes seem like a melting, a melting at a near-unendurable intensity of loveliness and truth. A great awe is felt, and simultaneously a great release. Time seems to stop, the moment feeling as if it has always been there and is never going to end.

Whether the two dancers are remaining still or have started dancing, a wonderful impersonal power is felt at the very centres of their bodies and going right through them, with all the bearing and movements of head, torso, limbs, hands and feet a continuous fresh rediscovery and redefinition of these centres, and of the vitality radiating uninterruptedly out of them into the surrounding space. In their depth and beauty those centres, deeper than the ordinary unconscious or subconscious, are like the very springs or fountains of life.

It is surely the profoundly moved and moist-eyed impression that the dancers or opera-singers have somehow contrived to be more than human that accounts for those feelings of the keenest gratitude, love and devotion that ballet and opera audiences are almost notorious for showing at the end towards those, after all, merely human performers, in their often remarkably enthusiastic, wild and prolonged applause and their demand for unending curtain-calls.

I realise that the very use of the word "beauty" is another satire on the English poetry 'scene', and that yet another is people's frequent use of the word "poetry" when describing heights of beauty in ballet.

4. ALL TOO ENGLISH: (ii) IDEAS ABOUT POETRY

At the beginning of a 1933 lecture on Plato's *Republic* (collected in his *The Unwritten Philosophy and other essays*), F.M.Cornford sketches a parallel between England after the First World War and Athens after the Peloponnesian War, seeing in them the two common features of a collapse in the belief in democracy and "what looks to us Victorians like a failure of nerve in the generation to whom the war came in their childhood":

> ...it is hard to keep that faith [in the essential goodness of common humanity] when you have seen humanity at war. And if men lose faith in one another, perhaps they must also lose faith in themselves.

Orwell was born in 1903 and Auden in 1907. Though F.R.Leavis was a little older, born in 1895, that war and the failure of nerve in that generation seem to me to show clearly enough in a certain weakness in his thought about poetry. And I turn to this now as the more significant for the fact that Leavis was so extraordinarily sensitive to poetry and intelligent about it and, more than an ordinary literary critic in his passionate ardour for it, approached being an 'all-out' writer himself, with some prophetic intensity of inspiration. It is true that there is no quite exact match between the vice of poetic style described in this chapter's second section and the weakness in this thought, and that this critic and the various poets affected by that vice hardly thought of themselves as a 'school' or even, necessarily, respected each other. But is there still a clear connection between this weakness in the critic and the nervous over-deliberateness in the poets?

The weakness can be found here, in an essay that is otherwise one of Leavis's finest. (The poem of Tennyson's commented on has been quoted by me, on pp46-47). The tears the poem talks about are clearly not unrelated to the tears at the beauty of all-out art.

> ...it is plain that habitual indulgence of the kind represented by *Tears, idle tears* – indulgence not accompanied and virtually disowned by a critical placing – would be, on grounds of emotional and spiritual hygiene, something to deplore. There is nothing gross about the poem; it exhibits its author's highly personal distinction; but it unquestionably offers emotion directly, emotion for its own sake without a justifying situation, and, in the comparison, its inferiority to Lawrence's poem compels a largely disparaging commentary. ("'Thought' and Emotional Quality," later collected by Leavis in his *The Living Principle*...)

That last sentence is a concluding reference to a sustained comparison Leavis has here been making between Tennyson's poem and this fairly early poem of D.H. Lawrence's, "Piano":

> Softly, in the dusk, a woman is singing to me;

Taking me back down the vista of years, till I see
A child sitting under the piano, in the boom of the tingling
strings
And pressing the small, poised feet of a mother who smiles as
she sings.

In spite of myself the insidious mastery of song
Betrays me back, till the heart of me weeps to belong
To the old Sunday evenings at home, with winter outside
And hymns in the cosy parlour, the tinkling piano our guide.

So now it is vain for the singer to burst into clamour
With the great black piano appassionato. The glamour
Of childish days is upon me, my manhood is cast
Down in the flood of remembrance. I weep like a child for the
past.

If Leavis's judgement between the two poems seems quite shockingly wrong – and continues to seem so even after all allowance has been made for the fact that unfairness to a fairly recent generation, especially to a powerfully dominant figure in it, is frequent in the history of the arts, and sometimes inevitable and even necessary – what can account for that shocking misjudgement?

By quoting "Tears, idle tears" where I did in this book, as an illustration of how poetry is revelatory, I have already suggested that its scope or ambition is quite different from what Leavis assumes and that it is simply not true at all, let alone "unquestionably", that the poem merely "offers emotion directly, emotion for its own sake". In its scope the poem is much more closely comparable with T.S.Eliot's "Burnt Norton" than with "Piano", which shows next to no general concern with the wonder and mystery and pain of an experience's being at once in time and timeless. While one mark of his generation's failure of nerve is the extreme wariness and suspicion of passion that this quotation from Leavis shows, so that it is hard, now, not to smile at his shyly clinical "hygiene", a still more serious mark of the lack of faith is its seeming simply not to occur to him that a poem, let alone a popular one, could be all-out and revelatory in the way that "Tears, idle tears" is. In this essay, as in much of his other writing in the first half of his career, he can with a blank unconsciousness put drastic limits on the possibilities of all poetry, suggesting that a poem is somehow only made up of the poet's personal "emotion" and his or her "intellect". That personal "emotion" gives the inspiration and drive to write the poem and is checked by the "intellect" from being treated too indulgently and thereby producing sentimentality, distortion or vagueness in the presentation of whatever gave rise to the "emotion". This is the idea of artistic impersonality that is put forward, and there is next to no conception of anything powerfully impersonal's being likely to be the more important part of the inspiration and drive to write.

Things Leavis writes about Milton are relevant here. In a list of subjects Jowett said Tennyson was constantly speaking about, the first is this: "A strong desire to vindicate the ways of God to man, and, perhaps, to demonstrate a pertinacity on the part of man in demanding of God his rights" (quoted in Hallam Tennyson's *Memoir* of his father). Though that last part can also make one think of another great poet, the author of the *Book of Job*, it is clear enough that Tennyson or Jowett was here echoing the lines in *Paradise Lost* where Milton expresses his hope and aspiration that in the poem he

> ...may assert Eternal Providence
> And justify the ways of God to men.

Such an ambition has also been a main inspiration for the work of other of the greatest English poets, not to mention the poets of the rest of the world. It may, to a degree, be peculiarly characteristic of Milton that he states it so boldly, but the same ambition is Chaucer's in central enough poems like *Troilus and Criseyde* and *The Knight's Tale*, is inevitably the ambition of Shakespeare in his tragedies, as of all the writers of great tragedy (see pp53-55), is unmistakable in all those main poems of Wordsworth's that handle the problem of suffering and of radical loss of faith and vision and is very much the ambition of Tennyson's *In Memoriam* and *Maud*. Yet Leavis writes as if Milton's having this ambition is simply produced by his "great capacity for unawareness", a kind of innocent though egotistic self-deception.

While not explicitly saying so, he implies that good poets don't do that sort of thing, or have that kind of ridiculously overweening ambition. And, because he sees nothing strong in Milton's ambition, he sees a merely personal motive, and an unattractive one, for his conceiving and pursuing it:

> He reveals everywhere a dominating sense of righteousness and a complete incapacity to question or explore its significance and conditions.

So, apparently, Milton wishes to vindicate the ways of God not because, like everyone else at times, he doubts those ways – and makes a powerfully moving representation of the reasons for doubting them a main part of his poem – but because he has no doubt about them at all. (The especially relevant paragraphs are on pp58-59 of his *Revaluation* and pp26-27 of his *The Common Pursuit.*)

The early Leavis's tending to work with so drastically limited an idea of poetry is the more significant because it is also so seriously at odds with his own fundamental inspiration. And this fact gets a strange but telling confirmation. For he himself comes not only to hold precisely the view that there is something powerfully impersonal in a gifted writer's inspiration and drive to write but also to express that view with eloquent conviction. Characteristic of his later writing is the much more prominent place he gives to the word "religious" when describing the inspiration of the greatest writers. It is true that earlier, too, he has written, for example, of Wordsworth's "preoccupation with sanity and spontaneity [as] working at a level and in a spirit that it seems appropriate to call religious" (*Revaluation*). But later such a recognition, like similar recognitions about the work that he has always been most impressed by, and goes on and on thinking and writing about to the end, that of Lawrence and Eliot, pervades his thought as it has previously failed to. On the other hand, though, this later writing is much more often about novels than about poems, and he never returns to most of the poetry he has previously written on, with a view to reconsidering his judgements of it.

His earlier failure of nerve about the all-out quality of poetry shows in further ways. One is his peculiarly strong valuing of "particularity". That is the main thing that makes him think "Piano" a better poem than "Tears, idle tears", for all the "banal phrases" he concedes there are in Lawrence's poem. What saves it is "the presence of something other than directly offered emotion, or mere emotional flow – the presence of something, a specific situation, concretely grasped," while, contrastingly, in Tennyson's poem there is "a complete absence of anything like the particularity" of Lawrence's, and his "emotion" is "emotion for its own sake" because it is "without a justifying situation". It is perhaps no wonder that Leavis becomes increasingly interested in realistic prose fiction rather than poetry and, even while his general ideas about literature are maturing and deepening in the way just indicated, tends to overrate novels. It can sometimes seem that to his mind the only thing a human being can trust to be real, instead of over-emotional and more or less seriously bogus, is the "concrete" that can be grasped by the hand, smelt by the nose or trodden on by the foot: in other words, that the imagination has no power to move except by such creeping along the ground, and is certainly unable to leap. Yet

> …in the gliding from one image, evocation or suggestion to another, so that all contribute to a total effect, there is created a sense of a supreme significance, elusive, but not… illusory…

The words fit "Tears, idle tears" but are written by Leavis about Eliot's poem "Marina". He is again becoming truer to himself as he goes on thinking and writing about the poems of Eliot and the novels, stories and essays of Lawrence, even if the recovery from the weakness in his early thought is never quite complete and certainly does not mean that the poetry of a Tennyson or a Milton gets reconsidered.[*]

Another way in which that failure of nerve shows is the extreme

---

[*] Dates may look as if they are against me here, since the essay with the comparison between Tennyson's poem and Lawrence's is actually printed after and not before the essay on Eliot just quoted from, which is in *Education and the University* (1943). But before its 1945 publication in *Scrutiny* that former essay's main substance was almost certainly in Leavis's lectures for a number of years.

wariness and suspicion not only of passionateness but also of poetic music, the thing in poetry that has so much to do with the imagination's becoming both sensitive and able to leap. Leavis actually dislikes the use of the word music about poetry, preferring to speak of the "movement" of a poem. And the "movement" of Lawrence's "Piano" he apparently hears as "subtler" than that of "Tears, idle tears": in the comparison, "we feel it as decidedly complex." Of Tennyson's poem he writes:

> It moves simply forward with a sweetly plangent flow, without check, cross-tension or any qualifying element. To give it the reading it asks for is to flow with it, acquiescing in a complete and simple immersion: there is no attitude towards the experience except one of complaisance; we are to be wholly in and of it.

I.e., it is all-out poetry, and with the fluency of all-out poetry? It is strange how strikingly close Leavis's second sentence here is, though there is no consciousness of the fact, let alone curiosity about it, to language in which profound religious wisdom has often been described. Similarly, in the later of his essays on Milton he writes of the 'music' of *Paradise Lost* (Leavis's inverted commas) as inducing "a feeling of exalted significance, of energetic effortlessness, and of a buoyant ease of command," and again his words are both a beautiful appreciation of the poetic music and intended, nevertheless, to be making a point against it: "The state induced," he has written in the previous sentence, "has analogies with intoxication."

Three further suggestions on poetic music. Leavis's valuing of the movement of the verse in "Piano" as "decidedly complex" sounds like a contentedness with not being whole but staying safely divided, distracted and on the ground, a contentedness coming from unconscious fear. Paradoxically, though, the wisdom well described by those phrases on the music of "Tears, idle tears" ("to flow with it… a complete and simple immersion… no attitude towards the experience… wholly in it and of it") is a wisdom that the older "religious" Leavis not only well knew to be wisdom but actually said was wisdom. In conversation he would sometimes, in a consciously challenging way, throw this off as the definition of all wisdom: that it is nothing but "living on the spot". Thirdly, to print the confident statement that a poem that includes this almost painfully crude and amateurish working of the vowel "a" –

> So now it is vain for the singer to burst into clamour
> With the great black piano appassionato, the glamour
> Of childish days is upon me

– is "subtler" in the way it moves than a poem that has this working of the same vowel –

> Ah, sad and strange as in dark summer dawns
> The earliest pipe of half-awakened birds…

– is to ask for a very big exclamation-mark to be written in the margin. And perhaps words: "All too English!"

An omission from this section will be unfair to Leavis if not repaired. The distrust of "emotion", of deficiency in "particularity", and of "flow" and "music", as also of "soul", does make a little more sense against the background it had when it was being expressed, of people's reading and loving much more second- and third-rate Victorian and Edwardian English verse than people read or love now.

This section also does not expand much on its suggestion that on his own account this mere critic approaches being an all-out writer, with some prophetic intensity of inspiration. Saying more about this, as I do in the review included in a chapter that is among this book's "Supporting Arguments" (pp184-191), may help further to bring out the truth in what could otherwise seem an improbable idea: that Leavis is among the later-twentieth-century's English English writers who have taken heroic steps towards all-out poetry – though incomplete ones.

5. SIGNS OF ALL-OUT POETRY: (iii) WORDS SAYING MORE THAN THEY LITERALLY SAY (Philip Larkin)

Philip Larkin most clearly shows himself to be another of these heroic English writers of the later twentieth century when he is bold enough to let a poem be beautifully and movingly meaningful without attempting to state in it all of what its significance is. He is rarely quite so bold in this way as in the closing two lines of "Cut Grass", a poem in his last collection, *High Windows*, though he achieves something comparable in "The Trees", in the same book. In their quite fresh way, even if less powerfully than Tennyson's "Tears, idle tears", and with a less fluent beauty (as also when compared with Weiss's "Last Summer Day", p80 above), both of these poems create something of a similar breathtaking knowledge.

> Cut grass lies frail:
> Brief is the breath
> Mown stalks exhale.
> Long long the death
>
> It dies in the white hours
> Of young-leafed June
> With chestnut flowers,
> With hedges snowlike strewn,
>
> White lilac bowed,
> Lost lanes of Queen Anne's lace,
> And that high-builded cloud
> Moving at summer's pace.

The last two lines are also unusual for Larkin, as is also, less markedly, the last stanza of "The Trees", because so much of the knowledge created in the lines is created by the simple-subtle change in the music, not merely by the meaning of the words.

How "Cut Grass" is nearer to being all-out poetry than other of Larkin's poems is also being felt in the fact that in this poem the poet, and his readers with him, are more *in* something than merely looking at or thinking about something. While it would be unfair to this poet to suggest that the latter is all he is doing in most of his other poems, in all the many good ones the degree to which his words are creating as against merely saying is less than it is in this poem.

Here a reference to that other relatively dull period of English poetry, the eighteenth century, could again be relevant, though this time I am thinking less of Wordsworth's criticism of that poetry than of Leavis's. About the best of it the latter is enthusiastic as Wordsworth is not, and he is concerned to distinguish what is stronger in it and much further away from being annihilated by Wordsworth's revolution against its "poetic diction". Yet he still suggests that this is a less creative period of English poetry and describes the virtues of its stronger poetry as the virtues of a poetry of "statement". In later-twentieth-century English poetry the vice of style that I have described as over-deliberate composition goes closely with the fact that so much of it, too, is only a poetry of statement. There is evidently more of ordinary everyday control and deliberateness in making statements than in creating.

Yet statements can still be made cleanly, without that vice of style, and, even if he is never completely free of the vice, Larkin becomes more and more free of it in the two collections of his poems that come after *The Less Deceived* (1955): *Whitsun Weddings* (1964) and *High Windows* (1974). He has more and more fully the courage as well as inspiration that have been there to an extent from the beginning of his career though in *The Less Deceived* they have been less acted on: to say things simply rather than either smartly or with nervous would-be smartness. And the increasing cleanness of his statements means that their 'poetry' or 'creating' is, if with some continuing uncertainty and incompleteness, increasingly evident and beautiful. For it is not that "Cut Grass" and "The Trees" are finally uncharacteristic of him even though they do carry the poetic boldness further than usual. *High Windows* begins with a poem, "To the Sea," that is more obviously characteristic in its quiet descriptive meditation on a familiar feature of contemporary life, but the poem has a general significance not so unlike that of those two 'nature' poems – about time and timelessness – and it has this significance the more securely and touchingly and beautifully because, while perhaps coming a little closer to stating it than those two poems do, it still doesn't strain nervously to try to state it all. In the final stanza the last detail of the description of the day, about the first few families starting "the trek back to the cars" from the beach, is followed by:

> The white steamer has gone. Like breathed-on glass
> The sunlight has turned milky. If the worst
> Of flawless weather is our falling short,
> It may be that through habit these do best,
> Coming to water clumsily undressed
> Yearly; teaching their children by a sort
> Of clowning; helping the old, too, as they ought.

That "If" clause, in its quietness, simplicity and brevity, and in its being only the initial subordinate clause of its sentence, may be found breathtaking. It occurred to me in one reading of the poem that what is said in the rest of this last sentence makes too questionable and simple a proposition to be a fully satisfactory 'conclusion' for the poem. But that only led me to become more fully aware that, though it has its weight and seriousness, this statement is not actually being offered as conclusive, let alone conclusive in any hard and absolute way: besides stating what it does, it is also suggesting or creating a larger truth than itself, to do with time and timelessness – quite clear and precise though not easy to paraphrase.

Even in Larkin's best poems there are still touches of the tight-nervous over-deliberateness in composition. The first sentence of "To the Sea" culminates in a line – "The miniature gaiety of seasides" – that sounds a little nervously smart and knowing, as if it were anxiously claiming to be more meaningful than it is. In the first stanza of "Cut Grass" the would-be precision of "exhale", in its rhyme as well as its meaning, makes it sound a little tight and fussy, as the second stanza's "snowlike strewn" perhaps does too. In "The Trees" the second stanza's way of combining the idea of the trees' yearly rebirth with the idea that they nevertheless share our mortality is unnecessarily and a little mechanically and wearisomely clever:

> Their yearly trick of looking new
> Is written down in rings of grain.

In "Show Saturday", a poem in *High Windows* that has much of the same kind of beauty and large significance as "To the Sea", I don't believe that Larkin finds so happy a way of ending. Compare

> If the worst
> Of flawless weather is our falling short…

with one of the final summarising references to the agricultural show, as

> …something people do,
> Not noticing how time's rolling smithy-smoke
> Shadows much greater gestures…

In "Cut Grass", besides its last two lines, I especially love the sudden excited emphasis of

> Lost lanes of Queen Anne's lace…

but the poem has to be read rather carefully for this emphasis to be felt, not having the full easy fluency in which it could not be missed.

Nevertheless, the would-be intellectual precision of "The miniature gaiety of seasides" is more the exception in "To the Sea" than it was likely to have been if the poem had been written earlier, and it is much less important to the poem's power and significance than are the touches of beautiful sensuous precision:

> The small hushed waves' repeated fresh collapse
> Up the warm yellow sand…

> The same clear water over smoothed pebbles,
> The distant bathers' weak protesting trebles
> Down at its edge…

As admitted, *The Less Deceived* does also show the poet's gift for words that say more than they literally say. "At Grass," for example, the last poem in it, creates a knowledge or wisdom not unlike those created in these poems from *High Windows*. The difference is that more than one would-be clever piece of phrasing and a corresponding greater amount of anxious tightness and awkwardness in the poem's music prevent that knowledge and wisdom from being created so clearly or beautifully. And, not being created so clearly or beautifully, they are in more danger of seeming to be mere sentiment, even sentimental.

6. TWO FURTHER HEROIC BUT INCOMPLETE STEPS TOWARDS ALL-OUT POETRY: BY TED HUGHES AND SUE LENIER

There is some penitence behind my discussing Larkin's poetry in the previous section and separating it from the poetry I now go on to discuss – as if it were more simply and fully an example of all-out poetry. I was badly unappreciative of it when I first read it while, when I first read Hughes's poetry and Lenier's, I believe I badly overrated both.* The confession is perhaps to tell the reader no more than that in late-twentieth-century England the parched thirst for all-out poetry could be such that, when a highly gifted and original writer made a dead set at it, as in their very different ways both Hughes and Lenier did (and in his indirect way Leavis), some people might have been – and I was – too ready to take the will for the full deed, and at the same time to take the absence of any such conspicuous will in Larkin for absence of the deed.

But I make this separation between these poets as a token of penitence without wanting to suggest that it finally expresses a serious judgement as well. Each of these three courageous steps towards all-out poetry (or four if that of the critic-prophet is included) has been rewarding and deserves great gratitude, and I don't pretend to be able to be precise about which kind of incompleteness in the step will finally turn out, with posterity, to be the least or the most serious.

---

* My mistake about Larkin still shows – and is not edited out of – a little review included in the second half of this book (see p198). But the full statement of the mistake had been in an earlier review, of the *Whitsun Weddings* collection.

This section hardly needs to be a long one, since the dead-set at the all-out is evident enough with both Hughes and Lenier, like the striking inspiration and power that give rise to it and support it, and like the question that there nevertheless is about the completeness of the success. One sign of that dead-set and of the power in it is the fact that each of these two poets, unlike Larkin, is from the beginning quite uninterested in that vicious style and completely free from its influence. On the other hand, the failure of nerve and faith in twentieth-century England that is shown by that style may be showing a little in their writing, in an element of desperate haste or short-cut-taking as each snatches at an alternative to that style – and at the chance each saw again for all-out art in poetry.

Already with "The Bull Moses" in his second book (*Lupercal*), as with a good number of other poems in his first two books, Hughes is evidently enough an inspired poet. In this poem he is describing himself as a boy looking into the impenetrably dark stall in which the bull is kept and seeing nothing. But

> the warm weight of his breathing,
> The ammoniac reek of his litter, the hotly-tongued
> Mash of his cud, steamed against me.
> Then, slowly, as on to the mind's eye -
> The brow like masonry, the deep-keeled neck:
> Something come up there onto the brink of the gulf,
> Hadn't heard of the world, too deep in itself to be called to,
> Stood in sleep. He would swing his muzzle at a fly
> But the square of sky where I hung, shouting, waving,
> Was nothing to him; nothing of our light
> Found any reflection in him.

It was also early in Hughes's career that a smart member of the London poetry 'scene' sarcastically called him the "Zoo-laureate", and in a similar spirit another member of it asked what Hughes would do as a poet when he ran out of animals to write about. Each was showing his own spiritual provinciality and ignorance. It was clear enough that Hughes's vision was a large and significant general one as well as inspired – of the awesome mystery and power of life, its divine mystery and power – and that in this vision of his Hughes was no rough bumpkin eccentric but joining up with, among other things in the poetic tradition, the great poetry of Chapters 38 to 41 of *The Book of Job.* ("Is the wild ox content to serve thee?") His abundant and ferociously radical religious inspiration then becomes clearer still in such later books as *Crow* and *Gaudete.* But here I have to admit that I praised these two books extravagantly when I published reviews of them, having in my first readings of them been completely bowled over. And it may be precisely the limitation of Hughes's writing that this is how it works when it does work. I now believe that he tended to take the short cut of putting his emphasis on hard-hitting at the expense of creating.

The reader of those lines about the bull can be thrilled and illuminated by the idea that is being put across, but there is almost nothing that he or she can stay with and possess in the poetry, and it is significant that the lines create little or no music to be still and suspended in. The apprehension that came with looking into the bull's stall is less created for its own sake, fully and disinterestedly, than described and staged in order to achieve simply the effect of the apprehension. And that means, among other things, that re-reading can disappoint. (The doubt whether this might happen with the many striking things in those two later books was a reservation I did express in my reviews of them.) While creation is for ever, effects don't continue indefinitely to make the same impact, even when they have been profoundly thrilling and illuminating ones. A part of the disappointment is that nothing new is found in later re-reading: the reader has 'got' it all when the effect is first made.

In this respect Lenier is almost the opposite. All her emphasis is on catching and creating moment after moment, and she can do this with extraordinary bold freedom and poetic resource. Consider the "Rainbuds" poem quoted earlier (p91) and this beginning of a poem from her second book, *Rain Following*:

> When love is in pale slender skeleton shape
> It winces and needs to fly, the air around it cannot help
> And nor can the sky,
> So love, in kimonos, rises and rests…

No English English poet of that time or later could put words together with this kind of quick and suggestive felicity, catching the most subtle and fugitive feelings. In both of her books Lenier seems to be overflowing with the ability to do it, and the quickness of her imagination's movements can even, for a moment, make the movements of Hughes's imagination look like those of a cart-horse and those of Larkin's like those of a permanent convalescent.

Yet the emphasis on ever-vivid 'creating' also seems to be somewhat at the expense of a clear interest in or knowledge of what such moments are finally all for or mean. And the poet herself perhaps admits to taking this short-cut to the all-out (though not saying that that is what it is) when, in the statement quoted in the publisher's prefatory note in her first book, *Swansongs*, she writes:

> I prefer movement to repose in poetry, and emotional action to contemplation.

Whatever the kind of combination they are in, doesn't every good poem have both, and have to have both? Excited and impressed as I am by such lines as I have quoted, part of me is also feeling, if not quite fairly, that they may be almost meaningless; and it seems significant that on that earlier page my starting observations on how the "Rainbuds" poem's fluent words slip and slide into each other are about the expressiveness of the sounds created – whereas my starting observations about how Weiss's fluent words in her four-line poem (p34) are similarly poetry working like poetry and not prose are all about how moving and significant what is created is.

May there even be some connection between what I have just quoted from Lenier's statement about her poetry and this second of the two paragraphs that make up a strikingly strong prose-poem called "The Scream" at the beginning of her *Rain Following*?

> Do you know I move all the time? Endless movement, endless and pointless, I walk not knowing where I am going. When I get there, I cannot stop, I turn around and walk back again. Sometimes when the sun is high and golden, and people are lying on the grass, warm and golden

asleep in the sun, I look upwards and think about waiting, think about stopping but then the sun starts to tick loudly again in my ears and the sky goes off like an alarm and I start walking quickly onwards again, never knowing where I'm going but onwards, onwards and I feel the scream rush backwards into my mouth and I hurry off back into the dark and a night where I cannot sleep.

This prose-poem is, admittedly, a dramatic monologue and not another personal statement.

But the quotation can also serve as another example both of Lenier's vivid creating and of the short-cut involved in it. The poem's own falling short of the wisdom that all-out poetry possesses is for me shown by the way in which it leaves the reader emotionally up in the air at the end, perhaps powerfully excited and impressed but with little or no artistic resolution and thus understanding.

This means that there is finally a resemblance to Hughes as well as the extreme contrast: both poets turn out to go all out for effects, though such very different ones – Hughes in his urgency to have poetry again reveal and celebrate the divinity in life and Lenier in her urgency to have words in poetry be fully dramatic again, creating life rather than merely talking about it.

It is a related point that both poets also, like Leavis, seem to overvalue the "particular" in poetry. In Hughes's writing vivid description can be there too much for its own sake, as if his hitting hard here too is supposed to help guarantee that there is creating of great vitality going on. In the first sentence I quote from "The Bull Moses" the vivid "particulars" are a part of the staging that can have the bull make his significant impression on the reader, but their vividness is somehow a bit more than their serving of that function requires. The "ammoniac reek of his litter" certainly tells us precisely of something real enough, and helps tell us that something invisible but of some size is alive in the black stall seen through this doorway. But does the little 'kick' we can get from its being at once so recognisable and so 'strong' a "particular" finally have anything to do with the more deeply thrilling apprehension the poem is about? In Lenier's writing the quick movement through a great variety of often contrasting vivid images certainly helps create the sensation of "theatre" she is avowedly after – "When I write 'nature' poetry, I'm writing about theatre not nature, conflicts and violence and sudden beauty" (from the statement in *Swansongs* already quoted from) – but the thrilling intense sensation of such 'life' tends to be too much and too exclusively the sheer sensation of it, somehow valued for its own sake.

Things that Hughes said in interview and wrote in prose confirm that he was a prophet and had something significant to say to the world, while the lack of such statements by Lenier tends to confirm that powerful general 'truth' has not quite been the all-important priority with her that one might have hoped it would be in so gifted a writer. Yet it is not exactly the case that she does not give such truth *some* high priority, or has little or nothing to say to the world. So extraordinary a poetic gift cannot very well come out of nothing: poetry of this kind and quality cannot be only fireworks for the sake of fireworks. The suggestion of many things in her poetry – of "The Scream" at the beginning of *Rain Following* and of "Killing Birds" at its end, or of two very early longer poems in *Swansongs*, "Cassandra" and "Harvest Festival" – is that for Lenier it is life that is finally meaningless, as well as abundantly and restlessly lively and lovely and cruel and violent and ugly. And another point that should qualify the criticism that is being made here is that, though her second book closely follows her first, there is already a development in it. I believe that some of the poems in *Rain Following* were written at the same time as poems in *Swansongs*, but that, nevertheless, the difference between the "Rainbuds" poem and the lines from "When love is in pale slender skeleton shape" represents some more general movement away from that "theatre" of nature. Perhaps in her relative silence since 1984, disappointing though this is, the apprehension of the black meaninglessness of life has been developing and being built on and, possibly by going with a deeper understanding of its relation to that touching figure of "Love", also met in one or two other of her poems, becoming a clearer wisdom.

7. BEAUTIFUL POETIC FLUENCY IN AN OLDER FOREIGN-BORN ENGLISH POET

I return to the quality of fluency that I was suggesting the importance of near the end of the previous chapter. I believe it is closely linked to the quality of poetry that the late William Empson was suggesting the importance of when in an interview he expressed disappointment at not finding "a singing line" in the poetry of any of his English contemporaries. Such qualities had obviously fallen into some discredit after the twentieth-century reaction against late Victorian poetry, but a proper *poetic* fluency and singing line can be possessed only by a poem that is also keenly and freshly imagined and thought through – as much of that poetry was not. Another point about these qualities is that they need the poet to have an artistic confidence that may have been more difficult to have when there had been some general failure of nerve in the country. I believe much of the poetry of F.T. Prince, born in South Africa though living most of his adult life in England, does possess a beautiful poetic fluency, and also that it was no accident that he also differed from many of his younger contemporaries by writing a good number of longer poems as well as short ones. His longest, *Memoirs in Oxford*, greatly struck and moved me when it came out as a book by itself in 1970, and it continues to do so. (But I don't remember its having been much noticed by reviewers, and I don't seem to have met many people who know it.) I quote the first seven stanzas from the 1970 edition –

> The sun shines on the gliding river,
>   The river shines and presses through
> Damp meadows and just yellowing trees;
> The tall trees left without a breeze
>   Stand up against the blue!
>
> And on one side a space for cows is
>   Fenced off with willow stumps and wires;
> While there the place of learning drowses –
> Churches and colleges and houses
>   Lifting their domes and towers and spires.

111

I can remember coming here
    For the first time, and in the sun
Of such an autumn, gold and clear;
I walked alone – it was the year
    Of 'crisis', nineteen thirty-one.

Frenchmen were wearing in lapels
    Ne me parlez pas de la crise!
Nobody could foresee what hells
Were waiting – some were forming cells,
    Others could be at ease:

But one could feel the chill on stricken
    England like an eclipse at noon –
A ghostly twilight come to sicken
The old bewildered realm, and thicken
    To darkness and disaster soon.

– Yet here am I, and forced to try
    Thirty years later as it is,
To find some way of telling all –
Walk by a mossy ditch or wall
    Thinking of opportunities

I missed! And can I now forgive
    Myself for having missed so much?
I was afraid to take or give –
Disabled or unfit, to live
    And love – reach out and touch!

– and I simply add that the poem continues in the same attractively easy way, with accumulating pleasure and reward for the reader, for a further 125 stanzas. (The later version printed in the Carcanet *Collected Poems 1935-1992* is two stanzas shorter. This is much the same poem as that of the first edition though with some larger changes in the first section and the beginning of the second, in addition to the small ones that there are made every now and then throughout.

Though my love of the poem as it first came out could well be prejudicing me here, I am not sure those larger changes are improvements.)

SOME SUPPORTING ARGUMENTS

Chapter IV
The grace of high comedy: a brief further note with two long appendices

It comes over me that that second joke-equation in this book's first chapter was incomplete, and this in spite of the use of the crucial missing term in that chapter's very title. If there was point in proposing that the sublime = the revelatory = the sacred = the holy, is the additional "= grace" needed? Perhaps this only comes over me now because it is so unmistakeable in the high comedy that is the exclusive subject of this note. And perhaps it is so unmistakeable here just because the outrageousness enjoyed in such comedy is not only an outrageousness that finally, if mysteriously, makes sense but is the outrageousness that there is in grace too. "How did we ever deserve this!"

There is plenty to justify what Shakespeare has one of his fairy immortals say at one point in *A Midsummer Night's Dream*, about the all too characteristic goings-on he is witnessing among human beings:

Lord, what fools these mortals be!

But this same immortal and others are helping these fools finally to get things right, and they end the play blessing them – after the newly-wed couples have gone off to bed. Something not so dissimilar is happening, and with a convincingness that similarly feels unaccountable or miraculous, at the endings of, for example, *The Wife of Bath's Tale*, *The Merchant of Venice*, *Così fan tutte* and *8½*. Again, too, in these comedies the final blessing is happening as night falls or has fallen. Night can so beautifully, because so naturally, represent both a magical respite from ordinary, often foolish human purposefulness and a magical healing of whatever sicknesses it has produced. It is also night when Mozart's *The Marriage of Figaro* and Verdi's *Falstaff* end, and it is night all the time both in the story we are

117

being told in *The Symposium* and, since its story is that of a dream at night, in Chaucer's *The House of Fame*.

It is again the shocking surprise and wonder of grace that are there to be felt in those light brief *prestos* that end *The Book of Job* and *The Odyssey*. On p60 I mentioned some details of the last page of *Job*. On the last page of *The Odyssey* the highly intelligent and resourceful hero is suddenly and remarkably much quicker-thinking and quicker-feeling than even he has ever been before. At one moment he is letting out a huge battle-cry, as he charges to certain victory against the group of the slain suitors' relatives and supporters that has come to hunt him and his son down (and who are thus, among other things, threatening his and their community in Ithaka with endless feuding); and the very next moment, after a quick intervention by Zeus as well as Athena, and in less than the single complete line that is the last line but one of the whole long epic poem, Odysseus is not only persuaded to halt his charge but absolutely delighted to do so.

The other joke-equation of my first chapter might also come in here. That outrageousness of comedy that has us continually exclaiming inside ourselves to some such effect as "What on earth is going on?" or "How on earth did we get *here*?" produces the catharsis of comedy. The mind is being blown with exceptional decisiveness and completeness, and this, as in the catharsis of tragedy,

> = the death of the ego
> = seeing 'God'.

The happy ending is no happy-complacent, wish-fulfilling fantasy but a matter both for joy and at the same time for profound and even chastening wonder.

I believe such a reference to catharsis makes more complete sense than Henri Bergson himself does of his own sustained and rewarding analysis of how the constant object of laughter is that we, as human beings, have the endless capacity for becoming stiff and mechanical and falling into "automatism", distracted from "the alert suppleness and living flexibility" that properly characterise a human being as against a thing. Automatism manifests ego just as that suppleness and flexibility manifest its divine opposite, life. Going with this is the fact, also not recognised by Bergson, that pure laughter is always finally, even if unconsciously, at ourselves, and accompanied by a feeling of love as well as of wonder. The more disappointingly because of all his lovely earlier examples of humour, particularly from Molière, Bergson ends *Le rire* with the conclusion that there is both malice and egotism in laughter and, with them, a secret bitter pessimism. Laughter evidently is a range of different things, and some laughter certainly does contain these elements, but pure comedy and laughter cannot. When someone slips on a banana skin, in conditions that allow it to be simply comic, uncomplicated by either concern for possible pain or dislike (whether of the person who slips or of the human race), the shock that is indispensable to the delight comes from our unconscious fellow-feeling with anyone walking in his or her dignity of control and purposefulness – and thus with that dignity's sudden collapse. When Bergson represents laughter as an instrument of social correction, with the community collaborating against the deviant, he is evidently right, but only, I suggest, in a narrow and incomplete way, drawing too simple a conclusion from his own just observation that the person in the theatre laughs more the fuller the audience is. Like Bergson, Yeats sees comedy as "passionless" while "tragedy must always be a drowning, a breaking of the dykes that separate man from man" ("The Tragic Theatre"), but he could just as well have written about drowning in comedy. We are all involved.

One proof that the outrageousness of good comedy is always in the end at our expense and thus cathartic is the fact that in some comedy there is no one else to laugh or smile at. The smile produced by the lines of Dryden's previously quoted (p61) is probably less a smile on the face than a smile deep inside, and it is a smile at nothing else but our own and everybody else's solemn self-importance. Even at our distance from the seventeenth century, which means that we can't get the full shock of such a quick, light throw-off as "Thy wars brought nothing about," we still have some serious feelings when we think of Charles I, Cromwell and the Civil War. On the last pages of *Job* and *The Odyssey* the protagonists are clearly not being smiled at, for doing something silly or wrong, and nor are all the wonderfully lively figures in Plato's *Symposium*. If in Chaucer's *The House of*

Fame the poet does occasionally have us smiling at himself, that is only one contribution to the extravagant outrageousness of the whole and is in any case itself part of the tease; and, if in his *Wife of Bath's Tale*, there may be some smiles at the knight who is the main character, it is we ourselves who are being much the more played around with by the story. Its beginning is a plain nasty rape by this knight and, of all things, its ending is this same man's finding himself in bed with his newly wed and wonderfully beautiful and loving young wife. In the poker-faced telling of the story one quietly bewildering surprise has followed another, starting with the fact that the rapist has initially been condemned to death and it has been women, of all people, who have pleaded for his life. Among the subsequent surprises is the fact that after this the rape is never mentioned again and, shockingly, can look as if it has actually been forgotten. Yet a beautiful combination of justice with grace is somehow, at the end of the story, felt to have been represented.

The great comedy created by Jonathan Swift's extraordinary way with irony is another example of there often being no butt for the comedy but ourselves (while it is also an example of the fact that great comedy, while always marked by delight and wonder, isn't always necessarily marked by laughter or even smiles). When in the last chapter of his *Travels* Lemuel Gulliver is indignant at some length at the tall stories other travellers sometimes tell, our minds, as so often by Swift's irony, are simply and impossibly cut in two:

> I could heartily wish a law were enacted, that every traveller, before he was permitted to publish his voyages, should be obliged to make oath before the Lord High Chancellor that all he intended to print was absolutely true to the best of his knowledge; for then the world would no longer be deceived as it usually is, while some writers, to make their works pass the better upon the public, impose the grossest falsities on the unwary reader.

With one half of our minds, as we go from this sentence to the next and to the next, we see the forceful indignation as completely real and reasonable, while with the other half we simultaneously know that that is impossible and completely ridiculous. Our minds are quite broken down – decisively, ruthlessly and quite unavoidably divided right down the middle – and, as our egos are thus annihilated, for a precious moment or two and with a delighted wonder we enjoy an extraordinary rare freedom.

The word "impossible" fits much that happens in *The Symposium*. In its outrageous and exuberant fun the impression of a special grace is marked and the characters are not only not the butts of the comedy but are actually being presented to us much more for admiration than for anything else. At its start the character telling the story of the great party is crazy-wild with his experience of grace. Words of Rumi, the great medieval dervish poet, fit him:

> I'm like an ant that's gotten into the granary,
> ludicrously happy, and trying to lug out
> a grain that's way too big.
> (Translated by Coleman Banks in his *The Essential Rumi*)

Then at the end, astonishingly and breathtakingly though very briefly, and being completely silent about what he is doing, Plato himself joins in the general crazy wildness. On his last page he tells of Socrates, Aristophanes and Agathon still drinking and talking, until just before dawn, with Socrates apparently persuading both this great writer of comedies and this great writer of tragedies that neither can really know anything about his art. Just as the persuasion is working and day is dawning, each of the dramatists in turn... falls asleep. Socrates' argument is that anyone who is able to understand and thus work in one of these two arts must also be able to understand and thus work in the other, and a part of the argument not given but clearly implied is that no one really understands either of those arts except the philosopher, who understands both. The breathtakingly bold, silent insinuation is that it is therefore Plato himself who is the only real master of drama in Athens. He has previously written both dialogues that are comedies and dialogues that are tragedies, and in *The Symposium* itself he has, in the speeches on Eros he has written for his characters, shown that he possesses both the art of Aristophanes and that of Agathon, as well as the philosophical art of Socrates. When such zestful and good-natured high spirits as the whole brilliant party has been full of are at their purest, in the true lover of wisdom, one result of the completer grace known by that lover is the freedom to compete, brag and exult with outrageous frankness and uninhibitedness – while at the same time being both serious and quite unegotistic. Here, of course, as in *The Book of Job* and *The Odyssey*, the ending is itself less any main part of the revelation than a delightfully unexpected but 'right' little topping on the cake. I describe it here because that can be done so briefly and at the same time suggest something of the extraordinariness of the whole work.

I have generalised about all good comedy, and I make the distinction "high comedy", for a kind of art that is rare, only to mark the double fact that the vision seen in the catharsis in these exceptional works is an unusually profound one and that their artists are openly offering to handle great mysteries in this extraordinarily bold way. There can obviously be bigger and smaller deaths of the ego and visions of 'God'.

THE TWO LONG APPENDICES

These appendices are as much to explain and support two possibly surprising inclusions in my list of examples of high comedy as to expand on the general idea of it. Most of the other examples are much more celebrated works, and I am addressing what I believe is a common underrating of both Chaucer's *The House of Fame* and Fellini's *8½*. Yet I hope that each appendix does also give some development to the idea of high comedy. Some of the underrating of each of these two works can be put down to people's not being prepared for this kind of art because the examples of it are so few.

The piece on *The House of Fame* is adapted, with some modification, from a review of a book on the poem. The piece on *8½* is extracted with some revisions from a longer article that was first published in 1967, four years after the film came out.

1. Chaucer's *The House of Fame*

This poem appears to break off, unfinished, at the very moment when an explanation of all that is baffling in it might seem to be just starting. In the poet's dream Jupiter's eagle has come to rescue him from illusions he has suddenly become terrified of falling into – after the shock of walking out of a beautiful temple of Venus into an endless barren desert. The eagle has hinted that he is going to learn news, both news about his neighbours and certain special news, from a distant country, about the gladness of "Love's folk", and for this he has taken him up to the sky's great house of fame. All that he has seen there has both impressed and disillusioned the poet, but he hasn't yet found the promised news and has now gone to look for it in a nearby building in the sky, the whirling and crowded and much less magnificent house of rumour. By this he is partly disappointed again: these ordinary noisy news-tellers seem to know more lies than anything else. But then he sees crowds rushing eagerly to a corner of the hall where news about love is being told, and he glimpses a man of great authority .

The text stops dead at this point. Some lines earlier the poet has indicated that he does now, as he tells his dream, know the special news. He says he won't tell it since there isn't any need to: other people can sing it better than he can.

In *Chaucer and the Tradition of Fame: Symbolism in "The House of Fame"*, which came out shortly before J.A.W. Bennett's *Chaucer's "Book of Fame": an exposition of "The House of Fame"*, an American scholar, B.G. Koonce, conjectures that the poem is not really unfinished. He speculates that it was a contribution to a festive Christmas 'ritual' or pageant put on in the Inner Temple, that the special news which some other person may have come on to declare was the good news of the Gospel, with the delivery of "a sermon or, more likely, a reading from Scripture or the liturgy." Some rather tenuous external evidence could associate the poem with an occasion in the Inner Temple, and the date which Chaucer himself gives his dream does fall within Advent. That does not sound very strong. But previously, in the main part of his commentary on the poem, Koonce has brought out many separate, unspeculative reasons for believing that this very light, witty and wild-dashing-fantastic poem is earnestly concerned with salvation and damnation, and has for its upshot something like this: that human wishes for success in this world are not only vain but spiritually dangerous traps, and men can consequently rejoice in the Christian hope. I do not find all of the detailed argument for this interpretation convincing, but I believe enough of it is, and I also believe that the interpretation has some very good poetry working in its favour. The passage in which the poet walks out of Venus' temple, at the end of the poem's first Book, is an example. After exclaiming over the fine representations of the story of *The Aeneid* that he has been looking at in the temple (and that have been described in the poem), the poet thinks to himself that he doesn't know who made them, nor where he is, nor in what country. He decides to go outside and see whether he can find anywhere

> …any stirring man
> That may me telle where I am.

Then:

>   When I out at the doores came
> I fast aboute me beheld.
> Then saw I but a large field
> As far as that I mighte see
> Withouten town or house or tree [*town=farm?*]
> Or bush or grass or eryd land [*ploughed*]
> For all the field nas but of sand [*was only*]
> As small as men may see yet lie
> In the desert of Libie,
> Ne no maner creature [*Nor any kind of*]
> That is yformed by Nature
> Ne saw I, me to rede or wisse. [*advise or guide*]
> "O Christ!" thought I, "that art in bliss,
> From phantom and illusion
> Me save!" and with devotion
> Mine eyen to the heaven I cast.
> Then was I war, lo! at the last, [*aware*]

124

That faste by the sun, as high
As kenne might I with mine eye,
Me thought I saw an eagle soar
But that it seemed muche more [*larger*]
Than I had any eagle seen.

Although we can slip past "That may me telle where I am" without necessarily feeling that the words carry any special weight, we can hardly do that with the words that follow – even though they, too, carry their load with a light step.

I give this prominence to the proposal of Koonce's that is mere speculation because I find it very taking, and even prefer it to some of the thoughts of his that he presses harder, but also for another reason. I think it might be a word to the wise, almost enough of a hint by itself to people who have hitherto been baffled and for that reason not very interested by *The House of Fame*. It does not matter, of course, whether or not it was the Inner Temple. The important suggestion is that the whole poem may have been leading up to the good news of the Kingdom of Heaven. And this is actually rather more than speculation. If the poem was doing this, then that news is a flash that lights up all that has come before. In the course of the poem Chaucer has only hinted at a central theme and has kept his hearers busy with the many surprises and changes of direction that he has sprung on them, all with his poker face, his light and non-committal verse and no explanation. Though he writes with an air of thoroughly knowing what he is about and of advancing towards a quite definite goal, no one could know in advance or even guess what that goal was. Even his first audience, supposing they had known beforehand that some celebration of the Christian good news had been promised by their poet, would have had little idea how he was going to fulfil that with the strange and often inconsequential-seeming though enjoyable and wonderful story-farrago that he appeared to be telling. In modern times readers have sometimes thought the poem confused. If Koonce's conjecture is correct, the light would suddenly have gone on at the very end, making a climax which would have been both convincing and breathtaking. It would have been bold but also beautifully polished and graceful, a fitting ending for a poem of such exuberant good spirits. Perhaps the nearest thing to it is the very different ending of Fellini's *8½*, a film that is another earnest handling of salvation and damnation through high-spirited comedy and fantasy.

For myself it was this coexistence of gravity with gaiety that first made the poem look worth more attention, at the time when Koonce's commentary came to make clear just how grave the poem is. Chaucer's art here is highly original, so far as I know, and it also seems to me to be of a rare and wonderful kind. Towards the close of his *Essay on Man* Pope describes that essential ease of poetry that he himself aspired to but that Chaucer's poem, as I believe, realises in a more remarkable way than any of his own.[*] (Pope is addressing his friend Bolingbroke.)

> Teach me, like thee, in various Nature wise,
> To fall with dignity, with temper rise;
> Formed by thy converse, happily to steer
> From grave to gay, from lively to severe...

If Pope's steering is that of a car-driver negotiating a pleasantly winding road with expert smoothness, Chaucer's, in comparison, is that of a pilot performing virtuoso aerobatics in the open sky. And his poem's wild bravura seems to me not only a power and a joy but a wisdom, and a kind of tact.

The poem has this quality whatever the truth about its ending. An exhilarated "Where on earth are we *now*?" or "How on earth did we get here?" is the reader's reaction again and again. I will take an example that Bennett makes a similar comment on. Before telling his dream, Chaucer invokes the help of the god of sleep. He does this in terms that are unexpectedly a little irreverent and sceptical, though not emphatically so, and continues in the same breath and same light-rapid verse with a solemn invoking of help from God:

---

[*] Yet, like the older Dryden of only a few years earlier, the younger Pope does have the idea and inspiration of outrageous high comedy. The idea is in the "Epistle to Miss Blount" about the works of the French poet Voiture, and the inspiration shows in *The Rape of the Lock*, which is so much more a piece of love-poetry than of satire.

> And he that mover is of all
> That is and was and ever shall…

With a further little equivocation or two he prays to God for blessings on those of his hearers who take his poem in the right way, and immediately follows this with a prayer to Christ for a thoroughgoing curse on hearers who take it the wrong way. As Bennett says, we are "being juggled between high style and low, jest and earnest." He says that the final curse "tips the scale back to pleasantry," but I am not sure that the juggling is not even faster than that. The curse is ridiculously emphatic, and it may be burlesquing a conventional admonition to the audience, but at the end of it are we left quite certain that there was no genuine sting in it? It concludes with a reference to the terrible fate of a man who misinterpreted a dream that was a matter of life and death to him… Might people who misinterpret this poem do so precisely because they themselves are on the primrose path, and blithely and blindly content to be on it? People do unwittingly pass judgements on themselves with the reactions they make to poems, and the history of comment on *The House of Fame* itself may supply some cases that are particularly piquant because of the warning. There are not only the consequences for this poem of a bad tradition in commentary on Chaucer's work, on which more later, but also indications that at least two great later poets, Ben Jonson in *The Masque of Queens* and Pope in *The Temple of Fame*, have responded to Chaucer's idea of a splendid hall of fame with more ambition than religious fear, and have apparently taken it for granted that that was what Chaucer intended. A train of thought like that in these last three sentences seems to come quite naturally, though the poetry is far from forcing it on us and quickly moves on, and our main feeling remains an exhilarated bewilderment at the joking. Later, if Koonce is right about the poem's ending, there seems to be a retrospective further delight from that opening curse. The doubt whether there may not be a serious sting in it for all its ridiculousness has probably carried with it – and left unresolved and hanging somewhere in the mind – a combination of amazement and some discomfort at the possibility that Chaucer, of all poets, could be showing such outrageous arrogance. But the tease of this is finally set to rest, and the powerful sense of grace thus given a further witty and pleasant reinforcement, when that news or "tiding" that is being quested for in the poem turns out to have nothing at all to do with the poet and is not even going to be given in his words.

Bennett probably would not agree about this sting, since he does not think the poem concerned with any life-or-death matters at all. He has a very different general idea of it from Koonce's: a version of the fairly common idea that in this poem Chaucer was thinking more about poetry than about anything else, and especially about his own future as a poet. The poet, as Bennett sees him, is presenting himself "as a seeker after fresh poetic inspiration." That is the barren desert from which he is rescued, and he is finally taken to the house of rumour in order that he may find new stories or subject-matter. Hitherto, as he himself says near the beginning of the poem, he has been a bookish man, ignorant of his very neighbours, but in the house of rumour he is to meet the ordinary people of the world and see that it is from the plethora of tales told by them that he should work his own things up. Later we are going to see him with these people, in *The Canterbury Tales*, collecting and working up their stories, himself transformed from a bookworm into a convivial fellow-drinker.

I believe that this idea is rather obviously questionable. But I will omit some immediate small objections made in my original review (*The Cambridge Quarterly* IV 3, on p306) and move straight to two larger ones. (1) Like Koonce, Bennett shows that at different places in his poem Chaucer is drawing on some impressive passages from Dante, Boethius, Cicero's *Dream of Scipio* and the Bible, but, unlike the American scholar, he has no account to give of why Chaucer is doing this. "...Dante's high purposes and allusions are half-humorously transposed into a different key, though never burlesqued." But, if Chaucer is not burlesquing Dante, it is not, apparently, that there is really any kind of seriousness in these passages. Bennett tends to assume that anything that is humorous could not also be serious. But in that case what is Chaucer doing? The only answer that comes to me from Bennett's book, and it only comes from between its lines, is that Chaucer was a very donnish literary trifler, lightly playing with echoes of famous and striking passages just for the sake of doing so. It is strange, in that case, that he should write such good poetry here. This is from the long sentence describing the Dantean eagle's terrible seizing of the poet, near the begining of Book 2:

> ...And with his grimme pawes strong
> Within his sharpe nailes long
> Me fleeing in a swoop he hent [*caught*]
> And with his sours again up went... [*upward flight*]

In a similar way Bennett brings out some of the reasons for identifying with the Christian God the Jupiter whose eagle is rescuing the poet but seems quite untroubled by the fact that, on his reading of the poem, either God is being represented as working to no very serious purpose or Chaucer is showing great personal presumption.

(2) Behind his idea of the poem lies a main distorting prejudice about Chaucer's work and, although he was unlucky to have sent his book to press before Koonce's had come out, I am not sure that that prejudice would not have resisted the American scholar's arguments. It is such a widespread prejudice, from so old and powerful a tradition, however bad. It appears when Bennett expresses his delight with all the liars in the house of rumour –

> Here in little is that "full tide of human existence" that Dr Johnson delighted to watch in motion at Charing Cross...

– and again when he describes as a "boon-companion" the character Chaucer represents of himself in *The Canterbury Tales*, even though the poet has another character in that work, the inn Host, call him "elfish"[*]. The prejudice appears again when Professor Bennett asserts that, when in Book 2 of *The House of Fame*, Chaucer borrows from Cicero the idea of seeing the world from far above, as an insignificant

---

[*] This is in the Prologue to *Sir Thopas*. Bennett does quote the passage from that Prologue but then bases his "boon-companion" on these lines from the *General Prologue*: "So had I spoken with them everyone / That I was of their fellowship anon." The entry on "elfish" in the Glossary of the edition of Chaucer's works that I have gives as alternative meanings "mysterious" and "elf-like, absent in demeanour, not of this world."

pinpoint, he is definitely not expressing any of the *contemptus mundi* that is in the Cicero. An earlier scholar expresses the general prejudice in these words:

> No strains from the music of the Dance of Death, which pleased certain ears in the Middle Ages and the Renaissance, no rarefied religiosity or unworldly melancholy mar [any of Chaucer's] lines.
>
> (H.R. Patch, *On Rereading Chaucer*, 1939)

On the same page as this are the usual remarks about the poet's health, sanity, good sense, good humour. The prejudice is a strong one that leads both of these scholars to fly so violently in the face of the facts. Mightn't Chaucer have had his sanity and good humour for the very reason that he thought that life on this earth has no secure good to offer and is only a pilgrimage?

> That thee is sent, receive in buxomness, [*What…submissively*]
> The wrestling for this world asketh a fall.
> Here is no home, here nis but wilderness, [*is only*]
> Forth, pilgrim, forth! Forth, beast, out of thy stall!
> Know thy country, look up, thank God of all, [*for all*]
> Hold the high way, and let thy ghost thee lead, [*spirit*]
> And truth thee shall deliver, it is no dread. [*there is no doubt*]

This is Chaucer, in his "Truth: Balade de Bon Conseyl". He also has his Theseus bring the action of *The Knight's Tale* to its final resolution with a long and grave speech about the inescapability of death, and about the fact that death itself is an escape from "this foule prison of this life." The deduction Chaucer has Theseus draw is that people should be joyful (and that two characters who have long been mourning the terrible death of another character should now marry each other):

> What may I conclude of this long serye [*from…argument*]
> But after woe I rede us to be merry [*counsel*]
> And thanken Jupiter of all his grace? [*for*]

130

Though the logic of this isn't obvious, it's neither unheard of nor necessarily unsound (and it may have much to do with Chaucer's being one of the most beautifully unegotistic of all the great poets). It is also the logic of *The House of Fame*. A realisation of the joyful news of grace would come after the exposure of the vanity and danger of human wishes, and after the clear vision *sub specie aeternatis* of the great confused mixture that human life on this earth is.

I don't believe the humour and wit of *The House of Fame* would be of so rare a quality if they were not in their extraordinary way coexisting with the great gravity. Here one specific test is the poet's conversations with the eagle in Book 2. Those who dwell on the supposed comic characterisation of the eagle – Bennett writes of this "garrulous and old-maidish bird" and of the bird's "slightly bossy, patronising good nature" – seem to have been led by their general idea of the poem to substitute a relatively coarse and complacent humour for Chaucer's. Isn't the fun finer, and also greater, if the eagle's manner of speaking doesn't make us think mainly about the eagle's character but about how completely the Chaucer he is speaking to is out of his depth? Seized by the powerful bird and carried up into the sky, he is terrified and bewildered, and most of what happens is quite beyond him, even when he makes desperate-silly attempts to grasp it. Yet he has the bird speaking to him in a thoroughly human voice, calmly and at great length, explaining things to him with an easy familiar confidence, vigorously reassuring him, being patient, kind, ironic – all with an incomprehensible authority and impersonality. Koonce suggests that Chaucer's very brief replies to the questions he is asked about the eagle's longest piece of exposition – he politely agrees that it is plausible and that its lucid straightforwardness was a good thing – indicates precisely that he has not been able to understand much of it at all. I think the humour and inexplicitness and complete absence of 'soul' help to make this one of the most felicitous accounts of the state of being out of one's depth, perhaps more than comparable with Diotima talking to Socrates in *The Symposium*.

That ending of the poem must be quoted, preceded by a further word about its polish and gracefulness. Throughout the poem some of Chaucer's serious play has been with allusions to *The Divine Comedy*, and there is some final play with them here. A much too unsympathetic reader of Dante's poem might say that on his last page Dante is awarding himself a unique, unprecedented personal interview with the Godhead, as the final reward for his devotion to Beatrice, admittedly erratic though that has been. Chaucer has been depicting himself as also being rewarded, by Jupiter, for his long and hopeless service to Venus. Yet the special privilege he is given of a flight up into the sky and a visit to the spectacular house of fame has brought more disillusion than reward. It is only when he has gone down to the house of rumour and is there among the crowd of deluded and deluding publicans and sinners that he hears the promised tiding of "some country". And at the moment when that news comes he can only be one of the whole crowd that is eagerly milling to hear it. Now, as he tells his dream, he doesn't need to repeat the news to the assembled company since other people can sing it better than he can. The joy and wonder of the poem's final brief *presto* are the more keenly felt:

> And as I altherfastest went [*fastest of all*]
> About and did all mine intent
> Me for to playen and to lere [*learn*]
> And eke a tiding for to hear [*also*]
> That I had heard of some country
> That shall not now be told for me -
> For it no need is, redely, [*truly*]
> Folk can sing it bet than I, [*better*]
> For all must out, either late or rathe, [*soon*]
> Alle the sheaves in the lathe - [*barn*]
> I heard a great noise withal
> In a corner of the hall
> Ther men of love-tidinges told [*Where*]
> And I gan thitherward behold, [*began*]
> For I saw running every wight [*person*]
> As fast as that they hadden might,
> And everych cried "What thing is that?" [*everyone*]
> And some said "I not never what." [*never discovered*]
> And when they were all on a heap

> Those behind began up leap
> And climben up on others fast
> And up the nose and eyen cast
> And trodden fast on others heels
> And stampen as men do after eels. [*when trying to catch eels*]
> At the last I saw a man
> Which that I namen not ne can
> But he seemed for to be
> A man of great authority.

The poet's touch is so light that his poetry vanishes almost as soon as it comes. It doesn't seem to have any great substance anywhere, even in the vivid encounters between the poet and the eagle and between Fame and her suitors. There seems to be nothing to hold us. Always the verse is moving rapidly on, and the strongest effects come through surprise and the fine timing with which unexpected things are being combined.

Some readers have thought that the poem doesn't really get going until Chaucer finishes describing the first part of his dream, when he is in the temple of Venus and seeing the representations there of the story of *The Aeneid*. For them one question is whether the light touch suits this material. The main emphasis falls on the grievously betrayed and bound-for-Hell Dido. But I have found, myself, that the brief Book 1's relative sobriety makes it a good start to the poem, and also that there is a positive felicity and truth in the way that the various catastrophes and deaths and the strongest notes of Dido's protest to Aeneas and tragic self-realisation come in and go out so quickly, as in lines like these:

> And after this was grave, allas! [*engraved*]
> How Ilion assailed was
> And won, and king Priam y-slain
> And Polites his son, certain,
> Despitously of daun Pirrhus. [*cruelly, lord*]

"O have ye men such goodlyhead
In speech and never a deal of truth?" [*never a bit of*]

"O sooth is, every thing is wist [*known*]
Though it be covered with the mist.
Eke though I mighte duren ever [*Also, could live for ever*]
That I have done recover I never..." [*What*]

Again the strongest and most significant effect is made by surprise, when the dreaming Chaucer wonders who made these representations and where he is and goes out of the magnificent temple into the terrifying endless desert that immediately has him praying to be saved from illusion.

The poem's peculiar insubstantiality is also its point and its exhilaratingness and its beauty.

2. Fellini's *8½*

I have described this film above (p126) as "another earnest handling of salvation and damnation through high-spirited comedy and fantasy." Everyone who has seen it will recognise the truth of the description "high-spirited" and of talk of its exceptional lightness, liveliness and élan. Perhaps all that is needed here is juxtaposition of the reference to this quality with some of the reasons for saying that the film is also dealing with matters of great gravity. I attempt this in two ways, first with a summary of the film's action[*] and second with a

---

[*] But from this I omit all reference to Fellini's decision to make his main character a film-director and to have it as a datum of his whole fiction that it is this director who has made the film the audience is now watching (the character's spiritual crisis becomes at the same time the 'creative block' that there is in his making of his film). This is scaffolding and not structure, an artistic device used in order to help create certain artistic possibilities, and the main character is clearly much more a representation of Everyman than Fellini's self-portrait. Sadly, when the film came out, some smart critics, at any rate in England, had no interest in artistic possibilities and purposes and couldn't resist the tit-bit of possible autobiography. Even Kenneth Tynan (*Right and Left*) called *8½* "a superb narcissistic film".

reference to Fellini's lifelong artistic interest in what he has referred to as "transfiguration".

(1) If *The House of Fame* alludes to *The Divine Comedy*, so does *8½*. Its opening alludes to Dante's opening lines. The main character, Guido, is having a nightmare of being in a huge and horribly deadly-still traffic jam on what looks like an intolerably hot Roman afternoon. Then he is being nearly suffocated in his motionless car, and desperately climbs onto the top of it and, from there, flies up into the air, only in a few moments to be brought crashing down to earth again – and to wake up. It is then slipped in that he is at the same point in his life as Dante's first line says he is. On waking, he is asked his age by the health-spa nurse and gives it, forty-three – a reasonable approximation for a modern Italian to the *mezzo del cammin di nostra vita*, the middle of our life's journey.

At the health spa this character seems to be taking a break because of mild illness but, even more, because he is at an impasse in his life. It has come to a stop as he is paralysed at once by a sense of his life's being a complicated irresolvable mess and by a teasing intuition, on which he hardly knows how to begin to act, of a possible hope for some resolution and for the simplicity of a new pure and free life. While definitely existing, his intuition is a woefully fragile and fleeting one, and in the film we watch him having to wait in a long, more than half passive and certainly not fully deliberate period of meditation, sometimes roused to observe with a musing fresh curiosity his wife, mistress, friends, colleagues and self, sometimes reminiscing in his own mind or dreaming or day-dreaming or brooding – allowing himself, altogether, to take in more and more of the truth about himself and his life. At the same time he and we are seeing in the spa crowds of other middle-aged and elderly people, queuing up with him for glasses of the spring water or, everyone uniformly stripped down like himself to wearing only a towel, going down the long stairs to the underground area where the steam-baths and mud-baths are. Each doubtless has his or her own trouble in life. Guido's plight is not only his own.

As he is assembling together main things in his life, the chance of his realising the new happiness and 'truth' that he is tantalised by the idea of seems more and more hopeless, though he hangs on to his intuition and holds out against cheating himself with any premature 'answer', let alone with any substitute contentment. For example, he has to take a bitter denunciation of himself from his wife, and has to recognise both how just it is and how fine a person she is even though she is being so unpleasant to him at that moment. He himself is only being ridiculous, listening without being able either to answer or to accept, grimacing with a fatuous mixture of helplessness and obstinacy. She denounces not mainly his infidelity, but the seemingly endless series of lies and half-lies that he tells her, himself and others. Yet he also knows, just about, that he has to be ridiculous like this in the face of her anger: he has to believe that those simple main facts and her understanding of them are not the whole truth about his life, and that it will turn out to make some sense and achieve some worthiness however unlikely that seems. And in all his seeming impotence he has to continue both to wait and to claim that he himself is the only person who can find out what that sense and worthiness are and only in his own way.

Finally, when he seems to have to confess complete defeat in the most humiliating public circumstances, his anguish and despair are at their height and he dreams vividly of suicide. Then in the magical silence which follows this moral 'death' the intuition at last begins to flower. Having gone to the bitter end and told himself all the truths, painful and less painful, he is at last free from all the inner pressure, confusion and flight, and free to see that what life has given him and is giving him is, in the whole, something wonderfully and beautifully pure. The break-through to this is not the literal escape that he has half thought it might be. It is a brief last day-dream, though here the kind of day-dream that is lucid vision, where he sees all the people in his life, the people he has been watching, remembering, dreaming about or running away from in the main part of the film, now calmly and happily walking nearby, smiling amiably and confidently and dressed in shining white. And he can join them, and everybody else at the spa, and the rest of the human race, because he is free of them as they are free of him. It is a swift vision of the essential beauty and grace of life that every human being may know.

A particularly touching moment is when, in the middle of the circus ring that is now there, he offers his wife his hand, to lead her into the large circle in which everybody else at that point is hand in hand walking or dancing round on that ring's low surrounding wall, and she, gently and soberly and with both a suggestion of reserve and all her independence, nevertheless takes it.

(2) So both the main character and the audience with him experience the death of the ego and the grace that follows. This final vision of the film is what Fellini means by a transfiguration.

Some years before *8½* he had written of another project for a film that it seemed a particularly suitable one for him "because it sums up all the themes that are dearest to me, and in the sympathetic depiction of this reality it carries along with it a 'transfiguration' that I have sometimes sought for painfully and laboriously in other films." (Translated from the French in Gilbert Salachas' handbook *Federico Fellini*, p173)

"And [He] was transfigured before them: and His face did shine as the sun, and his raiment was white as the light." The main character in any Fellini film is quite likely to meet a person with the special sweetness of a wonderfully shining face. Perhaps both the word and the idea, "sweetness", have lost their power in most of the Western World, and perhaps, in any case, on the evidence of painting, the idea has always been stronger in Italy. But anyone might be struck by the light in the faces of the nun in *La strada*, the crippled young woman in the last sequence of *Il bidone* and the girl who appears from nowhere at the end of *La dolce vita*. And, for all the pressure the other way in our culture, anyone might be slow to call this light sentimental. It is too unfamiliar for that. The quality that is seen in its sweetness is that of a complete and joyful inner stillness and self-possession. This seems to make the person pure of all covert egotistic fear or desire when she meets another person, and quite free therefore to go out to the other person, as to everything else in life, with absolutely open interest and curiosity and radiant good will. While it is true that the young woman in *Il bidone* clearly has a sudden hope for some miraculous help for her crippled condition from the senior ecclesiastic she believes she is meeting, she is never egotistically fixing the pressure of that on him or showing the slightest ill will when she is disappointed. With her the idea of this figure is so marvellously realised that its beauty is almost unbearable (and not only because of the cruel ironies that there are in the whole situation which the character cannot be aware of). In all these figures the shining water of life wells up from inside, into and through the face, and with a steady, ever-renewed flow. At the same time, they can also give the impression of having not the slightest fear of solitude – of space or of silence. On the contrary, space and silence in God's air are beautiful.

This is true even, and sometimes especially, when one comes out into them from a crowded, noisy and restless party. The movement from noise to silence, constriction to space, and crowdedness to emptiness is something Fellini often makes a wonderfully expressive use of, rendering an inner spiritual movement with great lucidity. The parties are frequent in his films before *8½*, especially in *La dolce vita*, and they seem to be showing another side of the subject of transfiguration: the fact that the human race's deep hunger for it is so often desperately blind and misdirected. Whether the party is a carnal-social debauch or a religious-social debauch, there we human beings are, urgently striving to lose ourselves in it. An example is the long sequence in *La dolce vita* about the false miracle that has gathered huge excited crowds and through a long night made a large open area outside Rome a very highly populated and busy one. An Italian writer, Angelo Solmi, who interprets this film as a whole in the simple severe sense against which Fellini himself protested, as denunciation, only sees in this "a social egotism masked by false piety" and has nothing to say about that powerful hunger that is also being vividly represented – all the more powerful just because it is being expressed in that partly egotistic and blind and therefore hopeless way. It is right that of the film's leading characters the one who is most involved in this sequence is the main character's mistress (Emma) and that here her 'blindness' is memorably and painfully seen in her characteristic tight emotional intensity and in the urgency of her searching. Correspondingly, the grave reality that comes back to the area with the bleak light of dawn and the people's beginning to disperse seems to me more than the accusation that that same writer says it is. It is moving and beautiful because, as it shows up the falseness in the night's emotion, it also shows that life has more dignity than that, and that people are greater than such false transfigurations make them. At the backs of our minds there may be a faint despairing sense of how wonderful that true transfiguration must be that might come about in this open light and air and quiet. The dignity which these human beings have at the painful dawn, in addition to their pathos, partly comes from the fact that they have been forced by the reality to retreat from their false togetherness and have each accepted their confirmed solitude and deprivation. And something of the same dignity is present even when, after more than one of the crude carnal debauches of the film, the dawnlight and space are exposing a more grotesque, cheapened and silly humanity. These human beings, too, are simply being returned to their hunger and, helplessly, are accepting this and cannot do anything but accept it.

In *8½* the crowds of health-seekers at the spa provide images of human beings in daylight and space (or, even when going downstairs to the underground baths, doing so in full light and with plenty of space and of white around them), and they are also images of human beings accepting both their need and each's being on his or her own with it, seeking neither any false transcendence nor any false togetherness.

The reference to *La dolce vita* and other earlier films of Fellini's, together with the artist's own statement that the transfiguration has sometimes been sought by him painfully and laboriously, can go alongside a French critic's account of why *8½* was "perhaps the first really honest film of Fellini's, the first which refuses to exalt the angel that the film-maker would like to be in order to acknowledge the human being that he is." Jean Collet finds Fellini succumbing to "this temptation of the angel", and at the same time straining too hard to exorcise "the brute", in both *La strada* and *Il bidone*, and writes that "The descent to the hells of *La dolce vita* was necessary for Fellini finally to venture, with *8½*, on intoning the chant of the depths" (translated from his contribution to the number of *Etudes Cinématographiques* that was devoted to *8½*). But Collet's observations may also help to suggest why the wonderful lightness and high spirits of *8½* are possible as they had not been for Fellini before (for all the many ways in which they had been anticipated in his earlier films), and also how they go so deep.

These are striking first of all, perhaps, in the overall rhythm of the film and of the movement and transitions in it, which is the rhythm of a circus show. The audience's attention is commanded by the dashing showman-like vigour with which any sequence or 'act' is briskly brought on, with little or no plot continuity that clearly links it with the preceding ones and to the accompaniment of circus music, of one mood or another but often a cheerfully extrovert one. Each separate 'act' in the whole brilliantly varied show therefore gets attended to and enjoyed for its own sake, simply and without *arrière-pensée*, and thus with an unusually full kind of attention and enjoyment. How this works in a deep way and helps bring about the sublimity of the film's ending is suggested by an observation that was made by André Bazin, remarkably, on earlier and much less comic films by Fellini and years before *8½* came out:

> The Fellini protagonist doesn't come to the final crisis, which destroys him and saves him, by the links of a connecting, developing plot, but because the circumstances that he is in some way or other struck by accumulate in him, like the energy of the vibrations in a body that is tuned to them. He doesn't so much evolve as get converted, and overbalance or tip over, to finish up in the way that icebergs do that have had the central point of their floating invisibly displaced. (Translated from Salachas' handbook on Fellini)

The fact gets obscured by Guido's own worry and anguish, and by the inclusion of enough real ugliness, pain and embarrassment, but there has been so much for the audience as well as him to be unconsciously delighting in, and to be "struck" by and have "accumulate" in them, that the film's final vision is only the suddenly possible full recognition of this, and thus feels absolutely right though miraculously so.

The film's very showman-likeness and bravura, like those of *The House of Fame*, work, among other things, as a kind of tact. Fellini's touch with the spiritual crisis and anguish is vigorous and yet also, and somehow as a result of this, light. Even the horror of the traffic-jam nightmare or of the vividly imagined suicide is at the same time witty, and even the bedroom scene of the wife's denunciation, or the scene on the following day in which she finally tells him that the marriage is over, doesn't, though powerful enough and constituting strongly different 'acts' in the show, really break the overall exuberant rhythm of delight.

And Fellini is a showman not only in the brisk-abrupt way in which he moves us from one sequence to another, but also in the way that, even while he is creating plenty of space in it as well, he can at other times be crowding the film with incidents and images. Many make a charged poetry, strongly and effortlessly suggestive of more than simply themselves and, without our consciously realising this, linking and cohering with other things in the film. They may be flashed before our eyes with an exhilarating rapidity, in a matter of seconds or split-seconds – exhilarating because brilliant and because so much is being seen so quickly. An example is the moment, which can hardly be more than a second or two, during which the audience catches a young bearded priest nodding and smiling his uglily and poignantly and amusingly earnest/unctuous/confident agreement with what his senior, a Monsignore, is saying to the enquiring Guido. And not only is this giving us vivid knowledge of the one individual: it is also combining with other telling images, involving other ecclesiastics, to be eloquent about the clear boundary within which the Church is enclosed – assured in perfect good faith and good will of her own mastery and centrality in the most important affairs of life, and also providing what are sometimes tantalisingly appealing and impressive images of such mastery and centrality, but nevertheless hopelessly ignorant and cut off, from Guido in his trouble and from almost everybody. Another and a more simply comic though still exhilarating example of such charged poetry is the one or two very brief moments in which the young girl-friend or 'bimbo' who is quite openly 'with' the mature, commanding figure who is the producer of Guido's film comes out in company with some opinion or wish and is each time, with an absolutely confident quick, curt and decisive callousness, told by him to shut up. Without realising we are doing so, we have this become a part of our meditation on Guido's more undercover relation with his own mistress, whom he isn't treating like this though he is embarrassed by her, and also has her intellectual limitations thrown in his face by his wife. And in this meditation it also combines with the image made by another couple. An old friend of Guido's turns up at the spa – he is marvellously well created in his conscious-defiant folly of flight from his years[*] – with the striking-looking and intellectually and spiritually somewhat pretentious young American Ph.D. student for whom he is giving up his longstanding marriage.

A final note on this dashingly light and high-spirited art comes with a reflection on how the very vision of its close is being handled quickly and lightly. Crucial figures in it are three arrestingly if pleasantly grotesque marching and music-playing circus clowns. It is they who are helping to marshal for the finale that whole great host of the characters who are already known and the crowds of the spa. The finale itself is a brief lively and loud *presto*. Then for a few moments at the very end it slows down and quietens. The audience suddenly sees that night has fallen and that that host of characters is disappearing and leaving on the screen only the three clowns, now spot-lighted – together with the figure who had joined these in their initial ushering in of the *presto*, marching with them and playing his own instrument, and doing so again now until, in the film's last second or two, he is spot-lighted on his own in the dark and with his little flute now the only instrument heard: the figure, with the black school uniform and cap he has been seen in earlier in the film now white, of Guido as a boy. The art partly *is* that of such enjoyably and fluently easy emotional transitions, and the easy transitions here at the end suggest something further about the art's poetic nature. To the lines of Pope quoted above in connection with *The House of Fame* (p126),

---

[*] In the article on *8½* from which this appendix is extracted and adapted (*The Cambridge Quarterly*, III 1, see pp17-21) I discuss those imperfections of the film that arise from the fact that Fellini's art requires more than acting from his players. Because it makes an unusually vivid expressive use of each player's individual physique and (as it were) inner physique, Fellini sometimes had to make compromises when it proved impossible to find anyone who could realise all of the idea of the figure being cast. So the Guido isn't as sensual-looking a man as I believe he needed to be, or his mistress as physically large as was wanted, or his wife as angular, and the mysterious figure who to an extent plays the Beatrice to Guido's Dante, and who is admittedly a more complex figure than those figures in earlier films, is less of a success than they are at representing what I wrote of above as the pure shining water of life welling up from inside, into and through the face, and with a steady, ever-renewed flow. Yet the figure of Guido's old friend seems perfect.

about the easy and effortless-seeming emotional mobility that belong to poetry, might be added the lines of Boileau that lie behind them, with their additional little suggestion, if it is there and *Heureux* does mean more than simply 'successful', of the joy of such mobility:

> *Heureux, qui dans ses vers sait d'une voix légère,*
> *Passer du grave au doux, du plaisant au sévère!* [*]

Such happy emotional mobility is at the same time an extraordinary freedom and wisdom.

---

[*] Happy the poet who knows how to move in an easy light way from being serious and solemn one moment to being soft and gentle the next, or just as quickly from being delightfully comic to being a stern critic!

Chapter V
Shakespeare's hatred of tragedy

I begin with two very short moments in *Macbeth*, neither of them a major one. The first is simply half a line spoken by Lady Macbeth in the first scene in which she appears. She has come in alone, reading her letter from her husband about his encounter with the three strange old women and their prophecy that he is going to be King, and she has been speaking eagerly about the crime that she believes her husband will need to commit in order to gain the throne. She wants him to come home so that she can use all her own conviction to overcome any scruples he might be beginning to have. A messenger comes in, to report that

> The King comes here tonight.

And her immediate words in response are violent:

> Thou'rt mad to say it.

She has been caught on the raw and betrayed herself and, though she immediately covers up and has an explanation for her words, we in the audience know her secret thought and are both thrilled and horrified.

Though we know her secret thought, we may not feel sure how far it goes: do the messenger's words accidentally touch a sensitive spot only because she has been thinking of her husband's usurping the throne by murdering King Duncan, though without knowing that so good an opportunity for that was going to be presented so promptly? or does the wild idea also flash through her mind that Macbeth has already killed Duncan and is himself the King whose arrival is being announced? Whether the shock is the single or the double one, it is almost too much for her – certainly, for a moment, for her self-control. And the reason why we are thrilled and horrified is that in this half-line we vividly feel the extreme state of excitement and disturbance that the character has actually been in all the time, and the fact that it is a more extreme state than she herself is aware. She believes both that she knows what she is doing and needs to do, and that she is quite happy about it. But in fact she is acutely sensitive to the evil of the murder that she and her husband are girding themselves to commit. When this evil that is inside her suddenly seems to be outside her too, in the messenger's innocent words, she momentarily breaks.

Towards the end of the play Macbeth is thrilling and terrifying as he also is caught on the raw by a messenger. His rule as King has quickly become a rule of terror, and now an army is coming against him from England, and a good number of Macbeth's Scottish lords are marching to join forces with it. He comes on, speaking with a desperate-forced defiance:

> Bring me no more reports, let them fly all:
> Till Birnam wood remove to Dunsinane,
> I cannot taint with fear. What's the boy Malcolm?
> Was he not born of woman? The spirits that know
> All mortal consequences, have pronounced me thus:
> Fear not, Macbeth, no man that's born of woman
> Shall e'er have power upon thee. Then fly, false thanes,
> And mingle with the English epicures,
> The mind I sway by, and the heart I bear,
> Shall never sag with doubt, or shake with fear.

A servant comes in, evidently with bad news, and Macbeth's speech is violent before the man has said a word:

> The devil damn thee black, thou cream-faced loon:
> Where got'st thou that goose-look?

The defiance is still there but is suddenly at a pitch that gives him away completely.

I think it remarkable that in each of these small moments Shakespeare has created drama of such power and depth, and also precision, with a few simple words. That by itself may be a first hint of the fact that in this play he has got further than ever before with tragedy. Hamlet, Othello and Lear (and also Titus Andonicus) do all catch, thrill and horrify us in not altogether dissimilar ways, as we are shocked to see these characters in quite different emotional places from where they seemed to be when we last saw and heard them, even just a moment before. But I do not think there is ever the same keenness and finality of revelation.

In both moments the characters are powerful and very much in command, yet also beside themselves and out of control. And the drama of this is more than simply a psychological or a moral one. Drama of either of these kinds would seem more definitely explicable than this drama is and inspire less awe. The precision is remarkable because what is being presented is a momentous spiritual drama, fully created and known though mysterious. Lady Macbeth is on the edge of selling her soul to the Devil, and Macbeth at this later point is a damned soul and more than half knows it. The extreme terror he betrays is evidently more than the fear that he may lose the coming battle.

This first part of the present chapter is mainly concerned with offering reasons for believing that Shakespeare's writing of his four main tragedies from *Hamlet* to *Macbeth* was extremely difficult for him. A provisional way of putting the belief, to be qualified later, is to describe him as like that hero of myth who, for everybody's sake, has to go into the dark underground place and single-handedly take on the most terrifying unknown monster there. The hero does eventually accomplish the task and save the community, but he inevitably feels considerable fear and reluctance as he embarks on that long quest that he may never return from. It seems an impossible task, and certainly no one else is taking it on. There may also, though, be some appetite for the task, since it will only be in accomplishing it that this hero will really know and enjoy all of his strength. Less provisionally, I suggest that the distinguishing feature of these four tragedies is their confronting by representing the appalling and heart-breaking power of moral evil.

A first reason for believing that Shakespeare partly hated his task is the fact that the full confrontation of moral evil is so marked in these tragedies but so rarely even approached in his many other plays. There is only one group of his plays in which it is confronted with anything like the same fullness and, interestingly, that is a group of very early plays – *Titus Andronicus*, the three plays about the reign of King Henry VI, and *King Richard III* – with which go the two narrative poems, also early, with the idea they together convey of there being potential destruction and evil at the very root of life, in sexuality. It is not, of course, that in other plays there is no handling at all of the moral evil that is the central matter of the great tragedies and of these early tragic works. The author of *Hamlet* and *Othello* can at any rate be recognised in both *King Richard II* and *Romeo and Juliet*, and the author of *Hamlet* and *Macbeth* in *Julius Caesar*. Also, moral evil is treated with more knowledge and a bitterer seriousness in the late comedies of *Cymbeline*, *The Winter's Tale* and *The Tempest* than it is in any of the comedies that Shakespeare wrote before he wrote *Hamlet*. But there is no full confrontation of moral evil in any of these plays, or in either *Coriolanus* or *Anthony and Cleopatra*. The plays that in this respect come nearest to those first and those main tragedies are *Troilus and Cressida*, the bitter satirical play that was probably written after *Hamlet* and before *Othello*, and *Measure for Measure*, the comedy that is generally thought to have been written after *Othello* and before *King Lear*.

In their fuller confrontation of moral evil the tragedies from *Hamlet* to *Macbeth* have further things in common with the tragic works from the beginning of Shakespeare's career. A fear or apprehension is expressed that life is evil at its very core and all innocence and goodness hopelessly doomed. It is striking that Shakespeare should have made a central figure of three of his earliest plays a boy-king who retains his innocence as he grows up but helps to bring ruin on himself and his country because the very beauty of his character – his wisdom and goodness and holiness – disable him from dealing with the world as it is. This fear is also there, as suggested, in the narrative poems and, though in the plays it is not based only on that idea about sexuality, that idea is itself never quite absent from them. For another common feature of these tragic works is the giving of a central place in the representation of moral evil to a woman or women – because of the evil in the women or because of the evil that

147

the men are drawn into by their sexual relations with them or because of both. Also striking in the three *King Henry VI* plays is the fact that the few main women characters who enter them are all physically beautiful and enter the plays only to cause trouble, managing between them to cause the most terrible trouble.

Not only is such tragedy relatively rare in Shakespeare's *oeuvre*. There also appears to be a gap of a good number of years between those first attempts at it, which were almost certainly completed with the publication of *The Rape of Lucrece* in 1594, and the second and final series of attempts that started with the writing of *Hamlet*, usually dated about 1600, and that even then was not immediately continued, since the next tragedy, *Othello*, may not have been written until 1604. And it is hardly that the years between 1594 and 1600 had been unproductive ones for Shakespeare. On the contrary, they may well have been the most richly productive ones of his whole career. They might even be thought of as his golden years, seeing the production of a good number of his most popular plays and also, unlike any other period of his career, of hardly a single play that is not popular. They are the years of *Romeo and Juliet*, *A Midsummer Night's Dream*, *Richard II*, *The Merchant of Venice*, *Much Ado About Nothing*, the two Parts of *Henry IV*, *Henry V*, *Julius Caesar* and *As You Like It*.

It may be significant that two of these plays, probably written near the middle of this golden period, tell the story of a young man who faces the gravest responsibilities but is giving a great deal of concern to his elders by seeming not to be facing up to these and to be, instead, playing around. Prince Hal then, as Henry V, proves that this has in fact been the best preparation for those responsibilities. Was Shakespeare here both preparing himself inwardly for the writing of further tragedy and showing some anxiety over the fact that he seemed to be putting the task off? And how much of the history of Prince Hal is then re-told, with variations, in the story of Prince Hamlet? In an article on the play (*Cambridge Quarterly* IX 1) I once suggested that we cannot properly understand Hamlet's much-discussed 'delay' unless we see that this is at the same time Shakespeare's; that is, that in *Hamlet* Shakespeare is both beginning on his task and still, in a sense, putting it off and playing around.

This leads to a second reason for believing that in his main tragedies Shakespeare was taking on a fearsomely difficult task: the uncertainty that he shows over how to go about it, and this at a stage of his career when he was so far from being a novice. With this uncertainty go signs of a slow and fitful growth in clarity and sureness as he composes each new tragedy in the series. In comparison with the last of the four, *Macbeth*, *Hamlet*, the first of them, may not be the artistic failure that two great critics have thought it (Matthew Arnold, in his late "Letters of an Old Playgoer", as well as T.S.Eliot). Among other things, the consistency of the play's outstanding success in the theatre must count for something against that view. But, if it is a great and extraordinary work, unique in its power and fascination and also perhaps uniquely characteristic (if that can be said) of its author, it is not so coherent or masterly a drama as *Macbeth*. For one thing, there is that playing around in it, by both the main character and Shakespeare.

There is quite a lot of this, and not only because the main character goes in for so much idleness and joking and even high spirits. There is also, among other things, the interest that both Hamlet on occasion and his author still more take in trying out various styles of passionate tragic speech – trying them out without being fully committed to them. However strange, it somehow does not seem irrelevant that in this play Shakespeare has his main character lecturing a group of actors on how and how not to play tragedy. The more obvious examples of different styles of tragic speech being tried out are the speech of the Ghost, the long declamation about Priam and Hecuba, the speech in the play that Hamlet has the actors put on, and both Laertes' rant at Ophelia's graveside and Hamlet's strange competing with him in it. Then, if not quite so obviously, there is the further trying out of a tragic style in such lines of Hamlet's as these:

> 'Tis now the very witching time of night,
> When churchyards yawn, and hell itself breathes out
> Contagion to this world. Now could I drink hot blood,
> And do such bitter business as the day
> Would quake to look on.

If it is often forgotten that Hamlet speaks such words, which do not sound like the words of the popular "sweet Prince", I do not believe they would ever be forgotten if, when he speaks them, there was any full conviction that he meant them. "Now *could* I drink hot blood..." By trying out speaking like this the character is, of course, trying out being evil; or his author is trying out having him be evil. What Hamlet immediately goes on to say at this point at the end of Act 3 Scene 2 indicates that one impulse he has, even though he is immediately checking it, is the impulse to go and murder not Claudius but his mother.

It is an example of what is strange and fascinating in the play and its main character that with a speech like this it cannot quite be said either that he means what he says or that he does not mean it.

> Fair is foul, and foul is fair,
> Hover through the fog and filthy air.

And, if in those lines about drinking hot blood we do not know whether he is evil or not, even though he is very much occupied with the thought of being so, it is a parallel fact that in most people's general impression of him he is not a murderer though actually he is one. "So Guildenstern and Rosencrantz go to't," as Horatio laconically remarks. He is also, of course, savagely quick to kill the person eavesdropping on his talk with his mother. Shakespeare's uncertainty over how to go about his task is showing again in the play's being as morally equivocal as it is, unclear about how far evil exists inside as well as outside its main character.

Another example of this is that Hamlet's grief, disaffection and despair are both *sympathique* – beautifully bitter-sweet – and at the same time the "melancholy" that was often for Shakespeare, if not a positive manifestation of evil, at least a fertile seed-bed of it. The villain of *Much Ado About Nothing* is melancholy, and in an earlier play melancholy as well as vengefulness is a state of feeling that King John wishes Hubert were in so that he would be receptive to the proposal that he murder a child:

> ...if the midnight bell
> Did with his iron tongue, and brazen mouth
> Sound on into the drowsy face of night:
> If this same were a churchyard where we stand,
> And thou possessed with a thousand wrongs:
> Or if that surly spirit melancholy
> Had baked thy blood, and made it heavy, thick,
> Which else runs tickling up and down the veins,
> Making that idiot laughter keep men's eyes,
> And strain their cheeks to idle merriment,
> A passion hateful to my purposes...

(This is also quoted for those characteristic lines about the natural disposition of human beings for comedy, which could well be used to support the great Samuel Johnson's view that that was very much Shakespeare's own disposition and that there was always strain for him in writing tragedy. The view being put forward here is partly a restatement of Johnson's: not that Shakespeare did not have a powerful and compelling inspiration for tragedy as well as comedy, but that it felt to him something like a curse.) Hamlet himself relates his melancholy to the possibility of his being taken over by the Devil.

> The spirit that I have seen
> May be the Devil, and the Devil hath power
> T'assume a pleasing shape, yea and perhaps
> Out of my weakness, and my melancholy,
> As he is very potent with such spirits,
> Abuses me to damn me.

But, if there is some self-knowledge here, with Hamlet recognising the possibility of evil in himself, it is not clear how *much* self-knowledge there is, and it certainly does not seem to be the complete self-knowledge that could mean that any such possibility is also being overcome. It may be significant that the plan Hamlet is making to test whether the Ghost was the Devil – by putting on a play and trying to catch the conscience of the King with it – looks a dubious plan in the light of the sensible warning that Shakespeare later puts into the mouth of Banquo, when he and Macbeth have met those witches: that the evil powers can deceive and take over a human being by revealing something true to him.

But, however much reason there is for taking a dark view of Hamlet's character and behaviour, the opposite view is also strongly given in the play. What Horatio says at Hamlet's death is a sufficient reminder of this:

> Now cracks a noble heart,
> Goodnight, sweet Prince,
> And flights of angels sing thee to thy rest.

But why should Shakespeare show uncertainty over how to go about his daunting task when he was coming to it not only from years of great success in the theatre but also with that previous experience of writing a tragic drama that confronts moral evil? And he had not been showing any similar uncertainty then. The task is now partly a new one and more difficult because the confrontation of evil can no longer be simply the showing of sympathetically presented characters suffering, in their innocence, at the hands of villains. It has to include the confrontation of evil inside sympathetically presented characters. The evil Richard III, like the Aaron of *Titus Andronicus*, is presented with fascination not sympathy, and he hardly has an inside in this sense – the ordinary conscience, heart and soul that we can know and feel with even if and as they are being corrupted. Towards the end Richard does have his nightmares and, waking from them, his conscience-stricken soliloquy, but this is supported by little else in the play. There has only been the new note of desperation in defiance that, Macbeth-like, he has begun to sound when news has come in of movements against his usurping of the throne. In that longer part of the play that presents his 'Machiavellian' soliloquies and actions there is nothing at all. The only villain in Shakespeare's early work who has this kind of an inside is Tarquin in *The Rape of Lucrece* – perhaps significantly a poem that both comes last, almost certainly, in Shakespeare's first confrontation of moral evil in tragic writing and so often reminds its readers of things in the great later tragedies. And the creation of such a figure in a narrative poem does not seem to solve all the problems with the creation of such a figure in a play. It also seems significant that the poem is divided in an almost broken-backed way between the rapist and his victim. The concentration on Tarquin's behaviour and inner state is intense and unbroken until he completely leaves the poem and there is a still longer concentration on Lucrece's. Is there later some combining of this criminal and his victim into the same figure, in each of Hamlet, Othello and Macbeth?

Some of the slow and fitful growth in clarity and sureness through the later tragedies shows in their dramatic movement. Paradoxically, it suggests the tremendous vitality of the inspiration in *Hamlet* that the play can be so powerful and so popular while doing so much wandering about, with some suspicion of capriciousness in parts of its dramatic movement and even of aimlessness. In *Othello* the powerful movement forward takes some time to establish itself fully but, once it does so, at the early point in Act 3 when Othello first doubts Desdemona, that movement is more or less unbroken and unrelenting and frightful. The much larger action of *King Lear* moves powerfully forward for great stretches of the play, as Johnson said -

> There is perhaps no play which keeps the attention so strongly fixed. So powerful is the current of the poet's imagination, that the mind, which once ventures within it, is hurried irresistibly along.

– but I believe it is common, in both performances and reading, to feel that the play comes a little too close for comfort to halting, and losing and disappointing us, in passages towards the end where the main weight is being carried by the blind Gloucester and the still disguised Edgar. Johnson's words are more completely true of *Macbeth*. Though I remember that, seeing a performance of the play as a child, I wondered why the action stopped for Malcolm and Macduff to have their long talk with each other in England, I now have no impression at all of the action's stopping in that scene and, on the contrary, find the scene working as powerful drama in both performance and reading. The whole play seems to me to move as compellingly from beginning to end as *Othello* does in its last three Acts – and to do so without that tunnel quality that distinguishes *Othello* from each of these other three tragedies.

A third reason for suggesting that Shakespeare both did and did not want this task is the moral violence in judgement in these tragedies. This is related both to the moral equivocation in *Hamlet* and to that crucial difference just mentioned from the early tragic work, and it is found in the extreme and somewhat questionable intensity of hatred felt towards certain characters, either by other characters or by ourselves in the audience and thus also (we are bound to feel) by Shakespeare.

> ...bloody, bawdy villain,
> Remorseless, treacherous, lecherous, kindless villain!

What is Hamlet doing working himself up like this? He himself goes on to ask that question, though not as searchingly as he might. What are we ourselves doing hating Iago as violently as we probably do when we are experiencing *Othello*, or Goneril and Regan as we certainly do in *King Lear*? There are words bearing on this in *As You Like It*, a play that Shakespeare had probably written not long before he wrote *Hamlet*. One of those refugees from the corrupt world of power and success who have gathered together in the forest of Arden, the "melancholy" Jaques, has expressed the wish that back in the ordinary world he could have the licence of the professional fool: if he could be allowed to speak his mind there, he would have a go at reforming and purifying that whole corrupt world. The good and wise Duke-in-exile tells him that what he would actually be doing would be

> ...Most mischievous foul sin, in chiding sin:
> For thou thyself hast been a libertine,
> As sensual as the brutish sting itself...

There are also the words King Lear is given to say as he himself rages against the corruption of that respectable world of power and success that he, too, is now a refugee from:

> Thou, rascal beadle, hold thy bloody hand: why dost thou lash that whore? Strip thy own back, thou hotly lusts to use her in that kind, for which thou whip'st her.

The issue of the "rascal beadle" and "Most mischievous foul sin, in chiding sin" is at the very centre of *Measure for Measure*. Why is Shakespeare so peculiarly interested in it in these years?

While the connection of this with the moral equivocation about the malcontent Hamlet is clear, more may need to be said about how such moral violence suggests Shakespeare's pain and difficulty with his task.

First, it is worth juxtaposing both Hamlet's unpacking of his heart with words of furious hatred (spoken to others, notably his mother, as well as in soliloquy) and Jaques' idea of freely speaking his mind to the world with the contrast that is made with them in two dramatic strokes in Shakespeare's early tragedies where powerful use is made of the silence of good characters. In the strong third Act of the best (as I think) of the *Henry VI* plays, *Part 2*, it is a great moment when the saintly young King silently turns away from his successful guilty Queen, hiding his face as he grieves for his leading good counsellor. The man has just died while under arrest on false charges, in fact, as Henry strongly suspects, murdered. The King has been hearing this much-loved Queen and wife of his going on and on fluently, forcefully and with an appalling Goneril-like self-righteousness professing her own grief for the dead man – while conveying nothing but extreme self-concern. The moment is sustained when she then, on his silently turning away from her, subjects him to a long speech that pulls out all the stops in taxing him with lack of love for her... and he continues to be silent. In *Titus Andronicus* the principal figure of innocence suffers the murder of her husband in front of her eyes and the double-rape of herself by his two murderers and is then on stage for much of the remaining three Acts of the play, silent and almost completely helpless because they have also cut her hands off and her tongue out. Perhaps there should also be a reference here to Cordelia's silence, not only at the beginning of her play but also at its very end.

It may be difficult to overstate the sense of imaginative helplessness that Shakespeare felt before the power of moral evil, or his repulsion and despair at the thought of what the full imaginative confrontation of it required of him: not turning away from it in silence but (to use what may be a cheap phrase here) getting his own hands dirty. Mainly this meant letting his sympathetic leading characters get their hands dirty, and even in the end, with the Macbeths, absolutely filthy. Something else that should probably be thought of along with the silences of Henry VI, Lavinia and Cordelia is the strength of Hamlet's wish for suicide.

In the moral violence in these tragedies we have Shakespeare raging and fighting furiously against the need to get his own hands dirty but doing so for the very reason that he is at the same time letting them get dirty. And there is the further paradox that the moral violence itself counts as a part of his letting them get dirty. A part of the moral evil allowed into the plays, to be fairly freely seen and felt there, is precisely the moral evil that there can be in chiding sin and ferociously hating other sinners. To use another phrase that may be cheap here, he is letting it all hang out and has to do so, and I believe that this is why it makes some but finally not all that much difference to the success of *Hamlet* that the play is unclear and equivocal at its centre. It can still be a great tragedy, if a faulted one. Even if it is uncertain in exactly what proportions the moral evil is distributed between the different characters in the play, and that is never going to cease being a subject of both debate and changes of mind, that evil is still powerfully there in the play and still wreaks its terrible and pitiful destruction. For similar reasons there are always likely to be debates and changes of mind about Othello's love and jealousy, and about, for example, the honesty or dishonesty of his final suicide-speech – whether there is real nobility in it or only cowardly self-concern – and again the unclarity both matters and does not matter all that much. An image comes to mind of two or more glass containers linked to each other in such a way that, if the level of the liquid goes up in one of them, the level in another goes proportionately down. All or most of the necessary total volume of the liquid is there in the whole apparatus. While there is some confusion and imperfection if the labels on the outsides of the different containers do not seem quite accurate in their record of the different levels visible but seem to record rather less evil than seems to be there in Hamlet, Othello or Lear, or even in Desdemona, Kent or Cordelia, and correspondingly rather more evil than seems to be there in Claudius and Gertrude or even in Iago, Goneril or Regan, and while there is some further confusion and imperfection if those levels also do not seem at all

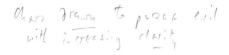

stable, nevertheless most of the appalling and heart-breaking power of moral evil is there in one way or another and being confronted in one way or another.

If Shakespeare often felt imaginative helplessness before his task, he must also have felt helpless against the extraordinary force of his tragic inspiration.

> ...why do I yield to that suggestion,
> Whose horrid image doth unfix my hair,
> And make my seated heart knock at my ribs,
> Against the use of nature?

It does not seem a coincidence that Macbeth (here), Hamlet and Othello – and also Tarquin – are all shown hating the path that they are being drawn into pursuing although they are all, to different degrees, pursuing it with the energy either of overwhelming desire or of something approaching that. It also seems no coincidence that in *Hamlet*, *Othello* and *Macbeth*, written in that order, the dirtiness of the main character's hands is successively clearer and clearer and more of the blame for all the destruction is seen to lie with him. Hamlet is given more excuses than Othello, but Othello is also given excuses, and Macbeth and Lady Macbeth are given none.

When beginning on the moral violence, I mentioned the hatred felt towards Claudius by Hamlet but the hatred felt towards Iago and towards Goneril and Regan by ourselves and Shakespeare. The distinction is intended but is only a rough one. For one thing, it might suggest that feelings towards Iago and towards Goneril and Regan are more like each other than they are. In all these three plays, as also in *Macbeth*, some of our feelings towards the villains are encouraged by being voiced in the hatred and indignation expressed by some of the other characters, but such speech has more to support and clarify it in the other tragedies than it does in *Hamlet*. If, to speak relatively and roughly still, Goneril and Regan are more hated because of what they are directly heard and seen and felt to be, and Iago more because of what he is seen doing and bringing about, it is doubtful whether Gertrude or even Claudius is actually hated much at all. The hatred expressed by Hamlet is almost the only reason given for hating them, along with references to what the two characters have done in the past and off-stage. In the second half of the play Claudius is admittedly shown plotting Hamlet's death, but that comes too late to make much difference, and is in any case, unlike his original murder of his brother, something he is doing in self-defence. Also, while it is always possible for an actor or reader to put a sinister oiliness into the plausible speeches Claudius makes on his first appearance in the play, Shakespeare gives little assistance to this in the actual lines, and such a reading of those speeches would reduce the dramatic power of that scene, where the dilemma for Hamlet is surely that everything feels wrong and probably is wrong but nothing at all looks wrong or sounds wrong.

> My tables, my tables; meet it is I set it down,
> That one may smile, and smile and be a villain...

This can hardly be worth Hamlet's setting down, in this later scene in which he has just heard the Ghost's revelation, if the smile of Claudius that he and the audience now remember had an insincerity that was obvious.

But what a strange thing this writing is, anyhow, for Hamlet to be thinking of doing! In the oddity there may be some hint of Hamlet's sense of impotence about being able to justify his hatred of Claudius either to himself or to the rest of the world, and of Shakespeare's sense of impotence on the same account. The violence of Hamlet's speech against Claudius seems to be in proportion to Shakespeare's failure vividly to create the evil of this adulterous murderer so that it can be seen, heard and felt, and properly known. With Goneril and Regan, as also, incidentally, with characters in some scenes in *Henry VI Part 2* and at least one scene in *Titus Andronicus* (with Saturninus in Act 4, scene 4), there is much greater success in making us feel and know their hateful evil in the very 'morality' and 'good sense' of their speeches.

A similar sense of impotence on Shakespeare's part may be betrayed by a quality in the representation of Goneril and Regan and even more in that of Iago that can be described as phobic. The fear that is part of the hatred of them is a little out of proportion to what they are, but in proportion to there being something missing in the knowledge of them. With Iago, as with Claudius, so much emphasis is laid on the fact that no one could possibly see through him. On-stage with other characters than Roderigo, the Iago the audience sees is the most honestly good-natured person possible, and the great effect made by the gap between his convincing appearance and what he is actually up to means that there is an element of panic terror in the hatred of him. Both Goneril and Regan have more substance and are more consistently vivid. I think it is in a good sense that they are less exciting: their evil is less theatrical. Yet even with them an emphasis on how terrible it is that they can get away with being what they are and have as much confidence about that as they do works just a little at the expense of their being seen quite clearly as what they are. Correspondingly, the moral militancy of both Cordelia and Kent in the play's first scene, which does so much damage, seems to have an element in it of giving up without trying.

In *Macbeth* other characters do not fail to speak strongly about the evil in the leading characters, be sometimes completely deceived by them, or feel sometimes weak and helpless when thinking of trying to resist their success, but less of the dramatic weight rests on these things, which are subordinate to what is created at the drama's centre: evil thoroughly and clearly seen and felt and known, in its mystery. And another difference is that, if this evil is hated and found appalling, a principal thing in it that is hated and found appalling is what Macbeth is doing to himself and Lady Macbeth to herself. Interestingly, there is a little of this with Claudius, but there is nothing of it with any of Iago, Goneril, Regan or Edmund, none of whom really has a soul. And the obvious reason why what the Macbeths are doing to themselves is hated and found appalling is that we are inside it and it is inside us. What makes Shakespeare's task in his tragedies such a difficult and painfully costly one is clearly the fact that the only real confrontation of the appalling and heart-breaking power of moral evil is the confrontation that is made in the full inward realisation of that power. That is not there in helplessly uncomprehending exclamation against moral evil seen outside oneself, however powerfully that exclamation is made.

Will you, I pray, demand that demi-devil
Why he hath thus ensnared my soul and body?

Then let them anatomise Regan: see what breeds about her
heart. Is there any cause in nature that makes these hard
hearts?

Compare with these speeches by Othello and Lear the speeches that
are made about Macbeth in the scene immediately preceding that first
entry of his in Act 5. The speakers are the Scottish lords who are
marching to join the army that is coming from England.

Great Dunsinane he strongly fortifies:
Some say he's mad: others, that lesser hate him,
Do call it valiant fury, but for certain
He cannot buckle his distempered cause
Within the belt of rule.
              – Now does he feel
His secret murders sticking on his hands,
Now minutely revolts upbraid his faith-breach:
Those he commands, move only in command,
Nothing in love: now does he feel his title
Hang loose about him, like a giant's robe
Upon a dwarfish thief.
              – Who then shall blame
His pestered senses to recoil, and start,
When all that is within him, does condemn
Itself, for being there.

It is impossible to imagine any of Claudius, Iago, Goneril, Regan,
Edmund or even Oswald being spoken of in their plays anything like
so clearly.

A fourth reason for believing that Shakespeare hated writing this
tragedy of moral evil is the partial evading of it that I believe there is
in the theatricality of both *Hamlet* and *Othello*. Both plays have had
especially good box-office success; both have provided famously

good parts for leading actors; both use the glamour and excitement of the theatre in a degree to which neither *King Lear* nor *Macbeth* does. The theatricality goes with the quite special degree of sympathy felt with Hamlet and Othello themselves, with how much there is in each play of backward-looking regret for the main character's lost innocent and popular self living in a stable world, with the sounding of notes of self-pity by him, and with a self-centredness in him that Shakespeare seems to an extent to share – as he does not so much share that of Lear or at all that of Macbeth. Not that these two very different earlier tragedies are theatrical in exactly the same way: it is more a matter of a dashing and restless liveliness in *Hamlet* and of emotional sensationalism in *Othello*, where the theatricality is closer to the acute pain. Shakespeare also seems to put himself at a greater initial distance from Othello than from Hamlet and not to let Othello run the play as Hamlet tends to run his. Yet Othello does take over at the very end, and it is a main example of Shakespeare's sharing some of a main character's self-centredness that with the great theatrical effect that Othello gains with his final speech and suicide the audience tends to forget and cease grieving for the two good women who have been murdered by their husbands and are there, dead, on the stage. Altogether, the speeches that Othello makes after Emilia has been killed by Iago and he has finally seen the truth lead the audience to grieve for Desdemona's death, insofar as we still grieve for it at all, not for her sake but for his. And this point about self-centredness remains even on the most unsympathetic interpretation of Othello's final behaviour: however cruel Shakespeare may have intended the exposure of his self-deception to be here, the audience's feelings are still not for Desdemona as much as they might be. Like anyone, Shakespeare can be self-centred in painful self-loathing as well as in self-justification and self-glorification.

In *King Lear* as well as *Macbeth* it seems to me that the tragic pain is purer – that we are harder hit and that correspondingly the tragic release and joy are deeper and less incomplete. Not only is moral violence and theatricality less seriously distorting than in *Hamlet* or *Othello* in the parts of *King Lear* in which they can be found, but they are also not found so much, anyhow, in the most important parts of the play. The centre of the play is not a powerfully good and attractive man, in or near his prime, being drawn towards or into evil with the help of the villainy of others, but two figures who have no equivalents at the centres of any of the other three tragedies: quite ordinarily sinful and unwise old men, one more sinful and unwise than the other, both put through extreme pain and distress. It is as if Polonius and Brabantio have been made the central characters.

Thinking about such main differences between these plays might lead to some fresh realisation of how tremendous Shakespeare's overall tragic inspiration was: that in *Othello* after *Hamlet* and in *King Lear* after *Othello* he should take such major and decisive new initiatives to make the confrontation with moral evil a more complete and honest one. The advance that he makes in *Othello* may be at the cost of some temporary narrowing of the scope, but there is still a courageous and brilliant-profound resourcefulness in it. And, if that is true, what is to be said of the further advance and artistic invention in *King Lear* and of the still further advance and invention in *Macbeth*?

***

In this second part of the present chapter a qualification of the above will eventually be offered but is approached slowly and indirectly.

Two good general accounts of Shakespeare's work could seem to contradict each other on the character of Macbeth. The first, much the shorter, is the five pages in which the Austrian poet and dramatist Hugo von Hofmannsthal describes a pervasive atmosphere of nobility as the most essential and valuable thing in Shakespeare's work, but the character of Macbeth as the great exception to this (pp320-324 in Oswald LeWinter's Penguin collection *Shakespeare in Europe*). So many of the other main, and not so main, characters of the plays possess "a noble consciousness – nay, deeper than that – an existence of almost conscious nobility," showing itself in a winningly expansive and gracious manner and in the radiant confidence and general goodwill towards life and people that this manner expresses. Among the many examples cited are Brutus' behaviour toward his boy attendant at Philippi, on the eve of his defeat and death, and Hamlet's welcoming to Elsinore of the troupe of actors. But

...I am deeply perplexed when perceiving a figure like Macbeth with almost nothing of this atmosphere around him. This suggests to me that Shakespeare meant to endow him with a peculiar frightfulness, meant to let him be shrouded by an icy air of death. It seems as if the ghastly breath of Hecate had eaten away from the world around Macbeth everything alive, everything that ordinarily unites mankind, leaving nothing of that which surrounds Hamlet as a breath of life.

This fits the thesis just argued about the four main tragedies, and that thesis is itself very much indebted to the second account of Shakespeare's work being referred to now, that in the late H.A.Mason's book on Shakespeare's *Tragedies of Love*. My debt is especially to the frequent reference that is made there, when other tragedies by Shakespeare are being criticised, to the standards set by *Macbeth*. Mason could seem to contradict von Hofmannsthal when, in his argument that in his fall the Anthony of Shakespeare's *Anthony and Cleopatra* "moves us less seriously" than Macbeth, he quotes the late speech of Macbeth's that begins "I have lived long enough" and says that it shows him to be, unlike Anthony, "swathed in an atmosphere of real human value-relations all fatally violated and destroyed," and goes on, "Macbeth, we feel, is a fine soul, who cares for real social relations ...". Earlier in his book he has placed this same speech and the later "Tomorrow, and tomorrow, and tomorrow" speech beside Othello's lines in Act 3 scene 3 from "Oh now for ever / Farewell the tranquil mind" to "Othello's occupation's gone!" to help show how, unlike Macbeth, "Othello is not a serious character" but "histrionic", "playing before himself as audience."

But that helps overcome this apparent contradiction between these two exceptionally good writers on Shakespeare. The "noble consciousness... [or] existence of almost conscious nobility" that von Hofmannsthal writes of and that becomes all too conscious in Othello may be elsewhere – and, as I believe, is – as deeply and potently winning as he claims it is, and also almost (at any rate) as central to the vitality of Shakespeare's work as a whole. But it has always had an element of fantasy in it, whereas, when in the lines from the speech

Mason twice quotes, Macbeth voices his knowledge that

> ...that which should accompany old age
> As honour, love, obedience, troops of friends
> I must not look to have, but in their stead
> Curses, not loud but deep, mouth-honour, breath
> Which the poor heart would fain deny, and dare not...

there is no element of fantasy about the "fine soul" that the character is showing himself fundamentally to be, even though he is now a damned soul too: it is altogether the real thing.

I have long had the idea that Shakespeare's relation to his many audiences resembles the Sphinx's relation to the people of Thebes: he sets us a riddle that we need to solve if we are only to prosper by his work and not also be a little damaged by it. Both the Sphinx's riddle and Shakespeare's have the same answer, "A human being," but Shakespeare's riddle is not "What is it that walks on four legs in the morning, on two at noon, and on three in the evening?" but "What do you think I am?" The question is a riddle as he asks it because two powerful things obscure the obvious enough answer: not only the almost universal and so frequently voiced impression of his being well nigh superhuman in his seemingly invisible creating of such a wealth of human life and character, but also – something that must have helped give rise to this – the fact that Shakespeare himself feels a similar wonder at his creations and can be a little seduced by a similar illusion about them. We do not know, though we may speculate, which member of his company first thought of calling their new theatre the Globe, but we do know that the canopy over its stage was called "the heavens" and that on its underside were painted the sun, moon and stars. And additional allusions besides this one to Shakespeare's own creation of theatre can be recognised in the following lines of Cleopatra about Anthony:

> Oh such another sleep, that I might see
> But such another man...
> His face was as the heav'ns, and therein stuck

A sun and moon, which kept their course, and lighted
The little O, the earth...
His legs bestrid the ocean, his rearèd arm
Crested the world: his voice was propertied
As all the tunèd spheres, and that to friends:
But when he meant to quail, and shake the orb,
He was as rattling thunder.[*] For his bounty,
There was no winter in't: an autumn 'twas
That grew the more by reaping: his delights
Were dolphin-like, they showed his back above
The element they lived in: in his livery
Walked crowns and crownets: realms and islands were
As plates dropped from his pocket...
Think you there was, or might be such a man
As this I dreamt of?

There are surely allusions here to the poetry in his plays, to the apparently unlimited imaginative travel possible in them and the socially lofty company often being kept and to the extraordinary abundance of them – and also, perhaps, to his own social-cum-moral shame about the world they involved him in.

It may be because he has now touched base in *Macbeth* that Shakespeare teases himself and us here, with the reluctant thought that there may have been too much of the dream in this idea of his work.

---

[*] Compare "to the dread rattling thunder / Have I given fire" in Prospero's farewell to his art near the beginning of Act V of *The Tempest*. There are sceptics about this play's being Shakespeare's farewell to the theatre, but I have not seen any of them explain what Prospero is referring to in this speech when he talks of having brought the dead back to life as ghosts. While there is no reference to this remarkable ability of his anywhere else in the play, Shakespeare's first audience would have recognised that their author had brought the dead back to life as ghosts, in *Julius Caesar*, *Hamlet* and *Macbeth*. There is, of course, no reason why, at the time when he was writing *Anthony and Cleopatra*, Shakespeare may not have been thinking of that as his last play.

Also, if his Cleopatra is partly his portrait of his muse, it is a bitter portrait as well as having its proud exultant moments like

> Age cannot wither her, nor custom stale
> Her infinite variety...

While there is plenty of wonder in such passages from *Anthony and Cleopatra*, there is no longer so much of the irresistible pulsing conviction in the verse that had been there earlier, a conviction being confidently shared with his audience and carrying all before it – as when, for example, Shakespeare has his Chorus figure in *King Henry V* more or less claim for him possession of that "Muse of fire" that can

> ...ascend
> The brightest heaven of invention...

Through this Chorus he is admittedly only expressing a wish, "O for a Muse of fire," but, in talking as the Chorus goes on to do about the things that cannot be created on those bare boards, he actually is creating them in his words and doing so vividly – and Shakespeare clearly knows that he is.

It must have been natural enough for him to associate lofty mastery in the theatre with lofty mastery in life. Macbeth himself is made to talk of the theatre both when he begins his journey to a supposed supreme greatness –

> Two truths are told [by the witches]
> As happy prologues to the swelling act
> Of the imperial theme.

– and when the journey is coming to its sorry end:

> Life's but a walking shadow, a poor player
> That struts and frets his hour upon the stage
> And then is heard no more.

Going along with there not being the same conviction about the reality of the supreme, almost more than human dramatist when Anthony is

being implicitly compared with him is the fact that there is not the
same sap of conviction and vitality as in, say, Henry V's in Anthony's
performance of the noble role of heroic leader – at the times when he
is performing it as opposed to evading it (and, like some of his
predecessors in the plays and like their author, playing around*).
When, shortly before his final defeat at Actium, he is being the
touchingly noble and gracious commander in the compliments and
strange farewells of his which are making his "sad captains" weep, his
Cleopatra does not know what on earth he is up to, and one of the
comments of his intelligent chief officer is that this is play-acting for
effect – though he, Enobarbus, is himself tearful. In earlier work of
Shakespeare's there are plenty of noble main characters who speak
with the effect of evoking others' tears and/or their own – Lucrece,
Richard II, Brutus, Hamlet, Othello, Lear – but it is difficult to
imagine any of them being so curtly cut down and half-distanced from
us as they do so. (Anthony is only half-distanced from us here because
in giving Enobarbus his tears Shakespeare is inviting us to be moved
by this reminder and recovery of Anthony's nobility – even if he is not
putting much conviction or power into that invitation).

All this has been going towards the qualification to the account
so far given of Shakespeare's main dealings with tragedy. For he
cannot simply be the great impersonal hero imaginatively tackling the
monster of evil, single-handedly but for everybody's sake, when much
of his hatred of the task and much of his difficulty and struggle with it
come from some narcissism in himself, the narcissism which is also
the source of the element of fantasy in that atmosphere of attractive
nobility that von Hofmannsthal persuasively describes as so dominant
in Shakespeare's writing overall.

It is not that the element of fantasy stops this atmosphere from
being profoundly beautiful and stirring as well as irrepressibly lively,
or from having wisdom in it. (A parallel point is that the narcissism in
Shakespeare's sonnets to the young man – the poet's consciousness of

---

* It is interesting that after writing *Macbeth* Shakespeare should return to the
central matter of the two *Henry IV* plays, with, on the one hand, Hotspur
reappearing to an extent as Coriolanus and, on the other, Hal and his father
and Falstaff to an extent as Anthony, Octavius Caesar and Cleopatra.

the beauty in his words, in the love he is expressing in them and in both his own selflessness and occasional self-deprecation – is far from destroying that beauty.) And Shakespeare here is wise with a wisdom it is not easy to see limits to. Playing around in the way that is so characteristic of him, especially in that golden period before his writing of his main tragedies, could well be argued to be living not just on a height of life but on *the* height. What wisdom could be greater? At the heart of the superior "noble" life is a beautiful insouciance, a great inner freedom that is the freedom to see all the involvements that people take so seriously as much ado about nothing, to see life as something to be lived as you like it and doing what you will, not necessarily going anywhere at all and perhaps only playing delightedly on the spot, and in what could seem a merely idle spirit if there were not such purity and vitality in it. (Alternatively, if you do have to be going somewhere, you make the necessary moves with the pure heart of a fine, charming and dashing aristocratic carelessness.) The *Henry IV* and *Henry V* trilogy is a wise fable about the necessity, certainly to people like Shakespeare who are spiritually kings and noblemen, of irresponsibility as well as responsibility.

But this great wisdom is finally limited in Shakespeare by the element of narcissism that goes with it. And this shows when he returns to tragedy, not only because that narcissism is a principal thing that is in the way of his fully succeeding in the task he is setting himself here, as I have suggested it especially is in *Hamlet* and *Othello*, but also in his very conception of the task. For why does that task have to be quite such a grim one, and why does moral evil have to be the central matter for tragedy? (It is all the stranger in a writer Johnson describes as "so much more careful to please than to instruct that he seems to write without any moral purpose" and normally has so much good reason for describing like this.) I think enough has been said for this question to answer itself. In the great Greek tragedies there is no ignorance of the moral evil human beings are capable of or playing down of the destruction it can wreak, but there is also no treating of it as if it was the only tragedy in life. In those tragedies we are living in a larger and a freer world though one that can still be terrible, and it is, I believe, a more divine world.

What I call the moral violence in *Hamlet*, *Othello* and *King Lear* is therefore still present, after all, in *Macbeth* even though no longer distorting any of the feelings and judgements about the individual characters. If anything, it may be still more present. If there is now no doubt about the right people getting the right amount of blame, there is even more of the intense concern with the assignment of blame. And, now going with that, through the creation of Malcolm and Macduff, there is also the intense concern with the moral effort to see how things can be put right. (These twin concerns may help to explain why the catharsis effected by the play does not seem to be so complete as it might be.)

I said that "get his hands dirty" may be a cheap phrase for what Shakespeare had to do to accomplish that task of his. But it does not seem simply cheap (and I therefore let it stand) because it is provoked by the coexistence with the truth in that inspiring and winning idea of the commanding noble-playful life of some denial by Shakespeare of ordinary knowledge of himself and of life. And the early tragic work that ends with *The Rape of Lucrece* shows that he has actually always had that knowledge – if anything, all too much of it. One can speculate that helping to get him away from it and thus release the high spirits and rich creative play of that golden period were a thrilled new consciousness of his own powers and the encouragement and reinforcement of that by greater success than ever – perhaps greater, for one thing, because distinct success with a socially lofty audience as well as with the general theatre audience. He could also have felt both that he had completed that tragic work and that he was now, at the beginning of this new period, just resolving and completing the more positive thinking out of love and sexuality that meets and at any rate considerably mutes that work's dark feeling and thought on the subject.

The confidently noble Shakespeare of that golden period has so very much that is both attractive and valuable that his continued strong presence in *Hamlet*, and to an extent in *Othello*, does give those plays a real advantage over *King Lear* and *Macbeth* as well as, for the task being undertaken, the serious disadvantage. The generally greater popularity of these two earlier tragedies of the series, as of many of the plays that precede them, comes of the fact that that Shakespeare is so extremely winning.

But the final conclusion to be drawn from Shakespeare's hatred of tragedy may be that, however great his writing, he never finally got everything together in it and achieved as whole a vision as some other

great writers have. Headings come to mind from a long discredited
late-Victorian reading of the plays as a kind of autobiography, but to
help make not a biographical but an artistic point: Shakespeare is just
a little too much "on the heights" in what I call his golden period and
is becoming a little too much "in the depths" during the period of the
great tragedies.

For a final suggestion on this I start from a remark made by a
good critic to me in conversation, on the excessive intellectuality of
Shakespeare's writing and its relative remoteness from the ordinarily
physical – and I would add, from the potential sacredness in the
ordinarily physical. Matthew Arnold said something similar when,
writing on Maurice de Guérin in the first series of his *Essays in
Criticism*, he observed that Shakespeare's "expression tends to become
too little sensuous and simple, too much intellectualised." I believe the
point is related to that fear or apprehension expressed in the tragic
writing of life's being evil at its very core and all innocence and
goodness hopelessly doomed. It is also related to both the startling
vehemence that there can be in statements of sexual disgust and
misogyny in the plays (and sonnets) and the fact that there is relatively
little beautiful bawdy in them though their bawdy double-entendres
can seem almost endless.

The intellect can play, and play beautifully and idly, and be
confidently in command when it does so – in ready punning and in
elaborate poetic conceits, and also in many scenes where little or
nothing of a play's action is going forward and we simply enjoy the
characters being their fine, dashing and charming selves as they talk
and play games. But the habit of writing with the intellect active
almost by itself, in partial dissociation, means that, when the
inspiration of a particular play is too urgent for such playing around,
the writing can become awkward and crabbed with a compressed-idle
cleverness. A randomly chosen example from the good number of
possible examples in *Macbeth* is

> His wonders and his praises do contend
> Which should be thine or his.

Then both the physical human body and the green earth tend to
be nasty when Shakespeare is writing about them most vividly. It is
the diabolically possessed Poor Tom in *King Lear*, the witches in
Macbeth and Caliban in *The Tempest*, the would-be rapist and a

170

Sh's lack of direct Shadows, pleasure in physical/worldly things

witch's bastard son, who are closest to the earth. I think they take us closer to it than the beautiful but a little more fanciful and literary 'pastoral' writing of either *A Midsummer Night's Dream* or *The Winter's Tale*. Shakespeare seems a long way, as Virgil does not, or Dante or Milton, from the Wordsworth who, early in his Tintern Abbey "Lines", is thrilled to see in the landscape before him that the farms are

> …Green to the very door.

Take that sentiment to the heaths of *King Lear* and *Macbeth*! The physical beauty that Shakespeare does memorably respond to is the beauty that in one way or another is taking off from being simply physical or of the earth. The martins or swallows that Banquo talks to his King about not only fly but also nest high and in churches, and their presence in a locality shows that "The air is delicate" and

> …the heaven's breath
> Smells wooingly here.

There is a similar feeling about the rose in the sonnets and about the other flowers in the celebrated passage from *The Winter's Tale*. On the page just quoted from, Matthew Arnold writes that earlier in his career Shakespeare does have the balance between the sensuous and simple, on the one hand, and the intellectual, on the other, but his example from the sonnets is

> Full many a glorious morning have I seen
> Flatter the mountain tops with sovereign eye…

Finally: for as comprehensive and universal a genius as Shakespeare is so often supposed to be it is remarkable that in his many thousands of lines I cannot remember a single beautiful line about meat or bread. Compare Homer!

Yet there *is* the small amount of beautiful bawdy, something that is in any case rare enough in English literature after Chaucer. It may be significant that much, or most, of it occurs in *A Midsummer Night's*

Only a little beautiful bawdy
(most of it in DND)

Dream. Titania is promising wonderful orgasms to the ass-headed Bottom after she has awoken to see him for the first time in Act 3 –

> And I will purge thy mortal grossness so,
> That thou shalt like an airy spirit go.

– and is immediately calling for help from attendant fairies whose names are lovely simple metaphors for different female genitalia. Bottom himself has his wonderful prose poetry of anxiety about premature ejaculation near the beginning of Act 4.

Chapter VI
Literary critics working for and against poetry

Here I venture to put together with little revision five separately written reviews. Although three of them were written a good number of years before this book's main argument, their relevance to it is clear enough.

The first piece was occasioned by the reprinting of Matthew Arnold's *St Paul and Protestantism* and *Literature and Dogma* as Volume VI, *Dissent and Dogma*, in Professor R.H. Super's edition of *The Complete Prose Works of Matthew Arnold.* (Here the comment on the volume's editing is omitted.)

The much more favourable comments on Arnold's writing on religion that come towards the review's end not only reflect the opinion of that writing that I've had most of my life, but would be given greater emphasis if I were rewriting the review now.

1. RELIGION, IRRELIGION AND MATTHEW ARNOLD

"Can there be anyone more irreligious than the articulate Christian? Who else, even if he tried, could match the impiety of that deliberate 'love', that deliberate hushed solemnity, that deliberate talking-to-edify? Among the host of people who go in so eagerly for serious 'Christian' talk is there no one who makes it the highest priority to feel and tell the truth?"

My sense of offence came back again recently, after I had sat through a Sunday-evening discussion on BBC Television. The topic was "Guilt". One member of the discussion-panel, the one who was in holy orders, kept on asking how he could help "Mrs Jones down the road" with "this problem". I thought the chances were that Mrs Jones wasn't so much in need of help as somebody else. But I also found myself asking how anyone who is not something of a poet dare offer to 'discuss' any of the gods or their workings. If every person can and perhaps must invoke the gods, in token or borrowed phrases, what man without a gift of words dare hold forth about them? How did the members of this discussion-panel suppose they could impart religious insight in impromptu speech that used some time-worn phrases and some cosy-churchy ones and was otherwise banal?

Is it true that holding forth about the gods must be impious unless the words make the truth both apparent and powerful, able to speak home to anyone who opens him- or herself to hear? Where do such words come from? These are some fairly random test-illustrations:

> The light of the body is thine eye. Wherefore if thine eye be single thy body shall be full of light. (*Matthew* 6.22)

> For that in us which is really natural is, in truth, *revealed*. We awake to the consciousness of it, we are aware of it coming forth in our mind; but we feel that we did not make it, that it is discovered to us, that it is what it is whether we will or no. (Matthew Arnold, *Literature and Dogma*)

> This non-faith is a denial of God's creativity. It is an attempt to find security in the limited me of which I am aware instead of in the unlimited me which issues continuously from the fount of Being, and of which I must be largely unaware. Non-faith is total reliance upon what can be grasped and held by conscious reflexion and implemented by conscious acts of will. (H.A.Williams, "Theology and Self-Awareness" in the 1962 collection *Soundings*, edited by Alec Vidler)

> Love alone, because, as it were, it has a built-in moral compass, enabling it to 'home' intuitively upon the deepest need of the other, can allow itself to be directed completely by the situation. It can afford to be utterly open to the situation, or rather to the person in the situation, uniquely and for his own sake, without losing its direction or unconditionally. (John A.T. Robinson, *Honest to God*, 1963)

We are jolted at one or two earlier points on the way down but it is the

174

final descent that brings the great bump. If the first passage is simultaneously intense thought and inspired poetry, so also, just about, at their successively much lower pitches, are the second and third. The fourth is a kind of guessing and hoping. The writer doesn't know what he's talking about – doesn't properly possess that truth – but insists on writing as if he did. The reader who tries to cooperate gets the untruth of a pious-sentimental forcing, which is impertinence to the imagined "person in the situation" as well as non-faith. Arnold explained the difference between words that speak and words that don't when he wrote, on the same page: "The real antithesis, to natural and revealed alike, is *invented, artificial.*"

The passages from Arnold and Williams go against my sweepingness about the articulate Christian. Readers may have guessed that I don't much frequent modern 'Christian' talk and writing, and some will be in a better position than I am to know what other passages could be quoted. My first paragraph was certainly too sweeping about them, but my reason for no longer much frequenting the articulate Christians is that, as a general rule, I have come to expect rather more truth from artists and poets and from other fellow publicans and sinners – and decidedly less risk of embarrassment and offence.

***

That is an attempt to establish one principle. With an abrupt shift I should like to propose a second (but related) one, by means of a short exam-paper for ordinands.

> 1. "You mustn't think that Christianity is a grim or glum affair. There's no reason at all why the Christian shouldn't be quite an exuberantly happy person."
> Why does this lower the spirits?
> (They sometimes put it higher, "Gaiety, lightness of heart, is just what the Christian knows all about," to sink the spirits lower still.)
> 2. The Cardinal is a revered, gentle, very frail old man. As we see him taking his ease in the spa hotel's dining-room,

175

with his attendant priests, we overhear them sharing a joke about a communist.

Is this the sort of thing they mean?

And was this a moment in *8 ½* when God refrained from smiling a little at the Cardinal's expense with Fellini and the rest of us?

3. The huge figure of Foolishness comes forward to praise herself to the assembled human race, and begins, "Whatever people say about me – and it's not as if I don't know what a bad name I have with even the most foolish of you – I am the force that is present, and I am the only force that is present, when gods and men are really overjoyed. I can prove it: immediately you saw me coming forward to speak to you now, all your faces suddenly lit up with a new and unusual cheerfulness..."

One man called out, "Nothing is sacred," and pulled the trigger. A second man hid his gun away, saying silently inside himself, "No, these few things must be sacred." Which was sinning against the Holy Ghost?

***

Quand on voit le style naturel, on est tout étonné et ravi, car on s'attendait de voir un auteur et on trouve un homme.[*]

I wish I could apply Pascal's words to Matthew Arnold, who strove hard to write a natural prose. However, his prose is always more or less unnaturally natural. The paragraph in *Literature and Dogma*'s first chapter that I have already quoted from begins like this:

> Now here, as we have already pointed out the falseness of the common antithesis between *ethical* and *religious*, let us anticipate the objection that the religion here spoken of is but

---

[*] When one sees the natural style, one is quite astounded and enraptured, for one was expecting to see an author and one finds a man.

natural religion, by pointing out the falseness of the common antithesis, also, between *natural* and *revealed*.

Sometimes, as here, we can see Arnold managing the rhythms of his prose in front of our eyes, those plain expository and hortatory rhythms which are always close to being banal. His language as a whole has an all-too-even, strained-pale simplicity, rising to a telling simplicity only sporadically: it moves forward quite confidently and often with a smile, as if it were whole, but it has actually been doctored; and it drains a little of our own vitality from us as we read it. I don't think there is anywhere in his essays where Arnold does strike us as thoroughly human. He is spontaneous and sincere in a phrase or a sentence but never for as long as a paragraph.

I should like to put forward two propositions about him, in the form of questions. (1) Do his good phrases and sentences show that he was born to be both one of the gods' poets and one of their fools? (2) Do his paragraphs show him evading full surrender to his inspiration, steering himself all the time in the direction of doing conscious good? That is, does he tend to spoil his thought, and his powers of thought, by expressing and organising thought too purposefully? Consider the rostrum-enthusiasm of the italics, written very much *de haut en bas*, as if to children:

> For that in us which is really natural is, in truth, *revealed*.

They weaken the truth that he is going to be bringing out in impressive nakedness in his next sentence, and betray that his own mind isn't filled by it. And consider what happens to the four-word flash of inspired wit here:

> …that formidable logical apparatus, not unlike a guillotine, which Professor Huxley speaks of somewhere as the young man's best companion; – and so it *would* be his best companion, no doubt, if all wisdom were come at by hard reasoning. (*Literature and Dogma*)

There is a valuable thought in the whole sentence, but by the end of it that special flash has not been built up into a blaze but pretty well damped out.

I don't think Arnold did ever make it his highest priority to feel and tell the truth. In every essay he writes he has one definite lesson or more to teach, and he is conscious of it almost all the time, putting much of his very strictly controlled energy into the effective addressing of it to his readers. He teaches the lesson, often (I believe) a true one, but doesn't think of pursuing its truth further and more exactly, for its own sake and also for his.

For this reason we can regularly get a strange impression that he is more and other than the writer we actually see, that in fact he is placed somewhere above the subject whose inside he is demonstratively showing us round.

If he does now and then let himself be wicked and his wit fly, it is only on a short lead and only when he has a definite good end in view. So that the wit tends to be a little corrupted. Some things were sacred, especially his own ends in view.

***

Though I think there was some tragic failure in Arnold's whole career as a writer, I don't want to say that the strict control under which he put himself through all his later writing-life – that is, very roughly, in his prose-writing – hadn't a great deal that was admirable in it, or that it gave him no strength. It did ensure his accomplishing valuable work, and he did forge for himself a firm public persona if not a fully human public self. And he might otherwise have done and been nothing. The pressures that led him to gird himself with some relentlessness seem to have been powerful ones: it was not radical personal success as a poet that his more public career as a writer of magazine-articles was following, and some thoroughgoing self-despair may lie behind that girding of himself.

Nevertheless, I believe there is some serious impiety in his self-discipline, and that in the end his prose work, also, is not as effective as it might have been, undermined as it is by the contradiction: he set himself resolutely and energetically to teach his contemporaries some good lessons; the pretension and conceit of that are always unavoidably there in his writing, however much he might have wished them away and however well he sometimes managed to mute them; yet what he set himself to teach as his main or central lesson was fundamentally a religious perception, that people take themselves too seriously and are too ready to assume that the good they think they have seen and are resolutely and energetically setting themselves to do will really give God pleasure. His assault on the crippling Victorian habit of cant was all the better because it was made with this understanding of the more general human folly in it, yet in the very act of making it he was another crippled-canting Victorian.

To try and illustrate this. T.S. Eliot seems to have found a different main or central lesson in Arnold, writing that "*Literature and Dogma* is irrelevant to Arnold's main position as given in the Essays and *Culture and Anarchy*" and describing *Culture and Anarchy* as "an invective against the crudities of the industrialism of his time" (*Selected Essays*).

> But, in truth, the free spontaneous play of consciousness with which culture tries to float our stock habits of thinking and acting, is by its very nature, as has been said, disinterested. Sometimes the result of floating them may be agreeable to this party, sometimes to that... but what culture seeks is, above all, to *float* them, to prevent their being stiff and stark pieces of petrifaction any longer. (From Chapter VI of *Culture and Anarchy*)

The idea about the free play of mind has general application, and a fair-minded reader of *Culture and Anarchy* would surely agree that it is much nearer the heart of the book than any ideas about "industrialism". There is also a clear relation to the idea in *Literature and Dogma* that I've represented by an earlier quotation: "We awake to the consciousness of it..." In *Culture and Anarchy* Arnold is quite explicit that by his not too happy phrase "the best self" he means the more impersonal life that a man may begin to enjoy when he loosens the hard tension of his will behind his cherished schemes and ideas. "In affirming them he affirms himself," whereas in our moments of more impersonal life and vision we feel we are governed by a power in us which is not ourselves. That brief quotation is from the Preface of *Culture and Anarchy*, while it is in *Literature and Dogma*, especially its first chapter, that he has much to say about the powers that are awe-inspiringly "not ourselves", both "in us and in the world around us".

Yet that contradiction: the free play of consciousness – how odd to make that a matter for sustained advocacy rather than something to be exercised and enjoyed. And the ineffectiveness: Arnold's poetry and wit could have freed our minds by themselves and without our ever thinking about it, simply making our blood flow and our vision clear itself in the way that all good poetry and wit do; his advocacy leaves us with a cold and inert idea called "culture" on our hands, perhaps with some good intentions about it. *Culture and Anarchy* is not all advocacy, but advocacy tends to dominate it. "Free spontaneous play" and "float" and "petrifaction" are poetic images set in sentences that don't move freely or spontaneously but tritely. In Chapter VI Arnold demonstrates the value of a free spontaneous play of consciousness by a deliberate illustrative performing of it. We see him in the act of floating stock ideas – that belong to his opponents. He makes much of "the best self", but the phrase's simplicity is not an intense simplicity, only a matter of the deliberate address to the reader: to show how attractively easy this saving truth is, he has forced himself to write about it with an impossible assurance and familiarity.

> But by our best self we are united, impersonal, at harmony. We are in no peril from giving authority to this, because it is the truest friend we all of us can have; and when anarchy is a danger to us, to this authority we can turn with sure trust. Well, and this is the very self which culture, or the study of perfection, seeks to develop in us… (Chapter II)

I think most readers of *Culture and Anarchy* do in fact find "the best self" uninspiring, sometimes to their considerable disappointment and unease, and they have plenty of excuse for not seeing that it is a religious idea. Can it be the depth of our nature when he seems to know it so well? And in affirming the idea is he not affirming more of what is himself than of what is not himself?

What I am trying to say is that a writer cannot recommend the power of God since he is immediately impious if he offers to: he can only worship it.

* * *

> And the word "God" is used [by a contemporary writer] …as if it stood for… an idea about which everyone was agreed, and from which we might proceed to argue and to make inferences, with the certainty that… the basis on which we were going everyone knew and granted. But, in truth, the word "God" is used in most cases as by no means a term of science or exact knowledge, but a term of poetry and eloquence, a term thrown out, so to speak, at a not fully grasped object of the speaker's consciousness…

> The language of the Bible, then, is literary, not scientific language; language thrown out at an object of consciousness not fully grasped, which inspired emotion. Evidently, if the object be one not fully to be grasped, and one to inspire emotion, the language of figure and feeling will satisfy us better about it, will cover more of what we seek to express, than the language of literal fact and science. The language of science about it will be below what we feel to be the truth.

These are further sentences from the first chapter of *Literature and Dogma*. Arnold saw the need for poetry and was himself something of a poet, again, as he explained it. The reader will see that my own idea comes from him although it is the idea by which I find him wanting and although his comparison is not the one made here between a full poetry and a partly held-back, half-stifled poetry. His comparison is between poetic language and the would-be 'scientific' language which he finds in "the astounding particularity and licence of affirmation of our dogmatists". I think Arnold's writing on religion is worth reading because I think his main position sound and much of his detailed argument sensible, and because he was the last greatly-gifted writer in

English who attempted to speak of the gods in formal Christian apologetics.

"But hasn't this writing been discredited?" I add a final note, not to argue the case in full but to say why that is hardly necessary.

> ...the thing turns upon understanding the manner in which men have thought, their way of using words, and what they mean by them. And by knowing letters... we become acquainted not only with the history, but also with the scope and powers, of the instruments which men employ in thinking and speaking.

Although T.S. Eliot tried to damn Arnold's writing on religion, in the two essays already quoted from, he never attempted to meet the ideas about language that *Literature and Dogma* is avowedly based on. He didn't even mention them; and, in fact, he invoked against the book the more conventional notions about thought and language that it questions. To my mind this marks not only obvious disqualifying prejudice but also some surprising philosophical naiveté and incuriosity.* And I am tempted to say that I find the same in the pages of F.H. Bradley that Eliot partly relied on: those on Arnold in the "Concluding Remarks" of *Ethical Studies*. Bradley equally disregards the fact that *Literature and Dogma* is an argument about language, and he seems to me philosophically naive and incurious when he does so in this manner:

---

* Surprising in the poet of:
> Words, after speech, reach
> Into the silence...
>
> Words strain,
> Crack and sometimes break, under the burden,
> Under the tension, slip, slide, perish,
> Decay with imprecision, will not stay in place,
> Will not stay still.
> ("Little Gidding," *Four Quartets*)

We hear the word "verifiable" from Mr Arnold pretty often. What is to verify? Has Mr Arnold put "such a tyro's question" to himself? If to verify means to find in outward experience, then the object of true religion can not be found as this or that outward thing or quality, and so can not be verified.

Incidentally, though Eliot asserted that Bradley "knocked the bottom out of *Literature and Dogma*," it is not certain that Bradley actually read it. The definite references he makes are all to two current magazine-articles, which Arnold wrote after *Literature and Dogma* and printed in revised form in his *God and the Bible*. The obvious and disqualifying prejudice that Bradley shows is the one he might be expected to show against articles in which, among other things, Arnold extended his ideas about language into a full-length assault on traditional metaphysics. (See Chapter II of *God and the Bible*, "The God of Metaphysics.") But to stick to Bradley's possibly not having read *Literature and Dogma*. He seems to have supposed that he was bringing out one of the positive truths that refuted Arnold's ideas on religion when he wrote this:

> Religion is more than morality. In the religious consciousness we find the belief, however vague and indistinct, in an object, a not-myself, an object, further, that is real.

The little I have quoted from *Literature and Dogma* is enough to deal with this. Again: when Bradley tries to expose as tautologous Arnold's famous description of religion as "morality touched by emotion", he makes no reference to those sections of *Literature and Dogma*'s first chapter where Arnold elaborates on his description by speaking of the awe, fear and gratitude that come with people's recognition that in the conduct of their lives they are so much in the hands of a power and an order not themselves; and Bradley's argument – "All morality is, in one sense or another, 'touched' by emotion... we see all that is meant is that morality 'touched' by religious emotion is religious" – has no force for the reader who knows that Arnold is not offering a rigorous definition of religion in that single phrase. In its context Bradley would also have seen that Arnold uses the word "touched" in one special sense, not "in one sense or another": he means "heightened, enkindled, lit up".

2. LEAVIS'S 'WORK'

There must be an ancient story, though I cannot remember where I read it: of a man who had to labour to pass a great treasure on to the people and couldn't pass it on. He tried, but the people didn't look interested, and he was filled with distrust, and he despaired of ever being able to carry out his task. He tried again and again, all his life, new effort after new effort, with a strenuous heroic force but never with much hope and often with the anger of his distrust, which was one of the things he became known by.

A few of the people visited him, and these were astonished not only by their thrilling glimpses of the treasure but also by the fact that the man himself, whom they had been more than half afraid to meet, was in fact no misanthropist but a man of a quite extraordinarily pure and compelling power and sweetness and beauty. They would have liked to help, and some did try to pass on to the rest of the people some small parts of the wonderful treasure, but that achieved nothing.

His despair only grew. His life was passing, and his understanding of the treasure's great value to the people was all the time increasing. The despair became black as he began to understand more clearly in his messages from the gods that the treasure had almost nothing of its great special value except when it was complete; and the despair became blacker still as he also began to understand what it was that he was bound to say to those willing helpers, what he did begin whispering half under his breath as they were drawn around him in love and admiration and with a sense of the sacred giftedness in him: "For the whole of the treasure to be passed on, my head must be struck off…"

***

There is a quality of absoluteness that an artist strives to give a work and that Leavis gives clear signs of seeking or half-seeking in spite of the fact that he writes 'criticism'. The very forcefulness of his writing – its marked and unceasing insistence on the statement it is making, its drive to make that statement complete and compelling – is one of the signs suggesting how the making of the statement it less an advancing and arguing of opinion than a labouring to create and incarnate truth: truth of a fundamental and permanent kind, truth of art rather than of specific literal fact. This may be clearer in his later books* than in their predecessors, but I should say that it is only clearer, not something new in them.

Another sign is the impatience of loose ends and the interest in binding closely together in one whole all the various themes and subjects of the writing. In these later books Blake, Dickens, D.H. Lawrence, life and creativity, the "spiritual philistinism" of the present age, the nature of any fruitful thought and use of language, all recur frequently and are forever being interwoven with each other. When Leavis writes of Dickens's "genius" as being "in certain essential ways akin to Lawrence's" (*Nor Shall My Sword*), that statement doesn't have for him the effect that it is bound to have for almost everyone else, that of flooding the mind with images of the ways in which these two writers are unlike each other and making it begin to weigh the issue, and the reason why it doesn't is that he is so possessed by the positive inspiration that makes him interested for the time being only in the kinship. It is the kinship that he senses there is between their inspiration and his own. That is almost what he means by "certain essential ways".

Here there is a further sign: the works referred to and recommended and discussed are brought in less for their own sakes than as part of the material out of which a new work is being made.

> I am no more offering a reading-list than a syllabus. [This comes from *The Living Principle*, which is partly concerned with the ideal university school of English – from a passage in which philosophical writing by Marjorie Grene, Michael Polanyi and R.G. Collingwood is being recommended.] Simply, the books I mention seem to me essential books,

---

* This review was occasioned by the appearance in 1976 of *Thought, Words and Creativity: Art and Thought in D.H. Lawrence*, but these "later books" also included *Nor Shall My Sword: Discourses on Pluralism, Compassion and Social Hope* (1972) and *The Living Principle: 'English' as a Discipline of Thought* (1975).

books that, associated in the given context, belong to my argument and help to define what I have in mind.

If the associating of "essential" with "belong to my argument" and "help to define what I have in mind" is unconscious egotism, it is the proper unconscious egotism of someone single-mindedly bent on his own work, *The Plumed Serpent* is the main novel of Lawrence's which Leavis likes least, but

> It contains abundant evidence of the great creative writer who wrote it; and in the course of my recent re-readings I have filled a large part of a notebook with felicities of thought-formulation that belong distinctively to a novelist's creativity and that one would wish to have ready in one's mind to use.
>
> *(Thought, Words and Creativity)*

Lawrence is a quarry, in one of the number of ways in which poets are commonly quarries for later poets. Another way in which they are, is is by telling stories that later writers are moved to take over from them and re-tell. Leavis's new chapter on "The Captain's Doll", the long story or *nouvelle* by Lawrence, is certainly a strong re-telling, with quotations from Lawrence's text but with very much its own narration, its own characterisation, its own management of suspense and emphasis. For some readers and certain moods it could well replace the original. Another way in which earlier writers provide material is by providing, in themselves or in their statements or deeds, some of the material out of which symbols can be created in the new work – in Leavis's case symbols of what are for him the fundamental truths and strengths and virtues, and symbols also of the opposite of these.

> Eliot matters in a major way because he is impressive enough as a creative writer to bring out by contrast the greatness and rarity of the genius who was not defeated – who demonstrates so marvellously what intelligence is. No one of course who has read him would suggest that Lawrence doesn't bring home to us that it is an essential condition of life-as-intelligence to know itself faced – ultimately, but not

remotely – with the unknown, and with the unknowable.

(Thought, Words and Creativity)

The giving of a symbolic value to material from the real world is a main part of what is being done in the repetition and interweaving of references.

The 'poem' made by these books and the others has something of the nature of a religious hymn, a tremendous, urgent affirmation of the divine creativity of life. It is an affirmation which has to be in part, as it often has to be, a self-affirmation. That life is known to Leavis, first and last, because it is what he himself is principally moved by. This is the reason why the notes that might otherwise sound like ordinarily egotistic ones are not simply that but have something magnificent about them and combine easily with the pervasive note that there is in the writing of an unusually strong impersonal pressure and authority. About this life Leavis is eloquent in manifold indirect ways – it is what he is writing about all the time, however improbably – but also directly, as when he writes of the "submission" to "the promptings to be gathered from the unknown – from which life and creativity enter us" that it is,

> ...of its nature, a very active matter, demanding self-knowledge, intense cultivation of the most delicate intuitiveness, and the courage to arrive at conclusions the precision and finality of which are not guaranteed: the responsibility for them is ours, and where it is not taken up there is no responsibility. (*Thought, Words and Creativity*)

***

This is a roughing-out of a proposition about Leavis. I am not sure that I wish, or should wish, to do more than that. To give to the proposition the flesh that I myself see on it after re-reading these three books (and that my reader may be able to see on it after reading them) would itself be a work of portraiture or drama or poetry rather than a work of ordinary argument. But the roughing-out is incomplete if I don't refer to one further sign of the books' making a 'poem': that they do *not* work and do *not* convince so well in the main way that they seem meant to do. What Leavis is avowedly offering is the truth of literal and specific fact rather than – or as at any rate having as much importance as – the general truth of art. And he is offering this as the basis for an urgent practical programme of combating the "spiritual philistinism" that he sees as so dominant.

> There could be in our time no more important preoccupation than that which brings us here. (*Nor Shall My Sword*)

This is the opening of a lecture in which Leavis was talking not about the seeking and affirmation of the divine but about… the university study of English literature. Or, rather, he *was* talking about that seeking and affirmation – evidently, from the special weight and force of the utterance as well as from the connections of thought actually made both in this lecture and throughout these books – but was taking this most peculiarly restricted and indirect way of doing so. University 'English' is another symbol but isn't acknowledged to be one. Leavis is partly denying his own inspiration, and deflecting and displacing the force of it, even as he is being governed by it. If the otherwise magnificent 'egotism' does ever become the ordinary failing, I should say that it was less when it was the egotism of pride than when it was that of fear and lack of faith – or that such fear is the source of any impure element in the pride. Truth, however powerfully uttered, isn't trusted by him to speak for itself – to be its own value and life, and to be the kind of life that inspires further life. He must also make it a concern with "practicality and with persuasion to directed energizing" (*The Living Principle*).

The main unfortunate consequence of this is that the compellingness of the utterance can become compellingness of the wrong sort, tending to close the reader's mind and spirit, and even to corrupt them in one way, rather than to do what in its nature it should be doing: stir and enlarge and liberate and purify. To take a small example: during my re-reading of *The Living Principle* I was asking myself why I have been so slow to act on its pressing recommendations of the books by Marjorie Grene, Polanyi and Collingwood. I believe the answer is that Leavis takes up the truths for which he recommends these books into his own work and makes his own forceful statement of them. The anticipation of the *déjà-vu* is off-putting and even upsetting because it not only dampens curiosity but is the anticipation of a quite radical inauthenticity in oneself. The books would be being picked up with some intensity of expectation but at the same time with a feeling that the crucial main things that were the reasons for this expectation were already perfectly well understood. By pressing the recommendations and making them part of a larger practical programme, Leavis is refusing to acknowledge the nature and self-sufficient power of his own utterance. And I believe that this same trouble affects all the other items in that programme: the repeated and emphatic recommendations of the study of Blake's work, Dickens's, Lawrence's and Eliot's and especially of certain parts of them, the insistence on 'English' in the university and on its function as a "liaison centre" among various specialist subjects, the insistence on the university thus centred as the country's and the Western world's only possible source of spiritual regeneration. It is all remarkably dynamic and remarkably static and depressing at the same time, all a great 'poem' of implicit self-affirmation that the reader is asked to take literally and that he cannot take literally without committing something like an intellectual and spiritual suicide. On the other hand, the 'poem' as a poem would be, and partly is, abundantly fruitful – even if not in any distinct or pre-determinable 'practical' way.

The part-refusal of his own inspiration can be seen in two interrelated prejudices in Leavis's thought: the rigidly confining historicism and the utilitarian bias in favour of a naturalistic art (notably in favour of novels as against poems). The truth is reduced, in statement if not in fact, to being the truth about our own very special time in history, and works of art are celebrated not for the power that they may have for all time but for their faithful representations and diagnoses of that special time of our own. It is as if the seeking and affirmation of the divine has been made necessary in an unprecedented way by a decline of civilization and only by that, and had somehow not always been needed in earlier and more fortunate periods:

> It seems to me that Lawrence's basic attitude is religious in the most vital, the most living, way: it is the way

189

compelled by a properly indocile perception of what our civilization is doing to life. (*Thought, Words and Creativity*)

It is probably in the nature of the case that Leavis's closest kinship should not be with any of the writers that he has been celebrating in these books. The character of his own writing from early on, weightily deliberate and considered and close-packed, with a fire of vehement conviction giving it always an edge of eloquence even when not a full and direct eloquence; his special awareness of being entrusted with a crucial and momentous task, religious in its fundamental character and at the same time a task to be carried out for the benefit and glory of his nation, and so that it can help show the way to other nations; his unresting effort and unquenchable spirit, and his 'egotism', assertive and intransigent and indocile and often magnificently so; his very literal-mindedness and his concern with making some kind of powerful practical effect, the great characteristic strength that these partly are in him; – the combination of these is surely matched in no other English writer so closely as in Milton. In dealing with his dissatisfaction with the religious thought of Eliot's *Four Quartets* – with the representation of human life as null and worthless – Leavis makes the sturdily and admirably Miltonic affirmation:

> ...there is no acceptable religious position that is not a reinforcement of human responsibility. (*The Living Principle*)

Compare the 'fallen' Adam and Eve:

> Thus they in lowliest plight repentant stood
> Praying...
> > yet their port
> Not of mean suitors... (*Paradise Lost*, XI)

The pity is that there is no work in which Leavis, like Milton, tests himself and his faith against the fullest statement he can make of all the reasons he knows for despairing of human nature. This means, among other things, that there occasionally creeps into the affirmation that he makes against the 'negativeness' he sees in Eliot's religious thought a note that belongs less properly to that affirmation than to Victorian muscular Christianity. It also means that the whole 'work' is a smaller thing than it might have been.

One trouble with a roughed-out proposition is that it tends to be diagrammatic. To say that the "practicality" is a denial of the true inspiration is not to say, as I have already admitted, that it isn't also a great strength. Nor is it to say that there isn't a resonant truth in the idea of the spiritual centre that a people has and needs, and needs to have renewed. Nor is it to say that a religious poet isn't naturally concerned with the unworthiness of statements made by members of a government and other prominent public figures – their unworthiness in their suggestions about human ends.

I append a later review (abbreviated), of the 1995 biography of Leavis, *F.R.Leavis: a Life in Criticism*, by Ian Mackillop.

When Leavis read poetry during a lecture, it could seem as if for the moment the world stopped. There was nothing staged about the effect. What commanded his audience was the rare purity of his deep and passionate commitment to poetry. The poet's words and nothing else came into the mind – say the opening lines of Eliot's "Ash Wednesday" – and did so as perhaps never before, however well known to the listener. What shone out was the wonderful and even sacred gift to the human race that poetry is. Nothing could seem more important or precious.

In his biography Ian Mackillop refers neutrally to the stress that Leavis placed on reading poetry aloud, almost as if it were a mere idiosyncrasy instead of something excitingly of the essence of poetry and capable of producing electricity. And, in general, Leavis's own electricity is missing from this biography. Leavis was the sort of person in whom that charge was felt simply by being in the same room with him. It was there, involuntarily, through the sheer extraordinary energy of his being. And more than this was felt. The accompanying sense of exceptional responsibility contributed to an unmistakable and beautiful impersonal weight that he possessed, in spite of the fact that he could hardly have been fuller of spunky and occasionally spiky character. Charming and unusually and even elaborately courteous in his talk, he was also vigorous in it – proud, assertive, combative, witty, confident in his insight into life and people as well as remarkably telling with it, always lively and sharp. Everyone else in comparison seemed more than half asleep. And there was this distinct sense of a special responsibility – in part a sense of a special calling – an unavoidable burden, yet not an unwanted one since much of the time it was sheer joyful inspiration. The concern that Leavis himself in his thought showed with the impersonal is something else that Mackillop makes neutral, cool references to, though it is again of the essence of the man, and surely everything to do with what makes art and literature capable of being awe-strikingly significant.

Anyone who knew Leavis will be grateful for things in this biography that help bring back the vivid person. For example: "Leavis said he could himself swim a hundred yards under water, but not manage a Swinburne stanza." His talk and teaching were full of such quick wit, also characteristic in its impish use of his personal experience and physical prowess. Other passages of the biography, reporting unique private statements, bring the vivid person back in a less direct but even more fascinating way. Most of the people who knew Leavis would not remember anything like them, yet they make perfect sense with what they do remember. A moving instance concerns the extreme, passionate scruple that Leavis had about talking of his experience in the First World War (with the Friends' Ambulance Unit) and perhaps seeming boastful. Yet I doubt that readers of this biography who did not know Leavis could feel either the same relish for the witty statements quoted or the same fascination with such things as that extreme scruple. Such things occur too briefly and sparsely to begin to create a living portrait, and Mackillop hardly attempts any portrait in his own words.

This book has a lot of work behind it, and it contains much of the raw material for a biography of F.R. Leavis. It also contains sensible observations and judgements, and is written in a sensible temper. Most of what has been written about Leavis by people who, like Mackillop and myself, were pupils, has tended to have more heat than light. Mackillop admirably resists partisanship. But was it impossible for him to be fair-minded and at the same time convey Leavis's electricity? I believe he made things unnecessarily difficult for himself with two unfortunate decisions.

First, he decided not to make any sustained enquiry into large parts of Leavis's non-professional life. While many readers might be pleased by the unfashionable good taste of a biographer's feeling some scruple about trespassing on his subject's private life, I think Mackillop feels too much. Leavis died in 1978, his wife in 1981, and this book [of 1995] is offered as a biography. It does give us something of the personal life, being fairly detailed on the childhood and family background, and on the final illness. But, if it gives other things in the life too, it does so in extremely slight and sketchy ways. Such are the indications that Queenie Leavis was both someone who in Leavis's mind had an even more important value than a good spouse normally does, as if he would have achieved nothing without her, and someone about whom he complained bitterly and often. On one occasion I know of, when he was about seventy, he said she'd never allowed him to have a friend. There had to be a vivid and significant story here. Mackillop's decision not to attempt either that story or comparable ones helps to deprive his biography of its portrait.

His other questionable decision is to devote so many pages to restating Leavis's ideas. These ideas are what is already known: it's the life that isn't. Many dull pages are given to the preoccupation Leavis had, from the beginning to the end of his career, with "cultural conditions" – and this at the expense of the burning faith in human creativity that Leavis also always had. That preoccupation with cultural conditions did involve both fresh historical insight and telling criticism of modern cultural barbarities, and it was full of Leavis's ardent idealism about what human life and society can be. But it always was faulted by a pessimistic determinism in which a powerful but unconscious prejudice seems to have operated, driving him to provide himself with something like an excuse for failure. In a half-secret but still evident enough way Leavis was an intense Shelleyan visionary, but he seems radically to have doubted his vision's power to effect anything and never expressed it directly. Indirectly he expressed some of it through his passion for the great things he knew to be eternal but that diffidence, or failure of nerve, led him to see and celebrate those things in the past rather than in the present or any possible future.

If restating a writer's thought must always be in danger of giving the letter of the thought at the expense of its spirit, that danger is the greater if the thought chosen for restatement was never the purest expression of that spirit.

But this is too simple to be altogether fair to this biography. Would it even have been realistic for Mackillop to have assumed that Leavis's thought didn't need restating, in the belief that his writing was still widely read and must have a strong future? It's not easy to divide what is prejudiced in that writing from what is timeless. And Leavis's diffidence not only affects his writing on cultural conditions. More pervasively, even while the intensity and delicacy of his thinking is manifested in his prose's peculiar syntactical complexity, his anxiety to cover his back is also showing here. The diffidence also means that Leavis himself tends to insist on the letter of his thought, as if any admission of fallibility in it would be surrender to the enemy. The letter of his thought is bound more and more, as time goes on, to become either what everyone has accepted or what everyone has come to see as mistaken – in either case a dead letter. May there be a law that, the more absolute its insistence on its letter, the less permanent any writing will be?

But this very doubt about how well Leavis's writing will last only increases one's disappointment with a biography that, by not supplying a living portrait of its subject, does not do all that it could have done to keep an extraordinary flame burning.

3. *WRITING IN ENGLAND TODAY: THE LAST FIFTEEN YEARS.* EDITED BY KARL MILLER (PENGUIN BOOKS, 1967)

"He had that confidence which the first thinker of anything never has" (*Estrangement*). Perhaps Yeats was not being altogether fair to the man. Perhaps he had that confidence which let him be prompt and regular in his everyday affairs and which he could properly have when his thinking had to take most or all of its principles for granted and had to be carried on in the front of his mind, busily and purposefully and with as little trouble as possible, and was yet effective in the main. In this state of mind a man is all, as it were, in his face, with his eyes looking straight forward out of it, seeing some things clearly and other things not at all. The disinterested and even naive look in the eyes of even the most unYeatsian poet is the look of a man who seems at the same time to be seeing with another eye, somewhere inside his head. It is not that he is not attending to what is in front of him but that he is not seeing it in the expected, clear-cut and small form that everyone else sees it in, and does not seem to want to do with it the expected, clear-cut and small things that everyone else wants to do with it. He looks almost naive because he thinks he sees something fresh and interesting, and does not mind showing that he is without an immediate answer. Into the conventional circle that is all facing inwards he will suddenly put a remark that seems to come from somewhere at the side or at the back; and it is the more disconcerting because he or she can do this in the purest candour, without a trace of either whimsy or pretentiousness.

The poet here is the figure of the person who is genuinely curious about things, not necessarily a writer of verse; and is in each of us, just as the non-poet is. This poet's proper sovereignty in the conversations we have in our leisure – with books, with people, with ourselves – is always tending to be usurped by the non-poet. The latter knows everything so readily.

The particular conversation that I have to report on takes place in a literary circle, though the poet isn't much in evidence. The particular non-poet who is very much in evidence excels in talk about recent books, and attaches a great deal of importance to it. He is no snob, and can be heard admitting that he also enjoys reading James Bond novels, but what he most likes doing and is most expansive over in this talk is 'placing' books, especially some books that are great current successes but, he thinks, hollow ones. (Perhaps the most prominent items in *Writing in England Today*, if only because their inclusion is so unexpected, are reviews of *The Alexandria Quartet* by D.J. Enright, of *Lolita* by Kingsley Amis, of Teilhard de Chardin by P.B. Medawar, and of the magazine *Encounter* by Conor Cruise O'Brien, and an article on 'Neo-Christian' literary criticism by Professor William Empson.)

On the other side of the conversational circle the silent poet does not look very interested. And there is no admiration on her face. In fact she is beginning to think that there is no kind of talk that interests her less than talk about books. She is thinking that this is all going on too confidently and too brightly and too long, and she feels oppressed because the talk is shutting out two things that would at any rate, if the talk has to be about those books, interest her more: "In which direction should we be looking then?" and "Even out of this possibly bad book, if only in its own despite, is there no general truth to be learnt?" She is restless.

Half-noticing this, the non-poet thinks that something more 'positive' might please her better. He mixes a generous sympathy into his 'placing' judgements of one or two writers who are not such great current successes (further items in this anthology of contemporary English writing are O'Brien, again, on Colin Wilson and Enright, again, on David Holbrook), and he speaks very enthusiastically about the artistry and humanity of a recently reprinted bawdy novel of the eighteenth century (Brigid Brophy on *Fanny Hill*). He then launches into his pleasantly informal explanation of what has been happening in English poetry in the last decade and a half, being able to show that there has been an advance over the previous decade, to something like this effect:

> In the 1940s the mistake was made of giving the *Id*, a sound player on the percussion side under a strict conductor, too much of a say in the doings of the orchestra as a whole.

(Robert Conquest's Introduction to the anthology, *New Lines*, is another distinguished specimen of contemporary English writing.)

"What is missing from my talk," the non-poet decides, as he sees the poet now looking thoroughly dejected, "is boldness, a flurry of the largest possible ideas, as if something had stirred me to think as hard as I have ever thought about the state of the world or about even more ultimate matters. Now I don't know that anything can really be said to have done that for me – I have so little time – but what do I know that *might* suitably have done it?" He has a go. (Another book-review, by Frank Kermode, on the novels of William Golding, is the third-longest piece in this anthology, three times as long as the extract from one of Golding's admired novels.) When she hears the name of the novelist, the poet looks dubious. But she listens and looks hard, to see whether the non-poet *has* been taken out of himself here. She looks down at the floor again as she sees that the eyes are glistening as sedately as ever, and she decides that there is no wrestling or that it is all being done in the front of the mind – that the books have moved the speaker no more than they have moved herself, that any wrestling is not with the matter but with the problems of giving a good-sounding account of the matter.

When the talk takes a new direction, the poet chokes. The boring-bright talk about books has washed over her mind and not really given any sharp pain. But now the non-poet's voice has risen and has taken on a feeling note as he has begun to talk seriously about his experience of life. He is looking out of the window and meditating poetically on some of the ordinary things of life. "Consider junk," he says –

> It lies there, vivid in its dereliction
> among fine ashes from combustion stoves…
> (Non-poem by Tony Connor)

He then stands up straight, juts his chin out and insists that, though he would be friendly enough, he would have something quite severe to say on behalf of our familiar humanity to Jesus of Nazareth:

> Should you revisit us,
> Stay a little longer,
> And get to know the place.
> Experience hunger,
> Madness, disease and war.
> You heard about them, true,
> The last time you came here;
> It's different having them.
> And what about a go

At sex, marriage, children…
(Non-poem by Kingsley Amis)

"Is there anything the matter?" he breaks off to ask the still choking poet. Without forethought, between coughs, the poet lets out: "Why on earth are you so *fond* of your boring little prison?"

"Ah!" with a suddenly deeper note. "But I'm not! Not *really*." And for a moment there is all the pathos of his and everyone else's life. Bravely he makes what his voice confesses is hopeless, a clutch at seeing some significance in the involving circle of birth, marriage and death, speaking of how moved he sometimes is by the church building he never worships in: "A serious house on serious earth it is." "Home is so sad," he says, and speaks of the ghastly quickness with which the order of his house and belongings falls into meaninglessness in his absence, after his death. (Two poems by Philip Larkin.) Once in the mood, he begins talking about the unexpected calamity that befell an acquaintance the other day: he had seemed perfectly all right, but then it had suddenly come out, that all the time he had been "not waving but drowning." (Poem by Stevie Smith.)

"Well!" the poet wants to exclaim but cannot, "Here I think you're trying, even though you're only managing to caress your own and everyone else's ordinary neurotic misery. But if, now that we have come down to it, you turn out to have so little to say and that so feeble, why don't you *listen* for a change, or simply enjoy God's silence?" [Though I did call Larkin and Stevie Smith poets, not non-poets, I believe I was being badly unjust to both of them here, letting my reading of their poetry be coloured too much by the use sometimes made of it. For my more recent view of Larkin see above, pp101-105.] She doesn't get this out and the talk goes on and on, with more variations than I have space or interest to describe. Besides the talk about books, its main staple – to help us forget our miserable prisons and avoid silence – is detailed, mindless anecdotage. (Endless extracts from what used to be called 'middlebrow' fiction, by sub-Galsworthy's and sub-sub-Galsworthy's.)

This anthology is an event of no importance. Someone in Penguin Books made a mistake. The Editor himself has made the mistake of forgetting that the masterful journalism which he makes it his normal job to provide is not necessarily literature. It is he, of course, who is the rampant non-poet. Not all of his writers can have supposed they were writing literature, and I dare say a good number of them are embarrassed. I dare say the writers of the one or two pieces, out of the fifty-eight, which do say something to our deeper minds and imaginations – as against the three pieces and fourteen pages of Amis there is one (already well-anthologised) poem of Ted Hughes, on two pages – are also embarrassed.

It is sad to think that some foreigners will look at this volume as a representation of writing in England today. But perhaps it does represent something rather more than a simple mistake by editor and publishers. Miller may have calculated, with a good deal of justification after his success with the *New Statesman* and *Listener*, that the non-poet is rampant in most of us.

Postscript What a different literary world we are in, moved by what very different inspirations and goals, when we open a book that begins with the following piece!

> Thou hast made me endless, such is thy pleasure. This frail vessel thou emptiest again and again, and fillest it ever with fresh life.
>
> This little flute of a reed thou hast carried over hills and dales, and hast breathed through it melodies eternally new.
>
> At the immortal touch of thy hands my little heart loses its limits in joy and gives birth to utterance ineffable.
>
> Thy infinite gift comes to me only on these very small hands of mine. Ages pass, and still thou pourest, and still there is room to fill.

This is the first poem in Rabindranath Tagore's translation into English of Bengali poems of his own, in the book published in 1913 under the title *Gitanjali*. An extra reason for quoting it here is the relative neglect of Tagore in the current English-speaking world. The contrast between this book's great success in that same world early in the twentieth century and the near-oblivion into which it has subsequently fallen there is eloquent about the severe decline in poetic taste that had taken place by the end of the century.

On a different matter: the description of the poet in the latter part of this review's first paragraph is partly, as I knew when I wrote it, a description of a particular friend, the late Tony Ward (the novelist, Anthony Ward).

4. PROPHETIC POETICS (A review of Ted Hughes's *Winter Pollen*)

In an episode surprisingly not reported before, Captain Kirk and Mr Spock have been beamed down to the planet Vatuity. The star-ship *Enterprise* is on an important mission to find out about a food grown on this planet that has quite exceptionally potent medicinal powers, possibly just the ones needed to save life in the universe from a disease threatening it with extinction. They have met inhabitants all too easily, immediately surrounded by crowds and crowds of them, all talking very loudly. But Kirk and Spock begin to notice that, as the Vatuous jabber away, each is also swelling enormously in size. They both become nervous, wondering whether they are going to be left with an inch to move or breathe in. And they also have the frustration of learning nothing of what they have come for – the more maddeningly because the jabbering is offered as talk about that food and is at any rate a *kind* of English. The Vatuous all talk simultaneously and, seemingly, only to each other.

Then Spock's tallness helps him to see that beyond the outer rim of the packed circles around them is a rather different-looking individual: silent and dignified and un-swollen. Spock gestures to Kirk, and together they slowly edge and elbow their way through to this person. To their intense relief, they now meet genuine interest in their questions, and are soon being given – in a plain, calm and business-like way – some clear and full and also encouraging answers. It turns out that this person and a few similar individuals are the actual growers of that special food. They have a different and older name: Vates.

The episode's crisis arises from a combination of the two facts: although the food is grown on this planet, that catastrophic disease is, strangely, much further advanced here and is soon going to make it uninhabitable; only the *Enterprise* is near enough to help, but has room for no more than a handful of refugees. "So," to cut the long story short with the last line of the English nursery-rhyme, "who do you think was saved?"

If six books of twentieth-century literary criticism in English are still being read a hundred years from now, this book of Ted Hughes's may well have a chance of being one of them. And his earlier book on Shakespeare could well be another. I ask myself whether this enthusiasm is exaggerated because of my impatience with the academic industry of 'criticism', but do not believe it is.

The distinction is one of reach. It is not that valuable work can't occasionally be found among the heaps of print piled up all the time by university departments of literature, for all the self-enclosure that tends to mark the thinking in those departments, the consequent gross self-overrating, and the disregard for literary criticism's only *raison d'être* except among writers, as a facilitating mediator between writer and general reader. The point is that none of even the best of this 'criticism' gives fresh answers to the questions, "Why and how does great literature, or art in general, get created? and why do that literature and art matter so much?", and it is such answers that do the fundamental critical work of awakening, nourishing and illuminating our basic passionate appetite for art. Those answers are given by the artists themselves, the people who have first made the imaginative and spiritual journeys involved and know about them. If, usually, the main things they have to say here are included in their actual work, it occasionally happens, most often in the case of artists with words, that for whatever reason – perhaps, as with Wordsworth's great Preface to *Lyrical Ballads*, because poetic power is partly failing – one or other artist may also say main things in discursive prose. *Winter Pollen* is a miscellany of reviews, talks and articles written by Ted Hughes over all the years of his adult writing life, but the essential thinking in it is strikingly coherent, and I believe is of this order.

About Hughes's own poetry there can be many opinions, though perhaps there shouldn't be about the moving and impressive endeavour it represents – or certainly not now that that has been made still clearer by the present book. I'm afraid I myself find that what he says in it, in the piece called "Poetry and Violence", about his frequently anthologised "Thrushes" poem is a more thrilling and satisfying piece of writing than the poem itself. This is how the nine pages end:

> The Thrush finding and killing its worm, Mozart's composing brain, and the Shark, at their incredible, superhuman speeds, are 'at rest in the law'. Their agile velocity is a kind of stillness. At peace with essential being. Only we humans – 'terrified' by what our debilitated sense of reality sees as negative 'violence' in the activity of the Thrush and the Shark, and renouncing any possibility of sharing Mozart's 'divine' facility – cannot attain that peace. We cannot attain it because we are divided within ourselves against such spontaneous allegiance to the 'divine' law. The cultivated split in human consciousness has exacted this price. As a result (and this is the gist of the last lines) that 'divine' faculty of spontaneous allegiance to the creator's law is trapped within us, and locked up. Deprived of access to life, it is therefore deprived of the possibility of any genuine adaptation to life. And so it is diabolised (in frustration) or invents a metaphysical bliss (in sublimation) or simply mourns (in despair and resignation). In other words, it has been 'violated' (and has suffered crippling 'violence') by our settling for too-easy substitutes that support our social contracts. It has been 'violated', that is, by 'our customary social and humanitarian values'.

An artist who may not have found the way to bring back the treasure perfectly intact may still have made the journey and have things of great value to tell about it to all the rest of us.

Fresh answers to these fundamental questions are unlikely to be new ones. Hughes's thinking is profoundly original yet also, as he himself understands better than anyone else, profoundly traditional. The freshness that matters is in any case less a matter of novelty than of feeling, requiring the passion of a rare individual inspiration (or call to the journey), supported by exceptional intelligence, clarity and stamina in meeting its demands. In this area, that of the fundamental poetics that is perhaps work only for someone like a prophet, cold thinking would be a complete non-starter.

Ted Hughes's manner here couldn't be quieter, soberer, more modest. He usually offers his exceptional insight as nothing but simple and plain matter of fact.

His essential thinking is presented as much in reviews like those of Max Nicholson's *The Environmental Revolution* and Mircea Eliade's *Shamanism* as in a talk like "Myth and Education" that is more directly about literature. The studies of individual writers tend to have less of it, probably because of the writers being written about, though the two remarkable pieces on T.S.Eliot and Shakespeare (the latter the early statement that Hughes has since expanded on at book length) are certainly central, and both an article on Singer's fiction and a long study of Coleridge's poetry also contain much of the essential thinking. Central in it, too, are the few commentaries on work of Hughes's own.

That thinking's reach is a matter of extent as well as depth. It seems that the depth enables Hughes to be almost unprecedentedly comprehensive in the knowledge he can draw on of the race's spiritual experience. It is with impressive ease, and complete unshowiness, that he identifies and expounds relevant evidence from all over the world and human history. That core of his thinking could not be less parochial, and among other benefits of both the depth and this extraordinary largeness of perspective is some radical insight into English and Western history. But the main benefit is for Hughes's understanding of poetry and art, making him classical here in the best sense of the word. While he doesn't himself use the word "classical", his thinking, in an excitingly unexpected and rewarding way, renews the whole idea of the standard it represents.

The little questionable thinking in the book comes when this standard is for the moment obscured by a temperamental sympathy he sometimes shows with the more assertively idiosyncratic kind of artist. It would be unfair to his long discussion of metres and rhythms simply to cite it as an example here, since it includes delicate pages on the classic poetry of Thomas Wyatt (pp346-364) as well as much on

Hopkins. Yet that essay does disappoint when compared with many other things in the book. Also, the essay's final emphasis, somewhat at the expense of the impersonality that marks the greatest verse-music, seems to be at odds with what can be found elsewhere in the book, for example in the short piece called "Inner Music".

The essential inspired idea is that all great art has to be understood in religious terms, and has as its fundamental work to heal and redeem. But everything is in Hughes's own various presentations of that idea.

Chapter VII
What Are We Doing When Enjoying Prose Fiction?
or
"Are you sitting *comfortably?"*[*]

This really ought to be the story of an Englishman, a Frenchman and an Irishman, but there is only space to tell some of the Irishman's part of it. But, first, the gist of the whole story can be given in fable form.

The Englishman, the Frenchman and the Irishman were bakers living and working in different parts of the same modern city, and they made a very popular kind of bread, almost the city's staple food.

But this bread, popular both then and now, has also been a trouble. It is difficult to make well, and the overwhelming majority of that city's bakers have either never understood this or never wanted to. The best of them have made fairly respectable loaves and rolls, nice to eat, providing some nourishment and not doing people too much harm. But even these bakers have made their job easier by adulterating their bread in one way or another, while others have done this so seriously as to deprive theirs of much or all of its food value. And this has been a grave matter, because people have filled themselves up with it and then not eaten the nourishing food they have needed. Some pretty worthless bread has been handed out to children in schools.

The Englishman, the Frenchman and the Irishman all saw there was something wrong, refused to adulterate, and worked hard to find out how to make the bread properly, each more or less on his own, receiving almost no help or encouragement – though each did receive

---

[*] This is adapted from a talk written for sixteen- to eighteen-year-old students in England. They had all been asked to read James Joyce's *Dubliners* beforehand.

some, indirectly, from the inspiration of the standards set by master-bakers a long time previously, in other cities and with older kinds of bread. And they did succeed.

But their arduous and lonely toil was not the only price they had to pay for their success. Everybody had been brought up on the more or less adulterated versions, and the taste of the real thing took some getting used to. It actually had more taste, just as it had much more goodness in it, but there was an initial slight bitterness that put people off after the blandness of the more synthetic products. Eventually this bitterness was itself enjoyed – people could feel they were actually tasting the goodness – yet at the beginning there was disappointment and resentment. While there was never a time when any of these three bakers was not recognised as unusually good at his job, each got a reputation for being something of a cross-patch, and unsympathetic. Because the Englishman refused to produce a thoroughly user-friendly loaf, people said he was an offensive cynic, and the Frenchman's and Irishman's potential customers went even further, calling the former a bitter misanthropist and the latter a thoroughly cold fish. In fact, each of the three had a heart of gold, and those who appreciated their bread knew this.

A happy part of the story is that, as time passed, more and more people came round to their bread, and to seeing that its awkward and obstinate makers had more generous hearts, finally, than even the best of their more immediately obliging rivals. Also, though all three have now been dead for some time, another good thing about the bread they were experts in making, as about the older kinds of bread made by those much earlier master-bakers, is that the pure product lasts better than the adulterated one, and, for all we know, lasts forever.

The city is that of modern literature. The special kind of bread is the realistic prose fiction of the modern novel and short story. The heroes are Thackeray, Flaubert and Joyce.

A measure of truth might be found in the fable yet surprise be felt at Thackeray's place in it. He is not often included, and understandably: unlike both Flaubert and Joyce, he has only one large masterpiece to his credit, though others novels of his are not so far behind it; even *Vanity Fair* is weakened by a little sentimentality in spite of its fight against it; and, like his English contemporary Dickens, he was not really so slow to find a large audience among his contemporaries. So was he not, after all, among the more obliging novelists? Unlike the others, and this time unlike Dickens too, he has never been thought of as a world-beater. Yet his best novels may still be the only English ones that are profoundly, even if not perfectly, wise books. Novels by Fielding, Austen, Dickens, George Eliot, Trollope, Hardy, Conrad, Lawrence and many other English writers contain wisdom, and a range and variety of it, reaching parts Thackeray does not, but that is not the same thing as their being profoundly wise books, and not so important.

These last two sentences are confined to England's fiction because of the audience this talk was originally written for. Partly for this reason, too, the preparation for the talk had not included a re-reading of all the world's most celebrated novels, and so no answer is offered in it to the question whether those three heroes should not be joined by at least one other Frenchman, Stendhal, and several Russians, and a few writers from other countries. Yet this hardly affects the talk's general proposition that it is an exceptional thing when realistic prose fiction is art.

When Satan is called the father of lies, what is mainly meant is not that long ago in Eden he introduced lies into a human life that had previously been innocent and truthful, but that human beings are all the time yielding to the temptation to lie, especially to themselves. Famous attempts that have been made to define what makes human beings different from other animals – as the animal that reasons, feels shame, plays, *etc.* – seem open to obvious objections. "We're surely not so distinct in that way," anybody might say, "since I know my dog reasons and plays, and I've seen her feeling shame," *etc*. But it may be true that human beings are the only animals who regularly lie to themselves. In other species animals may lie to escape danger, acquire food or protect their young, but in our species not only do we do this: we are also liable to be always romancing in our own minds, telling ourselves fairy-tales.

The old serious objection made to novels is that this is what is going on in them and they help confirm us in the general devilish habit. Though for many people the objection has long been discredited and forgotten, it is actually close to representing a position of Thackeray, Flaubert and Joyce, and potentially perhaps of all major artists. For these are most of all distinguished from most of the rest of our species by the exceptional intensity of their pursuit of the truth, and they would not have needed that intensity if it were not for everybody's partial subjection, including their own, to the father of lies.

Before I turn to Joyce's *Dubliners*, something else could help suggest why creating art out of the modern realistic novel and short story is difficult.

Many people have said how unfair it is to fairy-tales to refer to them in the way I did just above. While it may be all too characteristic of realistic fiction to tell lies, fairy-tales commonly tell the truth. An example, though not one concerned with fairies, is a little story short enough to quote complete, from among the *Household Tales* collected by the Grimm brothers: "The Mouse, the Bird and the Sausage."

Once upon a time a mouse, a bird and a sausage became acquainted and set up house together. They did well and became very happy and prosperous. The bird's job was to fly out every day and bring back wood from the forest. The mouse's was to bring in the water from the well and light the fire and lay the table. The sausage was the cook.

The person who is too well off is always on the lookout for something new. One day the bird met another bird and boasted about the wonderful living arrangements he had. But the other bird told him he was just a pathetic idiot for working so hard. He said the two who stayed home obviously had such an easy time. When the mouse had made the fire and brought in the water, she could go into her room and rest until she had to lay the table. The sausage just hung around the pot, making sure the food was cooking well, and then, when it was nearly time for dinner, only had to roll itself once or twice through the water and vegetables in order to butter and salt them and have them ready to eat. When the bird came home with his heavy load of wood, they all sat down to dinner and, after the meal, did nothing but sleep till morning. Yes, that was a wonderful life for the mouse and sausage!

Prompted by this, the next day the bird refused to go into the forest any more. He said he had been a slave to the other two long enough and made a fool of by them, and they must now take turns with the jobs. The mouse and the sausage argued back, but the bird insisted, and said this was what they must try. They drew straws and this decided that the sausage was now to collect the wood, the mouse to cook, and the bird to fetch in the water.

And what do you think happened? The sausage went off towards the forest, the bird lit the fire, and the mouse stayed by the pot and waited by herself for the sausage to come home with the wood for the next day. But it was gone for such a long time that the others became afraid that something was wrong, and the bird flew out to see if he could meet it on its way home. He had not gone far along the road before he met a dog who had eaten the sausage. The bird accused the dog of outright robbery, but that wasn't any use because the dog said he had found forged letters on the sausage, and for that reason it had to forfeit its life to him.

Sadly the bird picked up the wood and flew home, and told the mouse what he had seen and heard. They were both very upset, though they agreed to carry on doing their best and to stay together. So the bird laid the table and the mouse got the food ready. She wanted to season it, by getting into the pot like the sausage and rolling among the vegetables, but before she was anywhere near the middle of them she got scalded and in this effort lost her skin and her life. When the bird came into dinner, there was no cook. In distress, he threw the wood all over the place and shouted and searched, but there was simply no cook! Because of his carelessness the wood caught on fire and then the house. He hurried to fetch some water, but the bucket fell from his claws into the well, and he fell down with it, and could not get out, and so was drowned.

The story has to be imagined being told aloud and listened to with relish, by people who might know many such stories but were far from having thick newspapers delivered every day of the week, or endless further new stories continually coming straight into their living-rooms on television, or libraries and bookshops that might include among all their other books some thick collections of the whole world's favourite stories of all time. They naturally relished and made the most of the stories they had. What were they doing? Or what are we doing insofar as we enter into the spirit and enjoy the story?

It is safe to say that no one is being conned. No one is ever going to think this story true unless it is. Its outrageousness is part of the fun. Also safe to say is that the pleasure of the story is not the pleasure of being mollycoddled – of having any soothing flattery for the delicate sensibilities human beings have because, like all living creatures, we live in radical insecurity. It is a tough and horrific story – also part of the fun. This leads to the positive claim for the story, which is, of course, that its pleasure is its truth. What is only outrageous quickly palls and disappoints if it engages at all, but here the outrageousness challenges the imagination to come alive and work. It stirs it to feel for and recognise truth that is covered over by the ordinary everyday contents of the mind, and that would probably not be recognised so sharply if presented in a plain, literal way, in terms of those ordinary contents.

Human beings know an awful lot, and too much for our own good, it can often seem, because we do not really know what we suppose we know. Much of that – the readily available contents of the mind insofar as it is not just full of hopes and fears – is a mixture of what we have been told by other people and what we seem to have been told by our own experience. But this is all from the past, and no knowledge is real that is not new. Anything else is partly dead, just as clichés are more or less completely dead. A fresh moment in life is not the same as any previous one, and in it we neither are fully alive nor properly know anything unless we are all *there* – and not, instead, dragging something into it or over it from the past. It is a familiar irritation when somebody says the same old thing he or she has always said, and we think even the thickest numbskull ought to be able to see that in *this* situation things have changed.

That every moment is new is wonderful but terrifying. And the insecurity is always producing the wish to drag the past in, in order to control and run life from existing 'knowledge', partly or wholly dead but giving a sense of safety. The wish and project are perhaps the fundamental Satanic lie and pride, and the root of all lying. As the attempt is made to command life with 'knowledge', that 'knowledge' is easily put to the service of blinder hopes and fears and wishes, to help us see things not as they are but as we would like them. When it is part-dead and fading fast, what is there in it to resist the corruption? Then truths, even the greatest, turn into lies; marvellous rationalisations are made to justify any behaviour and much wishful thinking; people are comfortably on the side of the angels; the devil in the mind quotes scripture, *etc., etc., etc.*

And there is talk of the following kind about stories. After somebody has said that, while she feels "The Mouse, the Bird and the Sausage" is a true story, she cannot quite see how, she is told that that is easy. "The story is obviously showing that people need a *sensible* division of labour." If she hoped for enlightenment, she is let down with a bump. Something from the mind's ordinary contents and the dead past has been gratuitously brought forward, and momentarily made to kill what is alive in the story. The familiar idea of the division of labour is obviously present, but as an account of the story's truth it is simply a lie: probably told out of the anxiety to command life with 'knowledge', though with a positive wish to kill also possible – from an apprehension that that truth threatens more than it supports people's blinder hopes and wishes about life.

Somebody else comes in: "I agree it's a simple story with a moral, but that's surely the one stated in so many words: 'The person who is too well off is always on the lookout for something new.'" Another bump. In context those words of the story may contribute to its life and truth, and might even be used, at a pinch, to sum up what it tells as a whole. But why should anyone want to sum that up? The story is richer and rather more mysterious and, if in this hard way a 'moral' is fixed on and made its whole point, it is being killed again – probably for one of the same two motives. At the same time, that very 'moral' is being made a suspect one. In this hard form it is the sort of thing that can be imagined coming from a young person's very worst aunt or uncle – *i.e.* a thoroughly mean moral. "Some people don't know when they're well off," said in a dark voice to repress a perfectly innocent wish. Yet the 'moral' is not mean in the actual story.

The life and truth in the story are more in the bird's boasting, the ease with which it is influenced by the other bird's response, the terrible plausibility of the other bird's arguments, and the quick and neat thoroughness with which absolutely everything goes wrong. Some of the things the story may set its hearers and readers thinking about are pride and, on the other side, the frailty of anybody's faith in his or her way of living; how paranoid human beings are, ready to accept almost any suggestion that other people are doing us down; how easily we can be convinced of an idea and believe it an evidently and eminently sound and rational one, even though the adoption of it is going to turn out a complete disaster (the story of so many revolutions in history).

Not that the story sets us thinking about such things consciously. The recognition takes place at a deeper level and to a significant degree beyond our control – one of the reasons why no clear limits can be set to art's resonance and suggestion. Those of this story seem to be still more than what I have so far proposed. In its light way, it seems to be touching even more comprehensively our knowledge not only of how ridiculously wrong confidence in a decision can be, but of the close inter-connections between that terrible capacity of ours for error and our general and generally unrecognised condition of radical insecurity. That knowledge is not part of the mind's ordinary, readily accessible contents. Perhaps only a saint can live continuously in that order of truth. And the knowledge is not fully possessed by us until touched in this way, either by a work of art or by some other kind of revelatory new moment.

By bringing its freshly keen recognition of human frailty and folly the story evidently does not oppress us, even though for most of our lives we are doing so much to avoid recognising that frailty and folly. The comedy of them is there to be delighted in, and we delight in it because we are simultaneously, for the moment, liberated from them.

The lack of clear limits to art's resonance and suggestion is its generality or universality. Realistic modern fiction can sometimes deceive readers into thinking that truth and the truth of art are limited and specific: only showing what life is like for one particular kind of person at one particular time in one particular place. But that is not truth, and there is little if any liberation in it.

As it is kindled in the enjoyment of such a story as this, the imagination becomes creative, and we surprise ourselves. The point can be generalised: every new moment in life is an opportunity for the imagination to be creative and for us to surprise ourselves. And this is one of the reasons why art is highly treasured: while the great majority of these opportunities are more or less wasted, in art special help is given not to be wasting them for the time being. In the Grimm story we are not, as in most modern fiction, following from point to point a pedestrian, always reasonably consecutive narrative, one detail following on from another in a more or less expected sort of way. While the story is told as if it was all plain and consecutive, it is all the time taking jumps, with nothing in the least predictable. The ordinary 'sensible' mind is defeated and the imagination strides free, putting things together in the wiser way it does, and creating the story's delight and truth.

About James Joyce's *Dubliners*, I could just ask a question: is it not extraordinary that in these realistic modern stories – the plainest realistic stories, without the slightest touch of anything outrageous and with almost everything simply reading like sober fact – readers are nevertheless led to be creative and surprise themselves in the same way as when enjoying the story from Grimm? The only thing known in advance from one of Joyce's stories to the next, from one paragraph in one of them to the next, or even (often) from one sentence to the next, is that the matter is going to continue plain, matter-of-fact, steady and quiet, just as it is known in the Grimm story that the matter is going to continue fantastic. In either case where we are going to go in that matter we have no idea. It is not only that we do not know what is going to happen next in the story as a story. Predictability of that kind is normally an obvious weakness and disappointment in fiction, and most good novelists more or less succeed in avoiding it. But in *Dubliners* we often have no idea what kind of thing the imagination is going to be invited to do in the next sentence: whether, since there is no new paragraph, it is going to stay with the topic of the present sentence, or is suddenly going to move to something else, whether it is now to receive another piece of information about the character's past or to shift to something about the sort of person he or she is, or about the time of day or the weather or the place, or about something the character now suddenly does, *etc*. At the same time, it all feels perfectly natural, or it does when the imagination has got used to it. Every story establishes itself with us as we are led to create it, unpredictable step by unpredictable step, and, if anything mysterious is happening, it is not that Joyce is arbitrary, odd or wilful in the way he shifts from one thing to another. When each unpredictable next sentence comes, it feels right enough.

An artistic difficulty of realistic prose fiction is that a large part of its material is more or less immediately recognizable, so that it can often seem impossible for the mind, the writer's in the first place and then the reader's, not to go straightaway into the position of seeking to command life with 'knowledge'. The material seems to invite it, and the commanding seems to be not only temptingly attractive in itself but even a main point of such fiction. As readers, we quickly feel at home, and we enjoy feeling at home, and we are easily led to believe that we *should* be enjoying feeling at home, even though the reality of life, which is what we are supposed to be finding in art and do on the surface seem to be finding here, is actually so strange and frightening and wonderful. In this talk's subtitle, I quote (and twist) words that a BBC radio announcer used to say every day to introduce a story for very young listeners: "*Are* you sitting *comfortably*?" If the comfort all too often wanted in novels is that of having things our own way, a large part of that is having things the way they are already known. When the kitchen sink is mentioned, or the evening rush-hour traffic, or the way a certain kind of person parts his hair or holds her handbag, or the well-known ambitiousness of parents for their children, or the traditional pub-life of men, or the high spirits and hysteria of a big annual Christmas party, *etc., etc., etc.*, it is all too easy to imagine that we can have things the way we want them and already know. Joyce's artistic purity is such in *Dubliners* that he writes about nothing else but yet never produces this comfort for a single moment. The most ordinary life becomes strange and, instead of illusory knowledge of it being exploited, its reality is respected and created.

To come to his heart of gold. As with Thackeray and Flaubert, this is a point not about the personal life but entirely about the work, and about something in it that is not just one quality among many but essential and pervasive. It may be as simple as this: when human beings are not trying to run life with the mind, using the illusion of knowledge and making that serve hopes and fears, then the relation to life is one of love. The blessed fact seems to be that it cannot help being. The lie of Satanic pride is a lie against love. In *Dubliners* it sooner or later comes over readers that its stories about human life in its unglamorous pathos and absurdity, often unhappy and almost always foolish and sometimes vicious, are, surprisingly, quite beautiful stories, even with the kind of beauty that can hardly be borne. The beauty comes of the love, which is an exceptionally complete sensitiveness and, among other things, carries with it a liability to heartbreak after heartbreak. The story of the man who hates his work and drinks and beats up his children is terrible, but so is the lighter story of the boy who goes to the fair and does *not* buy anything for the girl who lives opposite. Whether mainly grieving or mainly smiling, we know exactly how each of these and Joyce's other characters feels, and there is nothing we can do about any pain involved. Yet the stories are wonderfully, even inspiringly beautiful.

The love is different from what must, in comparison, be called the facile 'sympathy' which fiction normally engages readers in with its characters. For example, in an enormous number of novels the writer, however good, only has to have an attractive unattached person meet an attractive unattached person of the opposite sex to have us beginning to hope for romantic love or a marriage. What is said by this about the novel as a form? At the root of the unpredictability of the stories in *Dubliners* is the fact that this kind of thing never happens in them. In none can it be known early on what the interest is going to turn out to be. It can never be completely known until a story's last word – and hardly even then, though it is felt. From this readers with habits formed by other fiction have sometimes concluded that the stories in *Dubliners* have no interest, are pointless. What will be the subject of a story that begins with a reference to boys playing cowboys and indians? We have no idea and, after finishing it, we know we could never have imagined it was going to be what it has turned out to be. And what is it anyhow? Though the subject and its interest are perfectly clear, as clear as in "The Mouse, the Bird and the Sausage", they are even less quickly recognisable than that story's. Again, there are no readily accessible ideas and words for them; that is one of the reasons why the disconcerting and frightening story is beautiful; also why it is a work of art, with a large subject and no clear limits to it.

Because Joyce does not give his readers the signals that let us know where we are and allow us to get going in facile 'sympathy', there is a distance and an effect as of irony. But he is never actually being ironic at the expense of a character. There is never that kind of knowingness. The writing is always impassive. Even when, in his book's first story, he has his narrating character exclaim, "Tiresome old red-nosed imbecile!", he is not, as Dickens would be, inviting us to be all on the boy's side against the old man. (There are wonderful moments with Pip and Mr Pumblechook at the Gargery dinner-table, but not such exactly true ones.) And it is not that there is any point being made against the boy either. If there is any irony, it is playing over the old man, the boy and all of us, and, as in Chaucer, is only the irony of life, something like God's irony.

The facile 'sympathy' with characters in other fiction does often mean being on their side in one way or another, and even having strong moral feeling about it. As in many places in Dickens (or Austen), marvellous indignation and hatred can be felt against a 'sympathetic' character's enemies. But moral feeling of this kind can all too easily be more or less immoral, serving the bent to have life only as we would like it. Joyce's rigorous abstention from facile moralising, as from all such 'sympathy', is far from being moral indifference, since it is difficult to think of any fiction in which moral points are felt so sensitively or clear-sightedly – as, for example, with the un-commented-on treatment of the woman by the "Two Gallants". On the contrary, his not being keen and quick to make moral judgements is the finest morality, and beautiful.

Yet love *is* also a kind of indifference. The love which is sensitive openness is a state where there is no subjection to any distorting partial view or desire. With other novels it can be asked: "What does it matter whether Elizabeth Bennet gets her Darcy, Jane

Eyre her Rochester, Pip his Estella, Dorothea Brooke her Will Ladislaw, Tess her Angel Clare, *etc.*? You win some and you lose some. So what? Why get so attached to the idea of the particular situation that you're in for the moment turning out to be a win? or make it such a big deal when it's a lose?" That is Chaucer's irony and indifference, and Homer's and Cervantes', and fundamentally, for all the great differences between all of these writers, Thackeray's, Flaubert's and Joyce's. It does not mean that any of them feels less for the happiness and unhappiness of their fellow human beings. It means they feel more.

The stories in *Dubliners* read easily enough. If something special is being done in them, there is no sense of strain. Yet the contrast with almost all other modern realistic fiction suggests that a prodigious imaginative and moral effort on Joyce's part must lie behind them. "Poems to which any value can be attached," Wordsworth wrote in his famous Preface to *Lyrical Ballads*, "were never produced on any variety of subjects but by a man, who being deeply possessed of more than usual organic sensibility, had also thought long and deeply."

This is a final note on what makes the Englishman, Frenchman and Irishman heroes. It is not that the other great novelists have not created, or do not enjoyably open their readers' eyes to truth we might never otherwise see. Almost anyone could happily go on and on about what a marvellous truth-teller Dickens is. But he has more an abundant artistic inspiration than a scrupulous artistic conscience. He cannot not delight himself and his readers with true image after true image after true image, and throughout his career he is hungry for ever new truth, but he also delights in lies, and is not rigorous in making the truth always his first priority or in understanding why he needs to. He actually criticised Thackeray for doing one of the things the latter did to encourage his reader to stand back from facile 'sympathy'. The other great Victorian novelist, George Eliot, is often thought of as a notably wise writer, and she was certainly wise enough to admire Thackeray and in her best storytelling learn from it. But from that very storytelling it appears that she, too, failed to understand his main artistic point. (On the other, almost non-fiction side of her work, the 'poetry' of some of its 'backgrounds', she is to some degree a different artist, and more thoroughly sound.)

Thackeray, Flaubert and Joyce stand out among the inspired creators of realistic prose fiction because they are the ones who fight systematically against the lie that, if they had not written, could have seemed almost inherent in the form. The purity of their inspiration was more complete.

Chapter VIII
What do we know about Andrew Marvell?
or
His poetry another twentieth-century mistake?

This long piece is included in this book because the invention that I believe the twentieth century's idea of Andrew Marvell's poetry mainly to be is not only revealing about the twentieth century but also contributed to its so often wearisome cultivation of a knowing smartness in much of its verse.

1. A SOUL THAT "ROUND IN ITSELF ENCLOSES"

> Stand who so list upon the slipper top
> Of court estate, and let me here rejoice
> And use me quiet without let or stop
> Unknown in court that hath such brackish joys:
> In hidden place so let my days forth pass
> That, when my years be done, withouten noise,
> I may die aged after the common trace.
>
> For him death grippeth right hard by the crop
> That known of all, but to himself, alas,
> Doth die unknown, dazed with dreadful face.[*]

You die known of yourself when you've been able to accomplish and be yourself, when you've really had a life and not that mere dream of one, all heady elation and anxiety. A life is what Thomas Wyatt

---

[*] The emendation in the penultimate line is the one made by H.A. Mason in his *Sir Thomas Wyatt: a literary portrait*.

219

wants, and what he wants to survive *for*.

When Marvell makes another English poem out of the same lines of Seneca, what does his poem show *him* to be interested in?

> Climb at court for me that will
> Tottering favour's pinnacle:
> All I seek is to lie still.
> Settled in some secret nest,
> In calm leisure let me rest;
> And far off the public stage
> Pass away my silent age.
> Thus when without noise, unknown,
> I have lived out all my span,
> I shall die, without a groan,
> An old honest countryman.
> Who exposed to others' eyes
> Into his own heart ne'er pries,
> Death to him's a strange surprise.

Mainly safety? I suggest that, paradoxically, something else that Marvell shows an interest in here is competitive success. The poem itself is partly an assertion of success, of having won superiority. The clever way in which the final trap of understatement is sprung confirms that, unlike Wyatt, Marvell doesn't think he's in much danger himself.

I find that the reverberation of that last line of the poem is strangely cut off before it gets properly started, with an effect of impotence, and that what should be a moment of tragic realisation and knowledge isn't.

Yet I don't find that the poem is one to be shrugged off. Its assertion of a superior general wisdom about life may be unsound and self-contradictory but it doesn't, somehow, seem fatuous; and there even seems to be something formidable in it.

Is the formidableness any more than the fact that the poet is giving so little away, is simple and perfectly assured but at the same time quite enigmatic? The reader might begin to find that "An old honest countryman" is something of a false note in the poem and a bit ridiculous but, even if he does, it's not clear that that matters. It's not at all clear that the poet is committing himself to that idea or basing anything on it. His assurance seems to come from somewhere else, behind.

In the same way it's not clear that it matters if the reader notices that the idea of lying still, settled in some secret nest, remains a fairly blank and negative idea, never growing into anything substantial, only getting repeated in the further negative phrases: "calm leisure... far off the public stage... my silent age... without noise, unknown." It's not clear that this matters because the assurance still seems to be both substantial and lively.

It's as if the poem presents an edge rather than a surface. Or as if it's being spoken from the secret nest where the poet, not exposed to others' eyes even in his own poem, can't be got at. Marvell's highly praised "poise"?

What does the man who does pry into his own heart find? what does Marvell suggest that he himself is seeing in his own? He isn't coming to know himself in Wyatt's sense, having the true current of his life able to flow at last without let or stop. It isn't Marvell's idea that anything is going to come from his lying still. That seems to be an end in itself, and the whole point...

I think that the reason why its relative negativeness or nullity doesn't matter is that it is his own knowledge of the nullity that is giving Marvell his invincibly superior wisdom and making him formidable. It is nullity that he finds in himself and that he says every other man would find in himself if he only looked:

> Who exposed to others' eyes
> Into his own heart ne'er pries,
> Death to him's a strange surprise.

Another poem of Marvell's, "The First Anniversary of the Government under O.C.," begins with these lines:

> Like the vain curlings of the wat'ry maze
> Which in smooth streams a sinking weight does raise,
> So man, declining always, disappears

> In the weak circles of increasing years;
> And his short tumults of themselves compose,
> While flowing time above his head does close.

I don't know how much I'm reading this into the poem from other poems of Marvell's, but I tend to find in that idea of lying still in a secret nest not only the nullity and absence of life but also a faint shimmering suggestion of a spiritual value, a certain cool purity. Not something at all separate from the idea of death: insofar as it's there, it seems to be partly expressing a feeling about death.

And that is the only thing Marvell puts into his poem besides his lively assertion of wisdom, superiority.

It isn't a formidable poem so much as a poem that reveals something formidable in the man who wrote it. He carries his perfect assurance so lightly because it doesn't cost him anything, because he's so single-minded... Because he seems to have hardly any of the usual human feelings?

I think something of this can be heard in the strangely anonymous voice of the poem and the pat way in which it moves. Especially by someone who hears them against the very different voice and rhythm of Wyatt's poem.

Before moving on to a different part of this enquiry, I stay with the present part with one or two notes on other poems of Marvell's and quotations from them.

First, "A Dialogue between the Resolved Soul and Created Pleasure," of which this is the first and longer part:

> Courage, my soul, now learn to wield
> The weight of thine immortal shield.
> Close on thy head thy helmet bright.
> Balance thy sword against the fight.
> See where an army, strong as fair,
> With silken banners spreads the air.
> Now, if thou be'est that thing divine,
> In this day's combat let it shine:
> And show that Nature wants an art

To conquer one resolved heart.

Pleasure
Welcome, the creation's guest,
Lord of earth, and Heaven's heir.
Lay aside that warlike crest,
And of Nature's banquet share,
Where the souls of fruits and flowers
Stand prepared to heighten yours.

Soul
I sup above, and cannot stay
To bait so long upon the way.

Pleasure
On these downy pillows lie,
Whose soft plumes will thither fly,
On these roses strewed so plain
Lest one leaf thy side should strain.

Soul
My gentler rest is on a thought,
Conscious of doing what I ought.

Pleasure
If thou be'est with perfumes pleased,
Such as oft the gods appeased,
Thou in fragrant clouds shall show
Like another god below.

Soul
A soul that knows not to presume
Is Heaven's and its own perfume.

Pleasure
Everything does seem to vie
Which should first attract thine eye,

But since none deserves that grace,
In this crystal view thy face.

Soul
When the Creator's skill is prized,
The rest is all but earth disguised.

Pleasure
Hark how music then prepares
For thy stay these charming airs,
Which the posting winds recall,
And suspend the river's fall.

Soul
Had I but any time to lose,
On this I would it all dispose.
Cease, tempter, none can chain a mind
Whom this sweet chordage cannot bind.

Chorus
Earth cannot show so brave a sight
As when a single soul does fence
The batteries of alluring sense,
And Heaven views it with delight.
Then persevere: for still new charges sound,
And if thou overcom'st thou shalt be crowned.

When the Soul says, "Had I but any time to lose," what is it supposed to be so busily engaged with? Lying still? Simply resisting life, and looking forward to its end? "I sup above..." The interest in life's end isn't so overtly heterodox here as it is in "Thyrsis and Dorinda" – the pastoral dialogue in which Marvell has an innocent young couple talking about the beauties of life in Heaven and deciding to commit suicide – but, like the version of Seneca, the poem is certainly short of suggestion about what the human soul has to do in its life on this earth. There is no impression, for example, that it has to make itself. It seems to be made and perfect before it starts.

Its word-perfect purity suggest a kind of frozen arrest. The poet's energy goes into the proud, vigorous and blank assertion of the beauty and rightness of that, made at no cost to him and therefore with the unfaltering witty-lively aplomb and assurance.

The mind's airy survey of life on this earth, in the speeches of Pleasure, together with its airy but total cancellation of it in the Soul's speeches, reminds me of some of Marvell's most famous lines, from "The Garden":

> Meanwhile the mind, from pleasure less,
> Withdraws into its happiness;
> The mind, that ocean where each kind
> Does straight its own resemblance find.
> Yet it creates, transcending these,
> Far other worlds and other seas,
> Annihilating all that's made
> To a green thought in a green shade.

And there is another feature of the "Dialogue" between the Soul and Pleasure that brings "The Garden" to mind, and also "Bermudas": the strange fine spiritualising of the senses. If the Resolved Soul's combat with Created Pleasure isn't much of a fight and gives the impression of being fixed, that is partly because the batteries of alluring sense aren't there. The Soul has more than half overcome the Pleasure before the fight starts:

> … the souls of fruits and flowers
> Stand prepared to heighten yours.
>
> On these downy pillows lie,
> Whose soft plumes will thither fly…

It seems in keeping that there is no sensual pleasure for the eyes at all, only:

> In this crystal view thy face.

Is there all that much difference between this temptation and what at other points the Soul actually boasts of doing, enjoying its own perfume and resting on "the thought, / Conscious of doing what I ought"? Again, if the Soul sounds as if it doesn't want to be active, it doesn't sound as if it's anything particularly active that Pleasure is tempting it to. Another reminder of "The Garden" and "Bermudas":

> What wondrous life is this I lead!
> Ripe apples drop about my head;
> The luscious clusters of the vine
> Upon my mouth do crush their wine;
> The nectarine, and curious peach,
> Into my hands themselves do reach;
> Stumbling on melons, as I pass,
> Ensnared with flowers, I fall on grass.
>
> He gave us this eternal Spring,
> Which here enamels everything;
> And sends the fowls to us in care,
> On daily visits through the air.
> He hangs in shades the orange bright,
> Like golden lamps in a green night,
> And does in the pom'granates close
> Jewels more rich than Ormus shows.
> He makes the figs our mouths to meet,
> And throws the melons at our feet,
> But apples plants of such a price,
> No tree could ever bear them twice.

I don't think anybody could get the impression that

> Where the remote Bermudas ride
> In th' ocean's bosom unespied...

there was hearty eating, any more than that there was farm work. It's with a special bright cold purity that those oranges' golden lamps shine in their green night.

In the short dialogue-poem of "Clorinda and Damon" the girl is tempting the religious boy to love. Having mentioned in vain the unfrequented cave

> In whose cool bosom we may lie
> Safe from the sun...

she tries to make it more attractive by saying:

> Near this, a fountain's liquid bell
> Tinkles within the concave shell.

He replies:

> Might a soul bathe there and be clean,
> Or slake its drought?

I turn to this because T.S.Eliot was impressed by it. He wrote (in a review separate from his famous and influential essay on Marvell, and reprinted in John Carey's *Andrew Marvell: a critical anthology*):

> In a conceit two things very different are brought together, and the spark of ecstasy generated in us is a perception of power in bringing them together. It is, in my opinion, a conceit of the very finest order when Marvell says, of a spring of clear water:
>> Might a soul bathe there and be clean,
>> Or slake its drought?
> Our pleasure is in the suddenness of the transference from material to spiritual water.

In the famous essay itself of two years earlier (*Selected Essays*), he quotes the same lines and says of them that "a metaphor has suddenly rapt us to the image of spiritual purgation." He finds in it the element of surprise that he says Poe considered of the highest importance for poetry "and also the restraint and quietness of tone which makes the surprise possible."

Does Eliot himself create the effect he is talking about, by

227

contributing that ordinary humanity which the poetry lacks? The surprise and the ecstasy are powerful and the reader is suddenly "rapt" to the image of spiritual purgation only if the reader's feet are on the ground in the first place. If they aren't, it's all too easy. And, in that case, what can the soul's thirst be, or its desire to be clean?

Much closer to matching the reality and gravity of "O wretched man that I am! who shall deliver me from the body of this death?" is Eliot's own use of the image of water:

> Here is no water but only rock
> Rock and no water and the sandy road
> The road winding about among the mountains
> Which are mountains of rock without water… *etc.*

"On a Drop of Dew" is worth quoting complete. Most of what I wish to say about it is already said.

> See how the Orient dew,
> Shed from the bosom of the morn
>   Into the blowing roses,
> Yet careless of its mansion new,
> For the clear region where 'twas born,
>   Round in itself encloses;
>   And in its little globe's extent
> Frames as it can its native element.
>   How it the purple flower does slight,
>   Scarce touching where it lies,
>   But gazing back upon the skies,
>   Shines with a mournful light,
>   Like its own tear,
> Because so long divided from the sphere.
>   Restless it rolls and unsecure,
>   Trembling lest it grow impure,
>   Till the warm sun pity its pain,
> And to the skies exhale it back again.
>   So the soul, that drop, that ray
> Of the clear fountain of Eternal Day,

Could it within the human flower be seen,
　　Remembering still its former height,
　　Shuns the sweat leaves and blossoms green,
　　And, recollecting its own light,
Does, in its pure and circling thoughts, express
The greater Heaven in a Heaven less.
　　In how coy a figure wound,
　　Every way it turns away,
　　So the world excluding round,
　　Yet receiving in the Day;
　　Dark beneath, but bright above;
　　Here disdaining, there in love;
　How loose and easy hence to go,
　How girt and ready to ascend.
　Moving but on a point below,
　It all about does upwards bend.
Such did the manna's sacred dew distill,
White, and entire, though congealed and chill;
Congealed on earth, but does, dissolving, run
Into the glories of th' Almighty Sun.

Again there is something blank and absolute in the poem: no sort of division within the poet's breast; all of his mind, will and feeling going in the one simple direction.

Though unable to reach their goal. At the same time as it gives a vivid account of a state of mind and spirit, does "On a Drop of Dew" also give a vivid account of its own manner and movement, and of the manner and movement of much of Marvell's most individual poetry? Of that peculiar enigmatic, uncommitted lightness? And of the secret sadness? "*Shines* with a mournful light." I think the most acute observation comes at the end, where Marvell's special cool-perfect purity is identified as a kind of impotence:

White, and entire, though congealed and chill.

On this aspect of Marvell's poetry I add two further notes and a third that makes the transition to another aspect of it.

(1) It may be worth pointing out how much the soul of "On a Drop of Dew" has in common with the soul of another famous stanza of "The Garden":

> Here at the fountain's sliding foot,
> Or at some fruit-tree's mossy root,
> Casting the body's vest aside,
> My soul into the boughs does glide:
> There like a bird it sits, and sings,
> Then whets, and combs its silver wings;
> And, till prepared for longer flight,
> Waves in its plumes the various light.

(2) "There surely isn't anything blank, absolute or all-one-way about the bitter debate of 'A Dialogue between the Soul and the Body'?" I think, on the contrary, that this may be the most impossibly single-minded of all Marvell's poems. Prevented from being much of a poem at all – however striking and powerful a document – by its sitting so extraordinarily tight and cool on its one simple assertion. Impossibly single-minded in that even the reader who does get some notion of what is happening hardly manages to make his or her own mind adapt to it and read the poem. What both the Soul and the Body are saying throughout their debate with each other is that by its sheer elementary nature living is intolerable and the poet wishes he had none of it.

Other notable poems that belong more or less closely with the ones commented on so far are "Eyes and Tears" and "The Nymph lamenting for the death of her Fawn."

(3) What doesn't occur in these but in other poems of Marvell's is the idea of an extreme and desperate violence being used: to try and force the soul out of its beautiful, impotent passivity.

> In how coy a figure wound,
> Every way it turns away,
> So the world excluding round...

> Had we but world enough, and time,

This coyness, lady, were no crime.
We would sit down, and think which way
To walk, and pass our long love's day…
    But at my back I always hear
Time's winged chariot hurrying near,
And yonder all before us lie
Deserts of vast eternity…
Now let us sport us while we may;
And now, like amorous birds of prey,
Rather at once our time devour
Than languish in his slow-chapped power.
Let us roll all our strength, and all
Our sweetness, up into one ball,
And tear our pleasures with rough strife
Thorough the iron gates of life.
Thus, though we cannot make our sun
Stand still, yet we will make him run.

2. "THE FORWARD YOUTH THAT WOULD APPEAR"

An Horatian Ode upon Cromwell's Return from Ireland

The forward youth that would appear
Must now forsake his muses dear,
    Nor in the shadows sing
    His numbers languishing.
'Tis time to leave the books in dust,
And oil th' unused armour's rust,
    Removing from the wall
    The corselet of the hall.

Here at its beginning Marvell's "Horatian Ode" sounds less like a poem of deliberation, of weighing up, than like a poem of decision, and possibly of persuasion. It could be a call to arms. But what is the decision? and what are the arms to be taken up for?

Two further questions: why is it now, upon Cromwell's return from Ireland, that the youth has to forsake his muses? and why is it

231

that up till now this ardent young man, with his ambition to take part in public life, has been in the shadows and has there been singing languishing songs? (Languishing with inactivity or with grief?)

I'll take this last question first because I think it's less difficult. The young man's being in the shadows and singing languishing songs doesn't need any explanation in the poem if he is a young man of Royalist connections and sympathies. In the England of 1650 where else could such a young man be and what other songs could he be singing?

The question "Why now?" may also not be so difficult, if the scholars are right who discern in these opening lines a definite and intended reference to Lucan's *Pharsalia*. One of these scholars explains the allusion in this way:

> Lucan described the desperate plight of the inhabitants of Ariminum, on the day Caesar crossed the Rubicon, when they awoke to the blare of Caesar's trumpets in the market-place. In Thomas May's translation,
>
> > With this sad noise the people's rest was broke,
> > The young men rose, and from the temples took
> > Their arms, now such as peace had marred,
> > And their old bucklers now of leathers bared,
> > Their blunted pikes not of a long time used,
> > And swords with th' eatings of black rust abused.
>
> Caesar had presented the people of Ariminum with a *fait accompli*. Their weapons, defective with "th' unused armour's rust," were rendered yet more futile by the surprise with which Caesar had struck... Instead of attacking Caesar, the armed but terror-stricken youths had been too frightened to complain, and they had silently bewailed the fate of their city, which bore the brunt of every new invasion. (John M.Wallace, *Destiny His Choice: The Loyalism of Andrew Marvell*)

After his success in Ireland was Cromwell likely to be crossing his Rubicon any day? And was it now time to leave the books in dust because soon it was going to be too late?

Marvell compares the course of action that the forward youth should now follow with the course of action that Cromwell himself in the past has followed:

So restless Cromwell could not cease

In the inglorious arts of peace,
   But through advent'rous war
   Urged his active star;
And, like the three-forked lightning, first
Breaking the clouds where it was nursed,
   Did thorough his own side
   His fiery way divide.
For 'tis all one to courage high
The emulous or enemy;
   And with such to enclose
   Is more than to oppose.
Then burning through the air he went,
And palaces and temples rent,
   And Caesar's head at last
   Did through his laurels blast.

The introduction of Cromwell's name with the word "restless" doesn't sound friendly. Two lines lower, "advent'rous" means hazardous, full of risk or peril. What the analogy seems to be pressing on the keen and ambitious young Royalist is the idea of somehow forcing the issue, taking matters into his own hands, not waiting passively on opportunity but making it: by doing something both violent and dangerous.

I've never found anyone explain why such an emphatic and large place should be given at this point in the poem to the rivalry and in-fighting among the leaders on the Parliamentary side. Yes, it could be an encouragement that Cromwell can't have too many friends. But does more of the explanation come from the other side of the analogy, that at this date, as at both earlier and later dates in the Commonwealth, any hot-headed young Royalists who contemplated daring action would be opposed by older and more influential Royalists?

The echoes of the *Pharsalia* that tend to identify Cromwell with Lucan's hated Caesar continue in this second passage that I've quoted. So that it is a surprise to come to the name Caesar being applied to Charles. Does Marvell do it in order to emphasise what the point is on the forward youth's side of the analogy? The laurels seem much more fitting for the head of Ireland's victor than for the head of the defeated

Charles. Without such an emphasis the reader could be losing touch with the fact that an analogy is being drawn, or he or she could be wondering how exactly it stands; and this is the last and the main point of it.

Or is it? Is this the decision and persuasion? Couldn't the opposite just as easily be the case, that the forward youth is being urged to join Cromwell and fight *for* him, in Scotland or wherever? The young man would still be a Royalist, in the shadows, but one seeing that the time has now come to acknowledge defeat and to compromise, and to begin looking after the career of his own that he is so fiercely ambitious for. Wouldn't this be enough to explain the youth's coming into conflict with other people on the Royalist side? I think this is a markedly weaker reading of the lines, and that it is also more open to particular objection. For example, that analogy would have to be either exceedingly vague and general or petering out and getting forgotten at some indefinite point before "Then burning through the air he went" (and doing this in spite of Marvell's conjunctions).

Without for the moment mentioning any other objections to the reading of the "Horatian Ode" that I've started to give, I should like to return to the poem and give a little more.

> 'Tis madness to resist or blame
> The force of angry Heaven's flame,
>   And, if we would speak true,
>   Much to the man is due,
> Who, from his private gardens, where
> He lived reserved and austere,
>   As if his highest plot
>   To plant the bergamot,
> Could by industrious valour climb
> To ruin the great work of time,
>   And cast the kingdom old
>   Into another mould.

It is madness for a young Royalist to resist or blame that force of angry Heaven's flame that would now, by his agency, burn through the air to blast Cromwell's head. And in any case Cromwell has certainly got it coming to him: after what he's done.

"As if his highest plot" is fierce sarcasm; and one editor of the poems mentions that the bergamot was known as "prince's pear" or the "pear of kings". Senses now obsolete of the word "industrious" fit better than its modern sense: skilful, clever, ingenious, careful, attentive, purposeful. Cromwell knew what he was about from the beginning, knew what he wanted. By this date this was a common allegation of his enemies, like the poem's later statement that he deliberately contrived Charles's flight to Carisbrooke.

In the next lines the abrupt change of tense is another sign of the fact that the poet is talking at least as much about the present and the future, for the forward youth, as about what has already happened.

> Though justice against fate complain,
> And plead the ancient rights in vain –
>   But those do hold or break
>   As men are strong or weak.
> Nature that hateth emptiness
> Allows of penetration less,
>   And therefore must make room
>   Where greater spirits come.

Cromwell's success is horribly wrong, but it's no use going on complaining and pleading to that effect, in numbers languishing: men of mettle should do something about it.

Then Marvell reminds his reader of the many men Cromwell has killed or maimed, and then of his trapping and murdering of the noble and innocent King. In *his* extremity Charles didn't do anything common or mean like complaining or pleading: he didn't call "the gods with vulgar spite / To vindicate his helpless right" but bravely went through what he couldn't avoid. Is the action being urged on the forward youth an almost suicidally desperate one, like joining other young Royalist hot-heads in an attempt to catch and assassinate Cromwell in London, in palace or church, away from his camp?

If Marvell was saying anything like this, it is no wonder that he didn't want to make it as clear as daylight. He would be glad to include the line "'Tis madness to resist or blame," where the most obvious reading would be so thoroughly misleading, and he would be glad to have all but his intended readers identifying "angry Heaven's flame" with the lightning and burning of the successful Cromwell, and seeing only Cromwell in the phrase "greater spirits".

Talk of Marvell's intended readers is, of course, speculation. All we know is that this is one of the political poems of his which he did not publish. There is a little evidence, but not compellingly strong, that it did circulate among Royalists.[*]

The speculation is that the intended readers would know that Marvell was a Royalist hot-head like themselves but no one else would. They would therefore know what to look for in the poem, while everyone else could be misled or baffled. Next to nothing is known about the Marvell of these or earlier years, but it is rather more than speculation to say that he wouldn't generally have been thought of as an extremist on the defeated Royalist side. Besides the fact that he was shortly to be employed by Fairfax, if he wasn't already employed by him, and later by Cromwell himself, there is also the evidence of Marvell's earlier and published poem to Lovelace. Whatever the mixture of fact and fancy in the story told in this poem's last paragraph, one thing seems clear from it: that already at this date Marvell could be taken by other people to have some connection – in whatever capacity, formal or informal – with the commonwealth government. (There are, by the way, among the extremely scanty records of Marvell's life at all periods – which scantiness may be no coincidence – some signs that he knew a lot about the work of secret agents. There is the possibility that at some point he himself worked as a double agent. There are also these two interesting personal descriptions of him by contemporaries.

> He was in his conversation very modest, and of very few words: and though he loved wine he would never drink hard in company, and was wont to say that he would not play the

---

[*] An echo of two lines about Charles on the scaffold – "But with his keener eye / The axe's edge did try" – has been found in "His keener words did their sharp axe exceed," a line in Robert Wild's poem on the execution in 1651 of the Royalist Presbyterian, Christopher Love.

good-fellow in any man's company in whose hands he would not trust his life. He had not a general acquaintance.

John Aubrey, writing after the Restoration and after the poet's death. In 1656 a Royalist who had seen Marvell in France had described him in a letter to another Royalist as "a notable English Italo-Machavillian."[*])

I ought to say that, as far as I know, there isn't even a minority of one who is entirely convinced by the reading of the "Horatian Ode" that I've been proposing. I only find it less unconvincing than any other reading. I'm not sure there will ever be grounds for a completely confident account of what Marvell was doing in the "Ode". (Or of what he was doing in some of his other poems, let alone in important parts of his personal and political career.) A charge that could be made against this reading is that the poem is spoilt by being made cryptic; but the extreme disagreements among the existing commentators don't suggest that it was ever, unless for its intended first readers, a very clear poem.

I'm still less confident about the second half of the "Ode", and perhaps it's therefore too tempting for me to say that Marvell doesn't seem to have been able to keep up – or not quite at the same pitch – the extraordinarily tight intensity of the first half, gripped so hard and with such ferociously definite passion and purposefulness. Perhaps it couldn't be kept up. It's already something unparalleled in literature.

In the section of the poem from "This was that memorable hour"

---

[*] J.Scudamore to Sir Richard Browne, 15 August 1656, quoted in the notes of the third edition of Margoliouth's *Poems and Letters of Andrew Marvell*, Volume II p378. In this same volume (p380) it is stated that, although Marvell is often described as Milton's assistant in Cromwell's government, "he was in direct subordination to Thurloe and should be described as Thurloe's assistant" – the John Thurloe who from 1652 had been a co-opted member of the Council of State and head of the department of intelligence. The possibility that Marvell worked as a double agent was put to me by my former colleague, R.I.V. Hodge. There are very brief references to intelligence work in two of the poems and, after the Restoration, as a member of the House of Commons, Marvell in 1668 criticised the inefficiency of English espionage abroad. He is also known to have been on a secret mission to Holland in 1662 and to have been in touch with Dutch secret agents in 1673-1674.

to the simile of the falcon the main idea seems to be that everything is making for the crowning of Cromwell. Restless, ambitious, nursing "his highest plot", he has also been as clever and "industrious" a politician as ever, proving himself "fit for highest trust" by showing what "one man can do", while at the same time playing to perfection the role of the republic's loyal servant. I don't know whether or not the praise and confession of the Irish are mentioned sarcastically: the scholars may be right to warn us against anachronism here. Nor do I know whether or not the lines

> And yet in that the state
> Foresaw its happy fate.

contain a separate small innuendo as well as the main scornful sarcasm, the innuendo that supporters of Cromwell were pleased when not only was Charles dead but some of their own colleagues (like Fairfax) gone into retirement.

With the idea of Cromwell's almost irresistible movement towards the throne there seems to be combined a suggestion or hint – no more than that – that he is, nevertheless, vulnerable. Charles's murder won't be forgotten, and the government must be living in fear. Given that weakness, the Irish are ashamed to have let themselves be beaten by Cromwell so easily. Is the shift here to moralising generalisation a similar one to the changes to the present tense in the first half of the poem, a signal to the reader that he should now be thinking not only of what Cromwell has done but of what some equally bold spirit might do in the present?

> So much one man can do
> That does both act and know.

A more definite hint of vulnerability comes with the reference to the sword being ungirt and then in the striking development of that in the simile of the falcon:

> …Where, when he first does lure
> The falc'ner has her sure.

About the next section, on foreign conquest, I say with not much confidence that Marvell could have been warning Royalists that Cromwell was only going to grow more powerful if he wasn't stopped straightaway, that after his performance in Ireland it was no use their hoping either for effective military help from abroad or even for any secure refuge and freedom there. The most serious point of these lines about Cromwell's prospects of further victory may be coming in their second half, on Scotland. It was there that at this date main Royalist hopes lay. But even if they could be trusted, which an English Royalist was bound to doubt after his previous experience of them, the Scots had no hope against Cromwell. They would be lucky if they saved many of their own lives; and lucky, also, if they managed to save the young Charles Stuart from falling into Cromwell's hands. Who else could "the Caledonian deer" be? I can't understand why no editor or commentator even mentions the possibility of there being a pun and a point in this line.

In the eight lines on Scotland the writing is intensely pointed again, as it also is in the eight lines of the final address to Cromwell himself:

> But thou, the war's and fortune's son,
> March indefatigably on,
>   And for the last effect
>   Still keep thy sword erect:
> Besides the force it has to fright
> The spirits of the shady night,
>   The same arts that did gain
>   A power must it maintain.

The prospect of unending foreign conquest has suddenly and fearfully shrunk, vanished: replaced by the image of a Cromwell hemmed in at home on all sides; tied to the post, on his own, haunted both by the ghosts of the slain and the murdered and by the fear of that sudden final attack. The phrase "for the last effect" sounds as if it's a pointed one. What can it mean but "in readiness for the final event and upshot of the career of yours that I've been describing"? And, given what follows the phrase as well as what precedes it, is it really possible to think that that final event is Cromwell's coronation?

Readers of the "Horatian Ode" could have known that Marvell was a Royalist hot-head if they had previously both read and attributed to him another unpublished poem, the elegy written on the death of the young Francis Villiers, Buckingham's brother, in the Royalist uprising of 1648. The poem has been attributed to Marvell, though it is an uncertain and disputed item in the canon. But they could also have known that he was a Royalist hot-head if, some months after the "Horatian Ode", they had read his poem on "Tom May's Death". May died in the November of 1650. The poem wasn't published in Marvell's lifetime and there is no external evidence to confirm the date of its composition, any more than there is to confirm the date of composition of the "Horatian Ode", but it, too, sounds like a poem written close to the event. May had been a turncoat and, after being in the court of Charles, had used his pen to praise the leaders on the Parliamentary side. Marvell has him meeting Ben Jonson in the after-life, with all the other great dead poets, and being rebuked by him and ignominiously expelled from the august company.

> But thou, base man, first prostituted hast
> Our spotless knowledge and the studies chaste,
> Apostatising from our arts and us
> To turn the chronicler to Spartacus.
> Yet wast thou taken hence with equal fate,
> Before thou couldst great Charles his death relate.

The striking lines, the ones usually quoted from the poem and the ones for the sake of which, perhaps, the poem was mainly written, are the lines immediately before this, where Ben Jonson is made to generalise about the poet's role in times like the present:

> When the sword glitters o'er the judge's head,
> And fear has coward churchmen silenced,
> Then is the poet's time, 'tis then he draws
> And single fights forsaken virtue's cause.
> He, when the wheel of empire whirleth back,
> And though the world's disjointed axle crack,
> Sings still of ancient rights and better times,

Seeks wretched good, arraigns successful crimes.

A speculation plausible to me is that one thing Marvell was doing here was trying to explain the "Horatian Ode" to Royalists who had misunderstood it. Was the whole poem an apologia, written to protest and vindicate the poet against the charge that he, too, was a turncoat, and that he had prostituted his pen and his classical learning by praising Cromwell and comparing him to Julius Caesar? No, he had been arraigning successful crimes. And the comparison with Caesar hadn't been intended to suggest that Cromwell was any the less a rebel, or that the poet had any love for a rebel or wish to dignify him. At the beginning of the poem Ben Jonson is found

> Sounding of ancient heroes, such as were
> The subject's safety and the rebel's fear;
> But how a double-headed vulture eats
> Brutus and Cassius, the people's cheats.

May had been the translator of Lucan, and in his *History of the Parliament in England* he had made parallels between Roman and English leaders. Early in his rebuke to him Jonson is given this to say:

> Go seek the novice statesmen, and obtrude
> On them some Roman cast similitude;
> Tell them of liberty the stories fine,
> Until you all grow Consuls in your wine;
> Or thou, Dictator of the glass, bestow
> On him the Cato, this the Cicero,
> Transferring old Rome hither in your talk
> As Bethle'ms house did to Loretto walk.
> Foul architect, thou hadst not eye to see
> How ill the measures of these states agree;
> And who by Rome's example England lay
> Those but to Lucan do continue May.
> But thee nor ignorance nor seeming good
> Misled, but malice fixed and understood.

Is Marvell the person who in innocence was misled and is this his apology for it? No, he now agrees, Cromwell is less a Julius Caesar than a Spartacus.

In the line "Sings still of ancient rights and better times" the phrase "better times" couldn't refer to anything in the "Horatian Ode" but it could refer to the opening lines of the published poem to Lovelace, another poem which could very well have been found equivocal.

The note of simple Cavalier gallantry that can be recognised in certain lines of the "Horatian Ode" –

> The forward youth that would appear
> Must now forsake his muses dear
>
> For 'tis all one to courage high
>
> Where greater spirits come

– isn't recognised there readily because it merges with something stranger, more individual. Among other things, the note is a more violent and more desperate one. Perhaps, too, it is both more formidable and less sane. In the Cavalier gallantry of those eight lines of "Tom May's Death" about the poet's single fighting of forsaken virtue's cause there again seems to be a personal desperation and violence, though here it may be less formidable because a little histrionic.

The poems to turn to next, for more of the fierce extremism and the almost suicidal desperation, would be some that present themselves as 'love' poems. But first I should like to glance briefly at another of the more overtly political poems that stayed unpublished until after Marvell's death, "Upon the Hill and Grove at Billborow: To the Lord Fairfax." The description of the hill in the opening stanzas makes it an emblem of Fairfax's moral and political virtues. In the stanza where it is contrasted with other mountains it is difficult not to see another deliberate, hostile reference to Cromwell:

> See how the archèd earth does here
> Rise in a perfect hemisphere!

The stiffest compass could not strike
A line more circular and like;
Nor softest pencil draw a brow
So equal as this hill does bow.
It seems as for a model laid
And that the world by it was made.

Here learn, ye mountains more unjust,
Which to abrupter greatness thrust,
That do with your hook-shouldered height
The earth deform and Heaven fright,
For whose excrescence ill-designed
Nature must a new centre find;
Learn here those humble steps to tread
Which to securer glory lead.

See what a soft access and wide
Lies open to its grassy side,
Nor with the rugged path deters
The feet of breathless travellers.
See then how courteous it ascends
And all the way it rises bends,
Nor for itself the height does gain,
But only strives to raise the plain.

Yet thus it all the field commands
And in unenvied greatness stands,
Discerning further than the cliff
Of Heaven-daring Tenerife.
How glad the weary seamen haste
When they salute it from the mast!
By night the northern star their way
Directs, and this no less by day.

I don't pretend to be confident about what those last lines about the
weary seamen are insinuating. The defeated Royalists, many in exile,
did nurse hopes of the Parliamentary general Fairfax after he had

retired, as of the Scots. I also don't pretend to know what Marvell was doing when he took employment under the retired Fairfax in 1650 or 1651, or when he then, in 1653, sought employment under Cromwell.

The American scholar, Earl Miner, has written about "hidden meanings" in mid-seventeenth-century English poetry:

> The Civil War saw a rebirth of the enigmatic poetry of the Renaissance, in which emblems, parallelism, beast fable, pastoral, parable, or allegory – "darke" conceits of various kinds – were employed to carry a hidden meaning for those who shared knowledge and assumptions with the author but not for others. In the middle decades of the seventeenth century, the enigmatic mode was commonly employed to support the Royalist cause (the parliamentary victors could speak more plainly) and also by men like Marvell with divided feelings. Lovelace's poem "The Grasshopper" is a notable instance of this kind, and it is highly likely that another poem by him, "The Falcon," possesses a similar significance. In such poems the styles of various poets in the first half of the century are blended into semi-opaque dark conceits dealing with events of the realm. (*Modern Philology*, 1957)

As long ago as 1940 a suggestion by R.H. Syfret about the hidden meaning of Marvell's poem "The Unfortunate Lover" was put into print (in a footnote in the book on Marvell by M.C. Bradbrook and M.G. Lloyd Thomas). It is strange that it hasn't been taken much notice of or followed up, because I should have thought that from the poem's second stanza it's obvious that there is some hidden and political meaning.

'Twas in a shipwreck, when the seas
Ruled, and the waves did what they please,
That my poor lover floating lay,
And, e'er brought forth, was cast away;

Till at the last the master-wave
Upon the rock his mother drave;
And there she split against the stone,
In a Caesarian section.

The poem goes on:

The sea him lent these bitter tears
Which at his eyes he always bears;
And from the winds the sighs he bore
Which through his surging breast do roar.
No day he saw but that which breaks
Through frighted clouds in forked streaks,
While round the rattling thunder hurled,
As at the funeral of the world.

While nature to his birth presents
This masque of quarreling elements,
A numerous fleet of cormorants black,
That sailed insulting o'er the wrack,
Received into their cruel care
Th' unfortunate and abject heir,
Guardians not fit to entertain
The orphan of the hurricane.

They fed him up with hopes and air,
Which soon digested to despair.
And, as one cormorant fed him, still
Another on his heart did bill.
Thus while they famish him and feast,
He both consumèd and increased,
And languishèd with doubtful breath,
The amphibian of life and death.

And now, when angry Heaven would
Behold a spectacle of blood,

>Fortune and he are called to play
>At sharp before it all the day…

Syfret suggested that the unfortunate lover was Charles Stuart, Prince of Wales, "cast away in the Scilly Isles after the failure of the Royalist cause in the West in 1646." The footnote goes on: "The mother of verse two would then be England, the rock religious controversy, and the cormorants Grenville and Goring."

The idea of a hidden political meaning had occurred to me independently, but the idea of the younger Charles hadn't. I am persuaded by it and gratefully adopt it. Not all the other suggestions persuade me as they stand, and I wish I knew what the grounds were for offering them. How can "A *numerous* fleet of cormorants black" be Grenville and Goring? And more important: the "Caesarian section" is surely the execution of Charles I? The best sense I can make of that conceit in the second stanza is that the new, young and uncrowned King of England has been forced into exile before he has even, on his father's being unthroned (and later killed), become King. There seems no need to assign the poem to as early a date as the young Charles's stay in the Scilly Isles; and, if the date is later, after the execution of his father, the cormorants "that sailed insulting o'er the wrack" could be the Scots. I suggest that the shipwreck is less the defeat in the West of England than the final success of the rebellion as a whole, "when the seas / Ruled, and the winds did what they please", that the mother may be less England than the state and constitution of the kingdom old, and that the master-wave is Cromwell.

In the quoted stanzas there are coincidences of image and phrase with the "Horatian Ode". There is also a coincidence with a poem called "Caroli" in the anonymously printed collection of 1649, *Monumentum Regale: or A Tombe, Erected for that incomparable and Glorious Monarch, Charles the First, King of England, France and Ireland &c.* Compare "As at the funeral of the world" with

>One so diffusive, that he lived to all,
>And one that died the whole world's funeral…

Other poems in the same collection have lines that could recall other poems by Marvell:

> Rebellious giant hands have broke that pole
> On which our orb did long in glory roll.
>> ("A Deep Groane, fetch'd at the Funerall of that
>>   incomparable and glorious monarch...")

>> Such a fall
> Great Christendom ne'er patterned; and 'twas strange
> Earth's centre reeled not at this dismal change.
>>> ("Chronostichon...")

For me the extraordinary intense single-mindedness of Marvell's imagination as he writes verse, verging on the inhuman, tends to turn this fairly obvious kind of hyperbole into something more than that, more real.

Another thing common to both "The Unfortunate Lover" and the "Horatian Ode", and also to "Tom May's Death", is the declaration of an ardent personal claim or ambition: "The forward youth that would appear." Strong personal ambition is expressed of the kind that is brooded on by a single exceptionally isolated individual, a strangely violent ambition, verging again on the inhuman. In the first stanza of "The Unfortunate Lover" the infant Love, cool fountains and green shadows sound a note characteristic enough of Marvell, but so also do the lines about time:

> Alas, how pleasant are their days
> With whom the infant Love yet plays!
> Sorted by pairs, they still are seen
> By fountains cool, and shadows green.
> But soon these flames do lose their light,
> Like meteors of a summer's night,
> Nor can they to that region climb
> To make impression upon time.

A note in one edition mentions the belief that if meteors "pass the sphere of fire and the moon they would reach a region of incorruptibility and timelessness." Those already quoted (pp221-222) opening lines of Marvell's almost certainly later poem, "The First Anniversary of the Government under O.C.," makes it more vivid what the opposite is of making impression upon time. But by the date of this poem, 1654 or 1656, it is the restless Cromwell's success in making impression upon time that has come to interest the poet:

> Cromwell alone with greater vigour runs,
> Sun-like, the stages of succeeding suns,
> And still the day which he doth next restore
> Is the just wonder of the day before.
> Cromwell alone doth with new lustre spring,
> And shines the jewel of the yearly ring.
> 'Tis he the force of scattered time contracts,
> And in one year the work of ages acts...

In "The Unfortunate Lover", as in "Tom May's Death" and the "Horatian Ode", the idea seems to be that the only glory to be won will be out of the very hopelessness of the Royalist cause: for the noble, desperate ardour of continuing to the death in spite of the impossibility of success, or of its near-impossibility. The end of the poem's seventh stanza introduces another character in an awkwardly abrupt way, another unfortunate lover:

> And all he [*i.e.* Charles] says, a lover dressed
> In his own blood does relish best.

I'm not sure, but it seems likely that the poet introduces this character not only to bring himself into the poem, by implication, but also to help turn the next and last stanza into a general statement about unfortunate lovers, Royalist hot-heads. The reference in it to dying makes it difficult to think that this is to be taken as exclusively, if at all, a statement about the young Charles:

> This is the only banneret
> That ever Love created yet,
> Who, though, by the malignant stars,
> Forcèd to live in storms and wars,

> Yet dying leaves a perfume here,
> And music within every ear;
> And he in story only rules,
> In a field sable a lover gules.

Against a black background a blood-red lover. From these terrible times he is the one who is going to have a good place in history and be remembered as one of the rightful leaders. And compare "Cromwell alone..." with "And he in story only rules..."

How many of Marvell's 'love' poems are poems in what Professor Miner calls "the enigmatic mode"?

> My love is of a birth as rare
> As 'tis for object strange and high:
> It was begotten by despair
> Upon impossibility. ("The Definition of Love")

Can the mixture of Cavalier gallantry with something violent and suicidal be heard in the following lines?

> Rather at once our time devour
> Than languish in his time-chapped power.
>
> ("To his Coy Mistress")

It could be said that, if a poet has a preoccupation with time, he is as likely to bring it into his love poetry as into his political and 'career' poetry. All I can say on the other side is that in any case, independently of my thought about any of Marvell's other poems, I don't find it easy to think of the coy mistress as a woman. 'She' could be the young Charles Stuart. The poem is the wittier if 'she' is. (This poem does seem to me one in which, as also in "The Garden" and "Bermudas", Marvell does particularly well with his strange inspiration. It seems no accident that the three poems are probably his most popular – before as well as during the twentieth century, admired by Tennyson as well as by Eliot.)

I'm not sure that all of the poems by Marvell which carry a hidden meaning were necessarily written, in Earl Miner's words, "for those who shared knowledge and assumptions with the author." It seems highly likely that the "Horatian Ode", "Tom May's Death" and "To his Coy Mistress" were written to be read, and it doesn't seem impossible that "The Unfortunate Lover" was too. But it also doesn't seem impossible that this last poem was written by Marvell as a meditation for himself. The poem "Mourning" gives the impression of being this. But I do not know what the truth here is about "The Unfortunate Lover", and am in more or less the same position with Marvell's three poems about the Mower's love for Juliana. If, as I believe, they are connected with Marvell's eventually going over to Cromwell, who could they have been written for? I'm not sure about all the detail of these poems' hidden meaning, only fairly sure that they have one. That may be most evident in these stanzas from "Damon the Mower", about the Mower's failure in courting "Juliana":

> Oh what unusual heats are here,
> Which thus our sunburned meadows sear!
> The grasshopper its pipe gives o'er,
> And hamstringed frogs can dance no more.
> But in the brook the green frog wades,
> And grasshoppers seek out the shades.
> Only the snake, that kept within,
> Now glitters in its second skin.

> This heat the sun could never raise,
> Nor dog-star so inflames the days.
> It from an higher beauty grow'th,
> Which burns the fields and mowers both,
> Which made the dog, and makes the sun
> Hotter than his own Phaeton.
> Not July causes these extremes,
> But Juliana's scorching beams. [*]

---

[*] Compare:

    'Twas when the raging dog did rule the skies,

Tell me where I may pass the fires
Of the hot day, or hot desires.
To what cool cave shall I descend,
Or to what gelid fountain bend?
Alas, I look for ease in vain
When remedies themselves complain.
No moisture but my tears do rest,
No cold but in her icy breast.

How long wilt thou, fair shepherdess,
Esteem me, and my presents less?
To thee the harmless snake I bring,
Disarmed of its teeth and sting;
To thee chameleons changing hue,
And oak leaves tipped with honey due.
Yet thou, ungrateful, hast not sought
Nor what they are, nor who them brought.

Is "The Mower to the Glow-worms" sad with the sadness that an ardent, if unusual, Royalist might feel after despairing and changing sides? It may be a similar bleakness that is felt in those opening lines of "The First Anniversary of the Government under O.C."

A final fling. I believe that those who have subscribed to the belief that Marvell's poetry contains a rare wisdom, or anything approaching it, have done the thing they may very well believe I have done, especially in the second part of this enquiry: made it all up. In the first chapter of his *Revaluation* Leavis writes of "The Dialogue between the Resolved Soul and Created Pleasure" that Marvell's

---

And with his scorching face did tyrannise,
When Cromwell, whelp of that mad star,
But sure more fiery than his sire by far,
Had dried the northern fife, and with his heat
Put frozen Scotland in a bloody sweat...
These are further lines from Robert Wild's "The Tragedy of Christopher Love at Tower-Hill", already quoted from on p236n above.

"seriousness is the finer wisdom of a ripe civilization", having previously invoked Eliot's "extraordinarily pregnant and decisive essay on Marvell". In that essay of 1921 Eliot has also written of the "wisdom" and that, for example, it is "the equipoise, a balance and proportion of tones", in the "Horatian Ode" that "makes Marvell a classic." (In fairness to Marvell, it should be mentioned the patness with which that "Dialogue" poem moves could be due to its possibly having been written not as a poem but as a libretto.)

Postscript In the years since the publication of the two articles this chapter is drawn from, at least three different scholars have written of "The Unfortunate Lover" as a Royalist poem. However, each of the three seems to me to read the poem less convincingly than Syfret did, identifying the unfortunate lover with the dead Charles I rather than with his son.

Chapter IX
Charlotte Mew and the Future of
English Poetry

I begin with a joke: a poem "1967" (written in 1867), at which readers are likely to smile although the poet would not have wanted them to:

> In five-score summers! All new eyes,
> New minds, new modes, new fools, new wise;
> New woes to weep, new joys to prize;
>
> With nothing left of me and you
> In that live century's vivid view
> Beyond a pinch of dust or two;
>
> A century which, if not sublime,
> Will show, I doubt not, at its prime,
> A scope above this blinkered time.
>
> - Yet what to me how far above?
> For I would only ask thereof
> That thy worm should be my worm, Love!

The joke is probably funnier for those who recognise the poet, and know how lugubriously frequent are his references to graves, dust, yew trees, worms, *etc*.

Here is another poem in which a loved one is spoken to about loss and time:

> *A Quoi Bon Dire*

> Seventeen years ago you said
> Something that sounded like Good-bye;

> And everybody thinks that you are dead,
> But I.
>
> So I, as I grow stiff and cold
> To this and that say Good-bye too;
> And everybody sees that I am old
> But you.
>
> And one fine morning in a sunny lane
> Some boy and girl will meet and kiss and swear
> That nobody can love their way again
> While over there
> You will have smiled, I shall have tossed your hair.

The shifting between past, present and future may bring to mind the opening lines of a famous later poem:

> Time present and time past
> Are both perhaps present in time future
> And time future contained in time past.

Eliot's "Burnt Norton" goes on to say a great deal about that saving reality that all human beings know, if only in tantalisingly brief glimpses: the precious short moments that seem timeless. His repeated "At the still point of the turning world" suggests how miraculously time can seem to be arrested even while it continues to move, and

> To be conscious is not to be in time
> But only in time can the moment in the rose-garden,
> The moment in the arbour where the rain beat,
> The moment in the draughty church at smokefall
> Be remembered; involved with past and future.
> Only through time time is conquered.

As in the moment on the fine morning in the sunny lane. Eliot's words help bring out the depth of thought and feeling and – really – of wisdom that there is in the simple delicacy of "*A Quoi Bon Dire*".

The depth is the greater, and perhaps only possible, by being all between the lines. Asking what the good is of speaking, the poem's title suggests not only that words will not literally overcome the separation, but also that they cannot express what is ineffable, the paradoxical living existence of that past experience. Yet, as I hope readers may agree, the poem's words do express precisely this.

I begin with these poems in order to ask whether something must be wrong. For the writer of "1967", Thomas Hardy, is so very much better known a poet than the young contemporary of his who wrote "*A Quoi Bon Dire*", Charlotte Mew. And not only that: Hardy did write a large number of poems, and some of his warmest admirers have acknowledged that the number of his really good ones is small (and, while finding strength in its first stanza, would probably only smile and sigh over the rest of "1967"); yet "1967" is one of the thirty-odd poems by Hardy included in *The Norton Anthology of Modern Poetry*, which does not contain a single poem by Mew. Must something at any rate have been wrong in 1973, when this *Norton Anthology* came out? Its second edition did differ by omitting "1967", but still had a lot of Hardy and no Mew.

Hardy, of course, could write much better poems about love, loss and time. His "The Self-Unseeing" is also closer to Mew's poem in subject, as it is to "Burnt Norton":

> Here is the ancient floor,
> Footworn and hollowed and thin,
> Here was the former door
> Where the dead feet walked in.
>
> She sat here in her chair,
> Smiling into the fire;
> He who played stood there,
> Bowing it higher and higher.
>
> Childlike, I danced in a dream;
> Blessings emblazoned that day;
> Everything glowed with a gleam;
> Yet we were looking away!

The last line might seem at odds with any idea that this was one of those moments when human beings touch the eternal – how could that have been what the lovers were enjoying when their minds were elsewhere? – but, if anything, this line only clinches it. It is often only afterwards and in memory that we realise. In Mew's poem, the "Something that sounded like Good-bye" mysteriously turned out not to have been that. "We had the experience but missed the meaning," to invoke "The Dry Salvages" this time, where Eliot also writes of "the moment in and out of time" as "the unattended moment."

In this new comparison with Hardy, though, is not Mew, still, more obviously the poet? Seeing the depth of thought and feeling between her lines is seeing how much more her words do of the essential work of words in poetry, creation, even though they could hardly be simpler – in this poem without a single metaphor. It is as if the whole of it is on a high metaphorical plane, evoking the mystery that is also a very plain reality. The lines

> And everybody sees that I am old
> But you.

cannot rest in the mind with only the prosaic poignant meaning that he is no longer there to see. That is made impossible by the existence of the parallel lines in the poem's first stanza, which, together with "sounded like Good-bye", have gently stirred the imagination to apprehend that something unusual is being said. Then the tense of her verb in the poem's last line is perfect. Imagining a different, quite possible line in which, confident of the love's eternity, the poet had written that he *will* still be smiling, she *will* be tossing his hair, may help bring this out. Even while being so intimate, that last stanza's five simple lines suddenly open up a vista: of young couples stretching back into the past and on into the future, each believing that their love-experience is unique and permanent and, heartbreakingly and beautifully, each couple both wrong and right about this.

In comparison, the language of "The Self-Unseeing" is pedestrian. With only the small exception of the poem's last line and the earlier "She", its words tend to say what they are saying straightaway and not to say anything more. Mew is also more obviously a poet because it is impossible to imagine what her poem says being said in any other words, while much of Hardy's expression seems relatively optional or arbitrary. A reader is aware of him choosing to put something one way when he might have chosen another, and some of his choices are not even particularly good ones:

> Here was the former door
> Where the dead feet walked in.

comes close to a comic bathos. In the line "Everything glowed with a gleam" so far is Hardy from giving an extra, poetic charge to his words that he seems actually to take away from their ordinary meaning and produce a bit of a blur, since a glow is a different kind of shining from a gleam. If it might be argued that this difference represents a movement the poet's mind makes in the course of the short line, from the glowing scene as a whole to the gleam of one specific thing after another in it, the two words still seem not to combine well, since separate things gleaming tend to suggest that the scene as a whole is a bit dark. In any case, such sensitive reading as that kind of quick movement of mind would require, with the reader finding almost every word unusually alive and suspenseful, potentially capable as in Mew of taking the poem in a new, unforeseen direction, is made difficult by another near-arbitrary-feeling choice of Hardy's: his pat, off-the-peg rhythms. If Mew's rhythms seem exactly right, the best that can be said of his is that they do not do too badly: the short, regular and mainly end-stopped lines have a rough-and-ready fittingness for both the first two stanzas' itemising statements and the third's exclamatory ones. The one place where a rhythm does positively well is at the word "Childlike" and its comma, which delicately supply a kind of musical punctuation to aid the transition.

It is Mew's being more completely a poet that gives her poem its wisdom. The rarer kind of creation she is effecting with her words is the creation of something new, perhaps not absolutely new but not of an almost everyday familiarity. The reader senses that the realisation the poem arrives at cannot be clearly known to the poet when she begins writing; and it is not even clearly known at the end, to either her or the reader, at least not in the sense that it can easily be put into words, other words. If this is true to a degree of every good poem, so that the difference here between these two poems is only one of degree, it is still a big difference. By letting his emphasis fall simply on the regret, Hardy is handling the subject in a more conventional way: "Oh those happy far-off times! And we didn't even appreciate them then!" The more difficult thing Mew does, the greater wisdom she reaches through courage and subtlety of feeling as well as intellectual power, is to do justice simultaneously to the heartbreak and to the knowledge that eternity was nevertheless touched. Emotionally as well as intellectually, it is easier to conclude, not to be forever suspended and balanced and teased between the apparently contradictory feelings but to decide, instead, that it is all and only a matter of heartbreak, or that such heartbreak is something simple. Hardy's poem is a fresh and touching one, not compromised by such comfortable and comforting cliché as everybody is tempted to resort to with painful experience, but it is not so unmistakably quite out of sight of such cliché as Mew's much more beautiful poem is.

It therefore does not linger in the mind in the same way. To the reader's secret disappointment, it fairly quickly cuts out. The emotional stop has been pulled, and that is that. Though emotionally the stronger poem, "*A Quoi Bon Dire*" is more than the pulling of such a stop. At the same time, it is something like a discovery. So the mind is more deeply satisfied, and more inclined to stay with the experience of the poem when its last word has been read. There is more for it to stay with. Also, through the rare purity and completeness of the poet's art, the mind is itself suspended for a moment in that place where time seems to be absent.

Another mark of outstanding poetry is its unusual authority. Rather more than Hardy, and than many other poets read more than she is, Mew has a special right to address her fellow human beings and to be heard by us because it is clear how thoroughly she knows what she is doing. There is no sense of anything being merely tried for, or worked up, or laboriously worked at. She is boldly into it and doing it from her poem's first word, and is able to do it with an easy economy and lightness, as if casually. There is a touch of this ease in "The Self-Unseeing", but in comparison Hardy treads heavily.

Her authority as a poet derives, too, from both her matter's and her manner's being, without eccentricity, fresh and her own. And that becomes especially impressive, of course, when she takes on something big. Assuming that few readers can know much of Mew's writing, I will confine my examples of her longer poems to ones not too long to quote in full. Here is the first:

Le Sacré-Coeur
(Montmartre)

It is dark up here on the heights,
    Between the dome and the stars it is quiet too,
While down there under the crowded lights
    Flares the importunate face of you,
Dear Paris of the hot white hands, the scarlet lips, the scented
                                       hair,
      Une jolie fille à vendre, tres cher;
      A thing of gaiety, a thing of sorrow,
      Bought to-night, possessed, and tossed
      Back to the mart again to-morrow,
        Worth and over what you cost;
While half your charm is that you are
Withal, like some unpurchasable star,
    So old, so young and infinite and lost.

It is dark on the dome-capped hill,
    Serenely dark, divinely still,
Yet here is the Man who bought you first
    Dying of his immortal smart,
Your Lover, the King with the broken heart,
    Who while you, feasting, drink your fill,
        Pass round the cup
        Not looking up,
Calls down to you, "I thirst."

"A king with a broken heart! *Mon Dieu!*
    One breaks so many, *cela peut se croire*,
To remember all *c'est la mer à boire*,

And the first, *mais comme c'est vieux.*
Perhaps there is still some keepsake, or
One has possibly sold it for a song:
On ne peut pas toujours pleurer les morts,
And this One – He has been dead so long!"

I confess that I did not always think this so strong a poem, misreading
it at first as a more conventionally moral and Christian piece of
writing than it is. In fact, the tender tribute to Paris and the worldly
world is genuine and profound as well as original, with the poet's
interest not in preaching at them in the first two stanzas and then
satirising them for their incurable deafness. She is not so much
delivering a message as representing something like a tragedy: the
absolute intransigence of those facts. One large, impressive and
touching human reality is quite cut off from another large, impressive
and touching reality, the two at such an immense, hopeless distance
from each other even though closely adjacent in the same place, and
with suffering and great mutual need on each side. My misreading
ought to have been prevented by the surprises at the end of the first
stanza, especially in "star" and "infinite".

Some comparison with Eliot is earned, and not only because this
poem and the fourth of the "Preludes" in *Prufrock and Other
Observations* have an intriguing similarity in their tripartite
constructions (roughly the worldly world, a challenge and alternative
to it, and a final negative).

I imagine almost no one who reads that poem of Eliot's ever quite
forgets it, if only because of the four lines that make its second section
-

I am moved by fancies that are curled
Around these images, and cling:
The notion of some infinitely gentle
Infinitely suffering thing.

- another poetic surprise, or series of surprises, and so beautifully
written. The clause, "that are curled / Around these images," is
followed exactly rightly, it seems, by the comma and two short-
vowelled syllables and colon; and "cling" by its sound and duration as

well as its meaning almost reverses both "curled" and the whole phrase "are curled / Around," in order to complement and complete them precisely. Mew's writing is never quite so magically sensitive as this, though "You will have smiled, I shall have tossed your hair" does perhaps invite some comparison. (In sound and duration as well as meaning, "tossed" and "tossed your hair" seem the perfect completing complement to "Smiled".) In Eliot's whole poem words are put together more potently than they probably ever are by Mew. Its first section is packed and vivid, with its final evocation of the hard, carrying-the-world-before-it confidence in the city's "blackened street" setting things up perfectly for the extraordinary turn that then follows in the lines quoted.

Yet, on the other hand, this "Prelude" may also be a more limitedly personal poem than "*Le Sacré-Coeur*". In it Eliot has a touch of the secretly glamorous Hamletising young man who is present in much of his *Prufrock* collection, disaffected and self-soulful. It is easy to imagine such a young man speaking the poem: vulnerably sensitive and ambitious, oppressed by much that he finds around him in the big early-twentieth-century city, with an intuition of there being somewhere an emotional and spiritual potential that could transform things if it could manifest itself, but also with an inclination to dismiss existence as anyhow meaningless. It is an attractive role to play, especially for someone who is or has been a young man, even though it has its less pleasant features (some tendency to a defensive conscious cleverness and to feelings of contempt, hatred, self-contempt, self-pity, impotence and, in other *Prufrock* poems, misogyny). It is not that this is a large part of either this poem or the others, or that this poem does not have a great deal of impersonal weight and force. But there is the touch of this role-playing, and nothing equivalently personal in Mew's poem. "*Le Sacré-Coeur*" is the poem of a larger imagination and a larger heart, and is not less but more tough-minded.

Similarly, if in some ways it is a less modern poem than Eliot's, in another way it is more modern, further away from the nineteenth century. Two points to consider are: (1) a secretly glamorous and self-soulful bitterness and scepticism are not the opposite of glamorous self-soulful Romantic illusion, only the other side of the same coin, the real opposite being an un-self-soulful tragic position like Mew's; (2) this "Prelude", like many other of Eliot's poems up to and including *The Waste Land*, contains *inter alia* a melancholy elegiac note associating it, for all its originality, with that later nineteenth century in which it can sometimes seem that to be poetic *means* to be melancholy-elegiac – which note is completely absent from Mew's poetry.

It is not, of course, that this elegiac note cannot make wonderful poetry. My own view is that the most beautiful and profound English poems of the whole of that previous century – perhaps more beautiful and profound than even Wordsworth's or Shelley's – are by Tennyson. (Eliot himself can sometimes seem less the beginning of a new English poetry than the last and, apart from its founder, the greatest poet in the school of Tennyson.) Also, it is not that many of Mew's own poems are not movingly sad ones. I'm speaking here of a special kind of elegiac note that is heard so much in English poetry from Tennyson to Eliot and then disappears – though it has already disappeared in Mew, and also in the Hardy she admired and learned from. It tends to go with a special musicality in the verse, suggestive of sighing, as in Tennyson's:

> Tears, idle tears, I know not what they mean,
> Tears from the depth of some divine despair...

The voice continually swells and lapses. Though they are different, something similar can be heard in those beautiful four lines from Eliot's "Prelude" – just as the absence of anything like this can be heard in the plain, matter-of-fact voice of "*Le Sacré-Coeur*".

The juxtaposition of two other passages from the work of these poets may reinforce the distinction. The Eliot here is the closing verse-paragraph of what has sometimes been thought the best poem in *Prufrock*, "Portrait of a Lady":

> Well, and what if she should die some afternoon,
> Afternoon grey and smoky, evening yellow and rose;
> Should die and leave me sitting pen in hand
> With the smoke coming down above the house-tops;
> Doubtful, for a while
> Not knowing what to feel or if I understand
> Or whether wise or foolish, tardy or too soon...

Would she not have the advantage, after all?
This music is successful with a 'dying fall'
Now that we talk of dying -
And should I have the right to smile?

Alongside this, the Mew may be seen as an extreme example of her plain matter-of-fact voice. Like "Portrait of a Lady", "In Nunhead Cemetery" is a dramatic monologue, but the person speaking is a man close to suffering a nervous breakdown through grief. Yet his voice is only a special development of what is heard in all of her poetry. Like "*A Quoi Bon Dire*", the poem was in her first book, *The Farmer's Bride*, published in 1916, a year earlier than *Prufrock*. These are the opening stanzas:

It is the clay that makes the earth stick to his spade;
    He fills in holes like this year after year;
The others have gone; they were tired, and half afraid,
    But I would rather be standing here;

There is nowhere else to go. I have seen this place
    From the windows of the train that's going past
Against the sky. This is rain on my face -
    It was raining here when I saw it last.

There is something horrible about a flower;
    This, broken in my hand, is one of those
He threw in just now: it will not live another hour;
    There are thousands more: you do not miss a rose.

One of the children hanging about
    Pointed at the whole dreadful heap and smiled
This morning, after THAT was carried out;
    There is something terrible about a child.

We were like children, last week, in the Strand;
    That was the day you laughed at me
Because I tried to make you understand

The cheap stale chap I used to be
Before I saw the things you made me see.

This is not a real place; perhaps by-and-by
    I shall wake – I am getting drenched with all this rain:
To-morrow I will tell you about the eyes of the Crystal
                                    Palace train
Looking down on us, and you will laugh and I shall see
                                    what you see again.

I can't resist quoting the poem's last two stanzas too, partly because the first of them, like the penultimate one just quoted, gives us the character's voice rising in excitement and speaking longer sentences, no longer those appallingly flat and deadpan ones. At the end of it, the flatness poignantly comes back again to interrupt the more expansive speech.

        When I was quite a little lad
            At Christmas time we went half mad
                For joy of all the toys we had,
        And then we used to sing about the sheep
            The shepherds watched by night;
        We used to pray to Christ to keep
            Our small souls safe till morning light -
        I am scared, I am staying with you to-night -
                    Put me to sleep.

I shall stay here: here you can see the sky;
The houses in the street are much too high;
        There is no one left to speak to there;
        Here they are everywhere,
And just above them fields and fields of roses lie –
If he would dig it all up again they would not die.

It seems likely that Eliot himself was struck by that interruption: "I am scared, I am staying with you to-night." In *The Waste Land* (1922), he has a long, expansively written passage followed by a similarly abrupt change of rhythm in the line: "My nerves are bad tonight. Yes, bad. Stay with me." And, if indeed he did have Mew's line somewhere in his mind at this point, it would be significant that his own begins a passage that is more dramatic in character. The dramatic quality of Mew's poetry is one of the main things making it modern. And perhaps another thing that makes this particular poem modern is that its voice is not so far away from that of a Samuel Beckett character.

Interestingly, *The Waste Land* is the first poem in which Eliot makes a prominent use of abruptly and shockingly contrasted voices. There is nothing in any of his preceding poems like another sudden shift he makes in the same section of this long poem, to the cockney dialogue in the London pub. *The Waste Land* came out after "*Le Sacré-Coeur*", with its last stanza's Montmartre café voice. This was one of the additional poems included in a 1921 reissue of *The Farmer's Bride*. Here, as elsewhere, Mew was an independent poetic innovator.

The stanzas from "In Nunhead Cemetery" could be described by the words I used of "*Le Sacré-Coeur*": again there is something like a tragedy, the absolute intransigence of the facts. The words describe a good number of Mew's works, a few of her prose stories as well as many of her poems, and they may justify the proposition that, if Mew is not an Eliot and there are great things in his poetry that are well beyond her, Eliot also is not a Mew and there is at least this one great thing in her poetry that is beyond him. His poetry's more beautiful musicality and what goes with this, the subtler and more intimate interrelating that his words can do, may finally open readers up a little more completely than Mew's poetry ever does, and in a poem like "Portrait of a Lady" or *The Waste Land* what they open readers up to certainly possesses tragic weight. At the same time, these poems have not Mew's bald and stark directness in tragic representation. If Eliot is more Shakespearean, does Mew's poetry have more in common with the poetry of Greek tragedy?

My general hypothesis here is that it may not be a case of a major figure in early twentieth-century English poetry, or *the* major figure, Eliot, and a minor figure with a curiously original way of writing, Mew, but a case of two major figures – perhaps *the* two major figures.

"The Farmer's Bride" was probably her best-known poem in her lifetime: another of the dramatic monologues that so many of her poems are, though unlike most of the others in its sustained closeness to ballad form.

> Three summers since I chose a maid -
> Too young maybe – but more's to do
> At harvest-time than bide and woo.
>   When us was wed she turned afraid
> Of love and me and all things human;
> Like the shut of a winter's day
> Her smile went out, and 'twasn't a woman -
>   More like a little frightened fay.
>   One night, in the Fall, she runned away.

> "Out 'mong the sheep, her be," they said,
> 'Should properly have been abed;
> But sure enough she wasn't there
> Lying awake with her wide brown stare.
> So over seven-acre field and up-along across the down
> We chased her, flying like a hare
> Before our lanterns. To Church-Town
>   All in a shiver and a scare
> We caught her, fetched her home at last,
>   And turned the key upon her fast.

> She does the work about the house
> As well as most, but like a mouse.
>   Happy enough to chat and play
>   With birds and rabbits and such as they,
>   So long as men-folk keep away.
> "Not near, not near!" her eyes beseech
> When one of us comes within reach.
>   The women say that beasts in stall
>   Look round like children at her call.
>   *I've* hardly heard her speak at all.

> Shy as a leveret, swift as he,

Straight and slight as a young larch tree,
Sweet as the first wild violets, she,
To her wild self. But what to me?

The short days shorten, and the oaks are brown,
    The blue smoke rises to the low grey sky,
One leaf in the still air falls slowly down,
    A magpie's spotted feathers lie
On the black earth spread white with rime,
The berries redden up to Christmas-time.
        What's Christmas-time without there be
        Some other in the house than we!

She sleeps up in the attic there
    Alone, poor maid. 'Tis but a stair
Betwixt us. Oh! my God! the down,
The soft young down of her, the brown,
The brown of her – her eyes, her hair, her hair!

The absolute intransigence again – in yet another place, literally and emotionally.

Her poetry's authority is also a matter of its being exceptionally out of its time. It is so little marked by period touches or period feel. Longer dramatic monologues like "In Nunhead Cemetery" have the occasional slight touch because the slang as well as the setting is Edwardian, but even here there is no period feel, which would be the more serious matter. At the present date, does "The Farmer's Bride" even look rather more timeless than Eliot's *Prufrock* poems? But fairness is difficult here, since poems read so often as the latter have evidently been put through the toughest test for what wears well, and Mew's poem has not yet begun to meet that.

Yet "timeless" would only be another way of describing that impersonality of hers which I have already suggested can be more complete than Eliot's. Because of his early essay, "Tradition and the Individual Talent," and because some of its ideas seem to be reflected in such features of his poetry as its use of ironic distance, impersonality is commonly thought of as having, with Eliot, gained a crucial new importance as a poetic principle, and a central place in a revolution against the principles of nineteenth-century English poetry. By my account, there is a deception in this. Eliot himself, of course, made his own famous deprecating remark about what a personal poem *The Waste Land* is – though, since he was being extravagantly unfair to it if he literally meant what he said, it is possible to speculate that here he had been provoked by the Philistinism in some of the celebration the poem has had: as one of an almost unique general significance, *the* statement of twentieth-century humanity's *malaise* and *angst*. He could have wanted to defend his poem, with whatever indirectness, against the false friend that a supposed eulogist is being who in this way takes its significance to be only of its time.[*] Yet may "personal" still describe an element in that poem, if a small one, that lessens rather than confirms its greatness? And in that "Tradition" essay may one reason why Eliot is so emphatic about impersonality be that in many ways he disliked himself and was urgent in his writing to get away from himself, and found doing this peculiarly difficult? The greater consistency and completeness with which Mew's poems achieve artistic impersonality seem to indicate that she found it easier.

It does not prove anything, but seems no coincidence, that in Eliot's dramatic monologues all the fictional characters who speak the poems, from Prufrock to the Tiresias of *The Waste Land*, are fairly transparent disguises for the poet, whereas there is no knowing where Mew the person stands in relation to that farmer, or that bereaved near-madman, or the sixteen-year-old boy of her second longest poem, "The Fête," or the 'loose' woman of her longest, "Madeleine in Church," *etc*. From knowledge about her life the guess may be made that another powerful dramatic monologue, "The Quiet House," is personally closer to her in its subject-matter, but this could not be known from there being any more personal quality in the writing, just

---

[*] "Various critics have done me the honour to interpret the poem in terms of criticism of the contemporary world, have considered it, indeed, as an important bit of social criticism. To me it was only the relief of a personal and wholly insignificant grouse against life; it is just a piece of rhythmical grumbling." Quoted on p1 of T.S. Eliot, *The Waste Land: a facsimile and transcript of the original drafts including the annotations of Ezra Pound*, edited by Valerie Eliot.

as it cannot be known whether "*A Quoi Bon Dire*" is fact or fiction, or whether its "I" is Mew herself or someone else. Writing about this poem above, I referred to the person speaking as "she" and the person spoken to as "he", but that was only for convenience. Not that the issue is that of the presence in the poetry or absence from it of biographical facts of the poet's life. If the speakers of Eliot's dramatic monologues are fairly transparent disguises, that does not mean that any of these poems necessarily contains literal autobiography. The issue is rather whether to any extent the imagination and feeling of the poetry are made less 'true' by the particular biases and hang-ups the poet happens to have. While a poet can make good use of such personal elements, it is only as material and by being for the moment free of them. Then they do not show as the poet's, and the poetry isn't limitedly personal.

This may be too long a way of coming to the central point: what a wonderfully liberating gift to human beings a poem is when in it the poet gives us something intensely felt and yet with the most complete and pure impersonality. We are out in the open air, absolutely free: moved and awed and in profound communion with another human spirit, but not in the least oppressed by or having to be bothered with his or her mere personality – to use this word as D.H. Lawrence did. When "The Farmer's Bride" was first printed in a magazine, one reader was, as she later reported, "electrified." (This was Alida Monro, who subsequently persuaded her husband Harold to publish *The Farmer's Bride* collection.) The rare impersonal power of the poem still makes it capable of electrifying.

A final, shorter poem, "June, 1915," before some words about Mew's reputation or lack of one, and her place in the future:

> Who thinks of June's first rose today?
> Only some child, perhaps, with shining eyes and rough bright
> hair will reach it down
> In a green sunny lane, to us almost as far away
> As are the fearless stars from these veiled lamps of town.
> What's little June to a great broken world with eyes gone dim
> From too much looking on the face of grief, the face of
> dread?

Or what's the broken world to June and him
Of the small eager hand, the shining eyes, the rough bright
head?

The remarkable balance and justice of this simple little poem tempt me to say that, if not the best of the many English poems of the First World War, it fails to be so only because Mew herself wrote others. It becomes, unlike most of that period's 'War poems', and apparently without even trying, a poem about every horrible major disaster in the history of the race. But I quote it to help with such more general questions as the following about Mew's work. Has she any main subject? If it characteristic of her to represent something like the intransigence of tragedy, specifically what sort of tragedy? And, if she has claims to being a great writer, perhaps the greatest twentieth-century writer from England after D.H. Lawrence, does she really possess her own large vision of life, the *sine qua non* of such stature?

I am struck, on reflection, and believe readers may be, by the range shown in the few poems I've quoted, but in all of them, as well as in many of her other poems, including all her longer ones, and also in almost all her short stories, the main intransigent facts are those of separation. There are insurmountable division and distance between farmer and bride, between Paris and Christ, perhaps between the two mourners in those other poems and their lost loved ones but even more between those mourners and everyone else, now between that "broken" world and the child. Often, on the one side of the division, it cannot even be imagined what it is like on the other side. While the subjects of the poems and stories are often sad and grim, what is created in them is inspiring. As readers, we can be struck with awe at how rich and deep the human spirit is when one person can go so far beyond where another can follow; and, at the same time, at how rich and deep our own human spirit is and also the bond that, after all, we find uniting all of us with each other when, nevertheless, the poet enables us to follow. It takes an extraordinary largeness of mind and heart to imagine and create simultaneously and with firm, calm clarity and full, generous passion, as Mew does again and again, both sides of such divisions, and to hold them in just balance together.

In her own lifetime Mew's poetry was admired by many, including Hardy, Pound and Virginia Woolf. The last described it (in letters of 25 January 1920 and 9 November 1922) as "very good and interesting and unlike anyone else" and Mew herself as "our greatest living poetess". One of her two longest poems was published by Pound in *The Egoist*, and in another issue of the same magazine the other was specially picked out by H.D. in an enthusiastic notice of *The Farmer's Bride*. *The Egoist* did not print or notice many writers, and was in those same two or three years printing Joyce and Eliot as well as Pound. Even the most significant rejection Mew is known to have suffered, when nothing by her was accepted by Edward Marsh for *Georgian Poetry* anthologies, might have been a rejection to help rather than hinder her reputation with posterity: posterity has more or less rejected those anthologies, and *The Egoist* proven itself much the better stable to come from.

So why does her writing not have a high reputation now? The main answer may be the perennial one: that poetry, however wonderful a possession and power of the race, is also a delicate possession and power. The sublime real thing rarely gives dependably immediate fast-food satisfaction, and is the more in danger of neglect as a result because there is always plenty of verse around that isn't the real thing but readily taken for it. But also contributing to Mew's neglect must be, first, that she seems to have written much less than she had done before in the years between *The Farmer's Bride* in 1916 and her death in 1928; secondly, that there was only that one small book of poems and one even smaller posthumous book of poems (the stories and essays appearing, if at all, in magazines and not collected until 1981); and, thirdly, that she was a woman. I wince at Woolf, of all people: "our greatest living poetess." Did she even consider that the correct description might have been "our greatest living poet"? Eliot and Pound were American, Yeats Irish, Hugh MacDiarmid (if she knew his work then) Scottish, Lawrence not at his best in verse. Hardy was the only serious rival among English poets. If Woolf herself suffered less from being a woman, that was probably because she was a central figure in the influential Bloomsbury circle – and also a novelist. Women had long been allowed to gain reputations in what for the greater part of its history has been a less prestigious form of writing.

What difference might Mew's poetry and its authority have made to English poetry? Or what difference could they yet make to its future? A great poet can help give confidence to succeeding poets, and can do so partly by renewing and purifying the language. When a language is corrupted by writers of verse, as with encrustations of would-be-poetic 'thickness', there is a lack of both confidence in it and respect for it. The influence of Mew could have been a strong ally to whatever influence the Eliot has had who, as both poet and critic, cared so much about the ideal, classic potentialities of the English language[*]: a strong ally because she is both a similar classic user of the language and a different one. If Larkin is another, at any rate when his phrasing is free of the showy smartness most marked in *The Less Deceived* (though, even there, not completely dominant), who else has there been in the middle and latter parts of the twentieth century? Auden very spottily indeed, F.T. Prince... But who else before the hardly known younger poets whose work attention is drawn to in this book's main argument?

If Mew had been read enough, there might not subsequently in England have been quite so much excessively cautious, 'clever', self-conscious, self-defensive, all too narrowly male verse: " ...I think the emotional content of twentieth-century English verse so far has been on the whole thinner than in previous centuries" (Larkin in a 1966 letter). Mew could have helped to teach poets, and now may, how to be powerfully direct, passionate and charged in the simplest and purest English language, lean and vigorous, and certainly without the use of words to pack and thicken lines with the idea that they will then have the appearance of poetry. Taken as a reference to 'thickness' in Ted Hughes's language, or Geoffrey Hill's, these last words might have a point but would also be a bit unfair.[†] Yet what about the work

---

[*] One page of Eliot's criticism that I've in mind here is the page in "What is a Classic?" (p63 when reprinted in *On Poetry and Poets*) on that "common style... which makes us exclaim, not 'this is a man of genius using the language' but 'this realizes the genius of the language'."

[†] But any inartistic 'thickness' in Hughes's writing has nothing to do with the specific vice of style discussed in Chapter III. From this, as I said towards the end of that chapter, his writing is notably free. What 'thickness' there is comes

of the contemporary of theirs who is now more celebrated than they are, perhaps because he comes from Ulster – even though, as a poet, he could hardly be more thoroughly later-twentieth-century English and 'establishment' London? A better-known Mew might either have helped Seamus Heaney be an almost unrecognisably better poet or have made it quite impossible for him to win the Nobel Prize.

If Mew had been read enough, there might also have been less deafness to the new American poetry this book's main argument draws attention to.

Note I am much indebted to the sheer existence of Val Warner's edition of Charlotte Mew's *Collected Poems and Prose* (1981). Also, it was in her Introduction that I found Alida Monro's "electrified" and the quotations from Woolf. Sadly, the book has now gone out of print, as has my own subsequent Penguin edition of the *Complete Poems* (2000). But Val Warner's separate publication, her edition of the *Collected Poems and Selected Prose* (1997), happily remains in print. The new 2003 edition of *The Norton Anthology of Modern Poetry* (in two volumes and now called *The Norton Anthology of Modern and Contemporary Poetry*) has twenty-eight poems by Hardy and none by Mew. On the other hand, *The Norton Anthology of Poetry* does contain two poems by Mew (to Hardy's fifteen).

---

rather through what can sometimes seem an excessively insistent crowding of his lines with striking metaphors and similes.

Chapter X
Lost and found: the paintings of Edwin Smith

How often does one come out of an exhibition of paintings with the feeling of being in love, one has been all at once seeing so much new beauty? It has just [May 1995], happened to me visiting the Edwin Smith exhibition at Sally Hunter's Fine Art in London. The pictures are small and not showy; most of them have traditional subjects (landscapes, flowers, still lives); and there are more watercolours than oils. Yet almost every picture is not only attractive straightaway. It also quietly grows in the mind, and more and more kindles, as an extraordinary warmth and freshness penetrate further. One can work steadily round to the other side of this gallery's double-room and then turn one's head for a moment and suddenly glimpse, away on the opposite wall, one of the pictures first looked at – and have one's breath taken away.

I write as someone who is already an enthusiast, having enjoyed paintings of Edwin Smith's for some years, though, like almost everyone else, having seen very few. Little may be predictable now of what is going to be thought and said about his work when it is better known, and attention to it has been increased in the huge way that must be likely to happen at some point. Yet it may already be clear that one claim is going to be frequently repeated and perhaps eventually accepted: that in the whole history of English painting there may be few finer colourists. It can sometimes seem that the distinction of almost any good English painter is indelibly associated with that painter's having developed a distinctive individual palette, which may be striking but is limited and can be cold. Edwin Smith's colour has no apparent limits and is endlessly various and, if there is anything special in it, it is simply that it is always warm, often glowingly so. In front of the pictures, literally or in memory, it seems completely unsentimental, only accurate, to think of the colouring as that of a quite exceptionally and thrillingly pure love. Look at the still life with oil-lamp in the far left hand corner of the double-room's right half.

I do find it amazing that in work most of which is forty to fifty years old the colour never looks as if it could begin to date. If one could think of anyone else who could have achieved it, one could suppose it was done yesterday.

Unsurprisingly, its lovely livingness tends to be most immediately felt in the watercolours. But it can be striking in the oils, too, certainly in two of the smallest landscape oils in this exhibition. One of them may be the only late picture here and the other is the little 9" x 5 1/2" miracle a photograph of which is given here. (It should be said that the late paintings like "Turning Away" are bolder and even more striking. A good number were shown in exhibitions of Edwin Smith's paintings and drawings put on in Clare College, Cambridge, the first some years before the exhibition at Sally Hunter's and the second a little after it.)

The particularly outstanding exception to what I say about relatively cold colouring in English painting is the early-nineteenth-century work in 'landscape' of John Crome. I've argued elsewhere that the warmth of his colouring is among the main things that may make Crome *the* classic in English painting (*Cambridge Quarterly* VIII 1).[*]

Edwin's Smith's own story is a remarkable one. He died in 1971, almost completely unknown as a painter. Though he had painted all his life, he had had only one exhibition and that a wartime and an unsuccessful one. Yet, at the same time, long before his death he was also well known, for the work by which he had made his living: photography, mainly for publishers. This is how I myself first met his work, buying a few photographs at an exhibition and then, some years later, impressed by the fact that I had been enjoying having them on my walls in the house ever since (though I would not normally expect to want to see so much of what are only photographs), eagerly going to a new exhibition and buying more. In this way I met Edwin Smith's

---

[*] When I began this review, I'd forgotten that in an attempted poem of a few years earlier I'd made a similar connection between warmth of colouring and love. For what it's worth, I print it at the end of this little chapter.

widow, the writer Olive Cook, and first learnt of the paintings and saw some.

Since 1974 the paintings and drawings have begun to be exhibited again and with increasing frequency, though not in London until fairly recently, while the fame of the photographs has grown only greater. In 1984 Thames & Hudson brought out a large volume devoted to them, and after the death of Olive Cook a national collection will hold all the huge number of his extant photographs.

But the paintings are even greater. And, if national collections are beginning to nibble, that, up to now, is all they are doing.

A few years ago a world-ranking foreign sculptor happened to be visiting Cambridge just before a small exhibition opened. It had already been hung and, since he had to fly abroad before it opened but had been struck by the two or three Edwin Smiths he had seen on my walls, he asked to be given his own special private view. He was, and was bowled over. But, besides almost jumping up and down with joy at what he was seeing, he also had some feeling of outrage: that these wonderful works should be not only unknown but also going to disappear into private houses, at ridiculously low prices. (The prices at Sally Hunter are not dissimilar.) It seemed to him blindingly clear that almost all the paintings in the room ought to go straight into a major public collection. In fact, he proposed to buy some twenty of them on the spot and present them to one such collection.

I am sure it would have happened if he had been able to stay in Cambridge the few days longer – and to be in the room again when the authorities of the collection in question had a curator go to see what it was being offered. His own abstract sculpture had only its excellence in common with Edwin Smith's work, but a good artist obviously has no petty prejudice. It is the scholar/curator who is more likely to be the prisoner of fashion, unless he has such an artist by his side to help him see. So it did not happen. (The sculptor then offered to present the paintings to one of the most distinguished museums of modern art on the continent, and the offer was accepted immediately, without their even being seen, with the museum also undertaking to publish a monograph on them. Olive Cook would not agree, unhappy that all these paintings at once should leave the country.)

"Oil Lamp, Furlongs" (18" x 12")

"Ffestiniog" (9" x 5½ ")

"Turning Away" (18" x 10")

Postscript Olive Cook died in 2002. Her collection of the photographs has gone to the Royal Institute of British Architecture in London, whose Trust in 2007 brought out, with Merrell the publishers, another large illustrated book on the photographs: Robert Elwall's *Evocations of Place: the photographs of Edwin Smith.* (But Mr Elwall doesn't share my or the eminent sculptor's view that the paintings are even more special.) Sadly, the many paintings and drawings still in Olive Cook's possession were sold at auction after her death, by Cheffins in Cambridge, along with much else from the house, and they are thus continuing indefinitely to be lost to public view. The only public collections I know of as having any paintings at all by Edwin Smith are ones in Saffron Walden and Chelmsford.

On the train back from Norwich to Cambridge, after a day-trip to look at the Cromes

Suddenly from nowhere high up and marvellous,
Steady but it comes and comes and comes,
– what on earth am I to do with it?

Trees and fields in evening sun radiance – rich-coloured, thick-
shadowed -

A gentle full perpetual ecstasy, unbelievably miles and miles and
miles,
- shake to find it unreal, can be fallen out of, but it isn't and can't.

Two college girls don't seem to notice (it or me)
but are themselves
so particularly beautiful (one a little more than the other)
so particularly beautifully dressed (same difference)
so particularly beautifully friendly with each other and happy.

At Cambridge
nothing for it
take down spirit from luggage-rack
stuff under jacket
bike home.

Half-peace.

A brief appendix.
More on 'simplicity' in poetry

I believe the main thing that has produced the extraordinary situation of almost all of Joanne Weiss's poetry still not being in print is her use of a radically simple and unpretentious language and overall 'attack'. In comparison, the language and attack of most other contemporary poets in English, when they have enough artistic ambition to come into the reckoning at all, show that they are only too self-conscious about being 'poets'. Weiss can accordingly, though much more of an artist, look artistically naïve. I am reminded both of what Wordsworth wrote in the Advertisement to the first edition of *Lyrical Ballads* –

> Readers accustomed to the gaudiness and inane phraseology of many modern writers, if they persist in reading this book to its conclusion, will perhaps frequently have to struggle with feelings of strangeness and awkwardness: they will look round for poetry, and will be induced to enquire by what species of courtesy these attempts can be permitted to assume that title.

– and of Eliot's generalising of the instance of Wordsworth's revolution in his *On Poetry and Poets* essay on "The Music of Poetry":

> Every revolution in poetry is apt to be, and sometimes to announce itself to be a return to common speech. That is the revolution which Wordsworth announced in his prefaces, and he was right; but the same revolution had been carried out a century before by Oldham, Waller, Denham and Dryden: and the same revolution was due again something over a century later.

And the same revolution was due again in our time, a further century later.

About Weiss's revolution there were suggestions when I brought out some of the wealth of meaning in the four simple lines of the poem quoted on p34 and pointed in contrast to both laboriousness and preciousness in her distinguished older contemporary, Heaney. But her poems contain even bolder examples of her radical simplicity and unpretentiousness – sometimes, for example, the use of extreme brevity, as in poems two lines long, sometimes the risking of looking soft-sweet late-Romantic, as in "Last summer day", quoted above on p80, sometimes the use of the form of children's verse, *etc.* If every now and then in a poem of hers a reader might find difficulty of the more familiar kind, always the main difficulty she sets her reader is not in her words, images or general attack but in the imaginative leap there has to be to new vision.

Such 'vision' is mainly conspicuous by its absence from recent poetry in English, but it is there in Weiss's. It is even rather evident. She is clearly, among other things, a passionate moralist. The idea of 'vision' is obviously related to that of the 'sublime', but both of these ideas are also closely related to a third one: that of the 'large' poetic voice. It is here, too, that Weiss seems to me exceptional. I hope I may get more said about her seeming 'simplicity' by trying to clarify this idea.

A 'large' poetic voice isn't normally a loud one, and has to do simultaneously with mind and breath. It is amazing that so much of life should get into one simple statement or part of one, and that this should nevertheless not feel at all crowded or breathless but, on the contrary, be sustaining its expression of its extraordinarily far-reaching thought quietly, steadily and with ease.

Another Weiss example is this opening of a poem:

> Where beauty and beauty of spirit are one
> There, we can say, moves a creature of God, wild, divine…

There may be different opinions about how comparable is the degree of such success here, but I suggest that a comparison can still be made with these openings of familiar poems:

> When to the sessions of sweet silent thought
> I summon up remembrance of things past…

> *Quand chez les débauchés l'aube blanche et vermeille*
> *Entre en société de l'Idéal rongeur…*

The generalisation suggested in each of these three short excerpts is an effortlessly powerful one because the large truth that is seen quickly is also seen with such sharp freshness: that the enjoyment of precious memories belongs to those deeper moments of safe and sweet self-communing that paradoxically have something of the awed solemnity of proceedings in a law-court; that, if only with a painful hopelessness, the beautiful colours of dawn can touch and nag at overhung debauchees, at the knowledge they have of everything in life that contrasts with the rottenness of their own conduct and present state of feeling; that in a living creature any beauty that is unusually complete, by being both an inner and an outer beauty, can seem miraculously to be at once entirely part of this world and something quite beyond this world. All this and more is flashed upon the imagination and deep understanding simply by the poets' using their plain ordinary words quite idiomatically but in a fresh way, making new and surprising connections which, once made, seem perfectly natural and inevitable. Shakespeare has his law-court metaphor. Baudelaire puts the debauched in one line with the beauty of dawn and then leaps to "*l'Idéal rongeur*". Weiss simply combines earthly and heavenly reference – with the result, among other things, that in her crucial last combination of "wild" and "divine" both words get quite surprisingly fresher and fuller meanings than they ordinarily possess. In the line that immediately follows, completing her sentence, there is another surprise as the large truth receives a moving further extension:

And one that we must lose to that divinity too soon.

Here "that divinity" seems to refer back more definitely to "divine" in the previous line than to "God", and it is difficult to be precise about the meaning created by that. Is the traditional consoling wisdom that the deceased loved creature had finally to be surrendered back to his or her Creator -

Yet all heaven's gifts being heaven's due,
It makes the father less to rue.
(Ben Jonson, "On My First Daughter")

- being combined with a deep awe at the perfection that such complete beauty is in a living creature, with some attendant acknowledgment that so rare a thing hardly belongs in life and therefore can stay in it only all too briefly? At the same time there are the beginnings of the intuition which the poem goes on to develop that, paradoxically, such a creature never dies.

In his "Life of Cowley" Samuel Johnson described the sublime in poetry as "that comprehension and expanse of thought which at once fills the whole mind, and of which the first effect is sudden astonishment, and the second rational admiration." That astonishment doesn't occur when some sublime apprehension is there but is, relatively, being laboured at, as in the lines preceding those quoted earlier (on p106) from Ted Hughes's "The Bull Moses":

> A hoist up and I could lean over
> The upper edge of the high half-door,
> My left foot ledged on the hinge, and look in at the byre's
> Blaze of darkness: a sudden shut-eyed look
> Backward into the head.
>   Blackness is depth
> Beyond star.

The contrast between that passage and those just quoted helps to bring out that the large easy-fluent voice of the best poets is at once of their lungs and of their minds and imaginations. Those three poets are writing there in fairly long and pregnant units of sense, but never does the reader feel the slightest oppression or the slightest hurry. On the contrary, there is some inclination to linger and expand indefinitely in each unit of sense. We are breathing, as we are thinking and feeling, absolutely freely, with almost a sense of floating and of having endless space around us. Contrastingly, in Hughes's writing there is some tight constriction. The voice and mind are less released into an unwontedly easy and free movement than frog-marched, with a touch of distrustful hostility to the reader: "*I* have been thrilled, awed and chastened by this experience, and the condition of your entering my poem is my making *you* be thrilled, awed and chastened in exactly the same way." There has to be the sudden arresting force, or forcible-feebleness, of "Blaze of darkness" and "Blackness is depth/ Beyond star". There is little of the sense the other short passages give that something common to all of us, which each of us can see and feel for him- or herself, is simply being opened up.

Incidentally, the religious vision that is the pervasive thing and the inspired thing in all of Hughes's writing (certainly separating him from the small voices of so many other recent English poets, and certainly thrilling me as his different volumes came out) seems to me to be all of it more or less present in those three lines of Weiss's, even in just her putting together in this context the words "wild" and "divine" – besides being present calmly and inevitably, sounding like the most elementary truth as well as a kind of absolute truth.

It is a similar easy-large sublimity that stops her "Last Summer Day" from being soft-sweet late-Romantic. The warm air written of is continuous in a partly chastening way with the whole of the vast universe, and the air's livingness, passingly felt but intimately, brings with it an apprehension of a mysterious livingness in the whole universe, felt in the same delicately fugitive yet intimate and eternal way. It is no wonder that, like those lines of Shakespeare's and Baudelaire's, and unlike Hughes's, the poem is also a markedly beautiful one.

The large voice of sublime poetry is a voice with a special moral and spiritual authority. If Hughes tends to assert such authority, Weiss simply has it. The absence from her verse of either the laboured or the self-consciously 'poetic' and precious *is* the greater confidence and urgency about what she has to say. Her vision is too strong for her to have to think of trying to force it. Even less can she be imagined thinking of overlaying it with nervously clever writing like that quoted above on pp89-90. It matters too much.